UNDER THE SIGN OF CONTRADICTION

UNDER THE SIGN OF CONTRADICTION

Mandelstam and the Politics of Memory

Anna Razumnaya

Peter Lang
Oxford · Bern · Berlin · Bruxelles · New York · Wien

Bibliographic information published by Die Deutsche Nationalbibliothek.
Die Deutsche Nationalbibliothek lists this publication in the Deutsche
Nationalbibliografie; detailed bibliographic data is available on the Internet at
http://dnb.d-nb.de.

A catalogue record for this book is available from the British Library.

Library of Congress Cataloging-in-Publication Data
Names: Razumnaya, Anna, 1979- author.
Title: Under the sign of contradiction : Mandelstam and the politics of
   memory / Anna Razumnaya.
Description: New York ; Oxford : Peter Lang, 2021. | Includes
   bibliographical references and index.
Identifiers: LCCN 2018038526 | ISBN 9781787070516 (alk. paper)
Subjects: LCSH: Mandel'shtam, Osip, 1891-1938. | Poets, Russian--20th
   century--Biography. | Literature and state--Soviet Union. |
   Mandel'shtam, Osip, 1891-1938--Trials, litigation, etc. | Political
   persecution--Soviet Union--History--Sources.
Classification: LCC PG3476.M355 Z894 2019 | DDC 891.71/3 [B]--dc23
LC record available at https://lccn.loc.gov/2018038526

Cover design by Brian Melville for Peter Lang.
Cover Image: Frans Snyders, *Boar Hunt* (ca. 1625–1630)

ISBN 978-1-78707-051-6 (print) • ISBN 978-1-78707-863-5 (ePDF)
ISBN 978-1-78707-864-2 (ePub) • ISBN 978-1-78707-865-9 (mobi)

© Peter Lang Group AG 2021

Published by Peter Lang Ltd, International Academic Publishers,
52 St Giles, Oxford, OX1 3LU, United Kingdom
oxford@peterlang.com, www.peterlang.com

Anna Razumnaya has asserted her right under the Copyright, Designs and Patents Act,
1988, to be identified as Author of this Work.

All rights reserved.
All parts of this publication are protected by copyright.
Any utilisation outside the strict limits of the copyright law, without the permission of
the publisher, is forbidden and liable to prosecution.
This applies in particular to reproductions, translations, microfilming, and storage and
processing in electronic retrieval systems.

This publication has been peer reviewed.

Little book – no, I don't begrudge you – you're off to the City
    without me, going where your only begetter is banned!
On your way, then – but penny-plain, as befits an exile's
    sad offering, and my present life.
For you no purple slip-case (that's a colour
    goes ill with grief), no title-line picked out
in vermillion, no cedar-oiled backing, no white bosses
    to set off those black
edges: leave luckier books to be dressed with such trimmings:
    never forget my sad estate.
                                        Ovid, *Tristia*, Book I

The notion is that life involves maintaining oneself between contradictions that can't be solved by analysis, e.g. those of philosophy, which apply to all creatures, and the religious one about man being both animal and divine.
                    William Empson, note to 'Bacchus'

Contents

Acknowledgements ix

Note on the Text xi

Preface 1

Exhibits 5
    I 7
    II 9
    III 11
    IV 13
    V 17
    VI 19

PROLOGUE
Biography Between Contradictions 21

CHAPTER 1
'The Stalin Epigram' and the Liberty of Protest 45

CHAPTER 2
A Moulten Falcon: *Poetry as Consolation and Dialectic* 89

CHAPTER 3
'Be Simple Answer'd, for We Know the Truth': *Of Protocol and Interrogations* 117

CHAPTER 4
Double Bind, 1934   131

INTERLUDE
Under the Stars: *Poetry as Courage and Resistance*   149

CHAPTER 5
In the Cross-Vault: *The Stalin 'Ode' as Metaphysical Poetry*   165

CHAPTER 6
Quarrels on the Witness Stand: *Posthumous Mandelstam*   193

EPILOGUE
Criticism and the Fate of Poets   213

References   227

Perspectives in English: *An Annotated Bibliography*   253

Acknowledgements

This book's foremost obligations are to critics and writers whose ideas I used, as recorded throughout the text.

Eight years have passed since the first incarnation of this work was defended as a doctoral dissertation at Boston University's Editorial Institute. The persons and institutions who had in different ways assisted the dissertation were noted at the time. I remain thankful to them, and especially to the Editorial Institute, whose programme in Editorial Studies has been the ground of many explorations of text and context in their fertile embrace. I cannot envision the present work outside of the environment that fostered it – without the exuberant discussions, the humour, the generosity of the faculty and the respectful interest and encouragement of senior colleagues within the ALSCW – the Association of Literary Scholars, Critics and Writers, whose ties to the Editorial Institute so much enriched student experience.

In the intervening years, the dissertation's principal advisor, Christopher Ricks, continued to be a source of encouragement, advice, illuminating and often chastening commentary, and nurturing support. Archie Burnett and David Bromwich have been reliably willing to bolster me with letters of recommendation during my search for a place within academia, indirectly sustaining my scholarship. Alessandra Anzani commissioned the work in 2016; her successor at Peter Lang, Laurel Plapp, shepherded the manuscript through peer review and other 'ages and stages', a reliable and supportive presence that defied the geographical distance between Oxford and Boston. During peer review itself, the stringent yet fair-minded and constructively detailed comments of my reader, whose name is not known to me, assured me that a book written in the New-Critical tradition could yet be favourably received by colleagues in the field of philology. As the head of the Mandelstam Society (headquartered in Moscow), Pavel Nerler was very kind to supply the two sets of images used in Exhibit V, together with a permission to reproduce them.

My beloved life partner, the historian of philosophy Peter Hanly, created all the conditions at home to enable my revisions; ever-ready to comment on the manuscript (which he has always done with the utmost discernment and tact), he supplied a number of references to Heraclitus, Fichte, Kant and other touchstones philosophical and artistic. The solidarity of my friends – especially Brad Hogg, Devin Johnson and Nathan Nielson – has meant a lot to me during the inevitable darker moments of working on the book. My son Leo has done wonders for my spirits, strengthening me with his love and trusting kindness: of all those mentioned here, he may be the youngest, and the last on this list, but never the least in his power to effect good things.

Note on the Text

In an effort to lighten the page, no superscript or any other signalling means have been used to announce the existence of a note: as notes are limited to citations, this would have been superfluous. The reader can instead expect to find the source of any quotation in the *References* towards the end of the book, where every quotation in the text is abridged to a choice of words that together amount to a running index of the voices and viewpoints sounded in the chapters that follow. Under the same rationale of resisting unnecessary clutter, two kinds of ellipsis have been used to distinguish between two kinds of elision within quoted text throughout. A spaced editorial ellipsis (. . .) signals text omitted from the quotation by the present author for the sake of brevity. Where the ellipsis belongs to the *author of the text being quoted*, a closed ellipsis with no spaces (...) figures instead.

All translations from the Russian, where not otherwise attributed, are my own, and where the cited source of quoted text happens to be in Russian (as opposed to a published translation), the English translation should automatically be attributed to the author. In translating verse, the sense of the original wording was the first priority; the line as a unit of sense was preserved wherever possible, and only on those occasions when this would have compromised either the syntax and the rhythm was the correspondence of sense and line sequence altered. ('Rhythm', in turn, should not be equated with 'metre' but understood only as loosely indicative of the poem's habit and intonations, conveyed to the best of the translator's skill.)

The book does not presume a reading knowledge of Russian: with very few exceptions where Cyrillic script was felt to be integral to a quotation, Russian words are either translated or reproduced in italics, following the author's best native sense of correct phonetics.

Preface

It has long been broadly understood that Osip Mandelstam's posthumous reputation is replete with contradictions. As a poet, he wrote both *against* and *in praise of* Stalin (under duress in *both* instances, not solely the latter – to foreshadow one of the recognitions this work will seek to corroborate). As a man, he was a faithful 'friend of his friends', and yet testified against a number of them to the secret police. This undeniable complexity continues to stimulate those who wish to resolve its inconsistencies, among which Mandelstam's composition of an 'Ode' to Stalin has occasioned the most critical dismay. Most judged it an aberrant, preposterous, even illegitimate phenomenon – a product of coercion according to some, or madness according to others. To survey the past half-century of Mandelstam scholarship is to be faced with a disparity between the contradictory manifold of Mandelstam's life and letters and the compulsive wish (shared by writers with otherwise divergent opinions) to eliminate the antinomies, reversals and paradoxes pervading the evidence, all in pursuit of a politically acceptable and, above all, 'tidy' narrative. Some such efforts take the form of whitewashing what is felt to be a tainted image; inevitably, they are compensated by attempts to expose the 'dark side' of a figure perceived to have been sanctified – or sanitized – at the expense of the truth.

Both tendencies represent but two phases of a single dynamic, within which the quest after a balanced view follows a pendulum's trajectory. The first phase was heralded by Anna Akhmatova, a close friend of Mandelstam's, whose 'Poem Without a Hero' is indicative of what she felt to be the best posthumous policy: 'he is guilty of nothing – not this, not that, nor the other'. Similar rhetoric was adopted by champions of Mandelstam in England, and all the more so in the United States, where a sentimentalized narrative of martyrdom at the hands of Stalin's regime turned Mandelstam into a 'political nonconformist' and thereby America's most unexpected ally in the Cold War. In Russian Mandelstam studies, whose development became possible with the fall of the Soviet system, nuanced conversation about Mandelstam's politics is made difficult by the prevailing sense that, if not carefully minimized, ambiguities within the poet's opposition to Stalin's regime would damage Mandelstam's reputation, felt to be dependent upon a strict interpretive hygiene.

The compensatory phase tends to manifest surreptitiously as glancing and insinuating misgivings about Mandelstam's 'less than saintly behaviour under interrogation' (as if nothing 'less' than saintliness *could* or *should* have been expected of a person under duress) and about the factitiousness detectable in dubious (and heartless) honorifics like 'literary martyr *par excellence*'. Though the impulse behind such calls for re-evaluation aims at achieving justice, the nuanced and balanced language necessary for a just and truthful valuation of a poet is by no means easy to bring into existence. Consequently, skilled and responsible criticism capable of meeting the puzzling evidence with both penetration and temperance is unlikely ever to become overabundant, even in a field as intensively worked as Mandelstam studies.

With this in mind, this book attempts to negotiate the contradictions of Mandelstam's biography without discounting any credible evidence whilst maintaining a grip on the critical language, its rhetorical ramifications, and the congruence of sensibility and manner of expression. This last requirement has long informed the English critical tradition, within which particularly the poet-critics – centrally, T. S. Eliot, William Empson and Geoffrey Hill – have tested the continuities and reciprocities of poetry and critical judgement. Their affinities with Mandelstam, who was himself not only a poet but also a critic, are rooted in philosophical dispositions that are not specific to any national literature. At the same time, the context of perennial literary ideas seems proper to Mandelstam in being consonant with his own professed longing for 'world culture'. That no further theory is brought to bear on matters of criticism is not an omission but a deliberate decision to be cautious in adopting theoretical concepts, whose applicability to literature is tested by their viability as literary language (as stringent particularity must precede induction). At the same time, no argument about contradiction could be possible without some analytical apparatus. This is borrowed largely from William Empson, whose concepts of *ambiguity, aspect, balance* and *deadlock* assist the analysis of contradiction as an organizing crux in both art and biography. Gregory Bateson's concept of the *double bind* proved to be another valuable tool in the analysis of Mandelstam's biography.

No artist of significance should be made a mascot of any, even the most benign, ideology *du jour*. In its pursuit of truths of thought and feeling, literature relies on a disinterestedness inevitably superseding political ends. The mistaken idea that its aims could be circumscribed by political interests is incompatible with an appreciation of Mandelstam's high achievement: the reconciliation of great dignity with great detachment. The truth of Mandelstam's biography is not, then, felt here to be a matter of deprecating the poet or dislodging him from his elevated place in cultural memory. It calls, rather, for the recognition that 'life involves maintaining oneself between contradictions that can't be solved by analysis'. One corollary to this principle is that if we are to understand a life, such understanding must involve locating and examining its salient contradictions – humanely, in keeping with the humanity we prize in literature itself. In Mandelstam's case, that crucial biographical paradox concerns the interplay of freedom and coercion. Much of what has been written about this crux in Mandelstam's life and art is in need of revisiting specifically because the relation between liberty and coercion is insufficiently seen as a paradox and as an interplay.

This first thing required by the kind of investigation the author has in mind is a sufficiently rich array of witnesses – textual witness, behind which stand real persons, with their individual voices. In order to preserve the distinctness of each testimony, from others and from the author's interpretations, they are presented, where possible, in direct quotation (as against paraphrase, which tends to absorb all voices into a single authorial voice). The coherence sought is that of a polyphony, a form whose political dimension is pluralistic, in contrast with the ideological univocalism of totalitarian and fascist states. This study does not claim to survey every piece of applicable evidence. What is attempted, however, is to marshal evidence sufficient for framing several significant loci of Mandelstam's life and letters under the aspect of contradiction. The array of rhetorical examples assembled here is intended to supply the grounds for comparative analysis of further materials. Apart from the pragmatics of book production, established authorities on a given question may not be invoked, for the very reason that they are already generally known and constitute the 'normal lighting' upon the subject of this book. Nevertheless, an effort has been made to maintain a balance among existing witnesses and commentators so as not to distort the critical implications of what is known, following a principle suggested by Empson:

> As a matter of literary criticism, to recover one lost historical fact no doubt does sometimes throw light all round, but only from one point; I tried to avoid too much disproportion from such lighting by simply adding what other lights occurred to me upon the poem. But anyway the reader is assumed to know the normal lighting already, and to judge the difference.

Beyond its positive critical aims, the work has the negative purpose of prophylaxis – the freeing of criticism, to what degree might be possible on the scale of a single study, from the misconceptions engendered by totalitarian tendencies of thought which, in criticism, compound the injustice done to Mandelstam through the very terms of its praise and through careless, though well-intentioned, attributions. There is no remedy for this problem but to be vigilant, alert to words and to their capacity to invoke more than what is intended. Finally, it is a critic's negative task, in the act explaining, to stop short of explaining *away* – at the boundary of what Fichte, and, after him, Emil Lask, Mandelstam's philosophical mentor, termed the *hiatus irrationalis*, meaning the unplumbable depths of individuality. Having led the reader to that threshold, the critic has done her job.

A narrative concerned with oppression must take care that the methods by which it is assembled do not violate the political principles it seeks to uphold. This entails, for the present book, a suspension of the impulse to settle the differences between witness accounts without sufficient grounds for doing so, and the corollary recognition of the limitations of our knowledge, limitations not always attributable to a shortage of evidence or surmountable through more 'research', as they are sometimes purely epistemic. We should not be surprised by this where the personality we seek to understand is a poet of genius, for whom the six chapters that follow are assembled as a loose memorial bouquet.

Exhibits

I

March 2, 1933
From the memoirs of Elena Tager:

> Mandelstam read with undiminishing pathos; as ever, he stood with his head tilted back, stretched to his full height – as if some sudden gale might at any moment pluck him off the ground. . . . But some odd, disgruntled people could be seen prowling about the hall. They exchanged ironic whispers, grimaced and shrugged. One of them passed a note to the stage. Mandelstam read it aloud: the note had a distinctly provocative character. Osip Emilyevich was being asked to express his opinion about contemporary Soviet poetry, and to define the significance of older poets who had been writing since before the revolution. Thousands of eyes saw Mandelstam blanche. His fingers crumpled up the note. The poet was being subjected to a public interrogation, with no possibility of escape. An anxious hush spread over the audience. Of course, the majority of those present listened with indifferent curiosity. But there were also those who blanched together with him. Mandelstam stepped towards the front of the stage; he lifted his head and his eyes sparkled. 'What do you expect of me? What kind of an answer?' Then, in a steady, sing-song voice: 'I am a friend of my friends!' A half-a-second pause. Then, a victorious, ecstatic cry: 'I am Akhmatova's contemporary!'

II

November 1933
'The Stalin Epigram'

> We live without sensing the country beneath our feet,
> Our voices die down at ten paces away,
> And wherever there's even a half-conversation,
> The Kremlin highlander will be remembered.
> His thick fingers are fat as worms,
> His words sure as kettlebells.
> The cockroach eyes snicker,
> The tall boots polished to a shine.
>
> Surrounded by a rabble of thin-necked chiefs,
> He toys with half-men's favours,
> As they yowl, whistle and moan –
> He alone prods and probes and points.
> Like horseshoes, he throws out decree by decree –
> One will hit in the groin, the next in the brow.
> Every death is as sweet as a berry,
> The Ossetian chest mighty and broad.

III

May 19, 1934
From the protocol of Mandelstam's interrogation by Nikolay Shivarov:

QUESTION: To whom did you read or give copies of this poem?

ANSWER: I did not give out copies but read it to the following persons: to my wife, to my brother, Alexander E. Mandelstam, to my wife's brother, Yevgeniy Yakovlevich Khazin, a man of letters and author of children's books, to my wife's friend Emma Grigoryevna Gerstein, employed in the research department of All-Union Central Council of Professional Trade Unions, to Anna Akhmatova, a writer, to her son Lev Gumilyov, to the man of letters, David Grigoryevich Brodsky, to Boris Sergeyevich Kuzin, employed at the Zoological Museum. . . . In supplement to my prior testimony, I must add that among the persons to whom I read the above-mentioned counter-revolutionary poem was the young poet Maria Sergeyevna Petrovykh. Petrovykh wrote down this work as I read it, promising, however, to destroy the copy later.

IV

January – March 1937
'Ode'

    If I were to pick up the charcoal in high praise,
    For the indisputable ecstasy of drawing, –
    I would section the air into cunning angles,
    Both carefully and anxiously, so that
    The present would resound in every feature,
    Verging on impudence in art,
    I would speak of him who found a fulcrum,
    Honouring the custom of a hundred and forty tribes.
    I would raise that eyebrow's little corner, and
    Would do so again, resolving differently:
    Prometheus has blown alive this ember –
    Behold, Aeschylus, how I draw – and weep!

    I would gather in a sheaf of thundering lines
    That whole youthful millennium of his,
    And tie up manliness into a smile,
    Untying once again in unharsh lighting,
    And in the friendship of these wise eyes, I shall find
    The countenance of a twin, the one one cannot name,
    In whom, upon approach, one discerns the father,
    Smothered at once by the proximity of all.
    And I am filled with gratitude for the hills
    That fostered this bone and this palm:
    He came down from the mountains and knew the pain of prison.
    I want to call him – not Stalin – Jugashvili!

    Artist! Protect and guard the warrior:
    Surround him with that tall, that gray-and-blue
    Forest of moist attention. Do not disappoint
    The father by an unkind likeness or a dearth of thought;
    Artist, assist the one who is all with you,
    The one who thinks, feels, builds.
    Not me, and not the other, but his kin,
    His Homer-people triples praise upon him.

Artist, protect and guard the warrior:
The human forest sings behind him, thickens,
Future itself the army of that sage,
And listens to him frequently and bravely.

He leaned out of the tribune as from a cliff
Over the hills of heads. The debtor overpowers the credit.
His mighty eyes are resolutely kind,
The thick eyebrow beckons someone near,
And I would like to point out by an arrow
The firmness of that mouth, the father of staunch speech,
The sculptural, complex and convex eyelid works
Out of a million frames.
All – candid honesty, all – confession's brass,
His hearing sight tolerates no falsehood,
Towards all who stand, ready to live and die,
Run, rippling, his severe wrinkles.

Crushing the charcoal intersecting all,
Voracious hand imploring a resemblance,
The likeness-axis preyed upon by the hand-carnivore,
I shall crumble the coal in hunting for his features.
I learn from him, but not for my own sake.
I learn from him to know no self-pity,
Misfortunes will obscure no portion of the picture,
I shall uncover him in the accidents of their form . . .
Though I remain unworthy to have friends,
Not yet replete with bile and tears,
He shows himself to me, in his coat and his cap,
Amidst the wondrous square, with happy eyes.

The eyes of Stalin part the mountain-side,
The valley squints into the distance.
As an unwrinkled sea, as tomorrow from the past –
The great plough's furrows reach up to the sun.
He smiles with the smile of the mower
Of handshakes in a conversation that,
Incipient, goes on without an end,
Within the space sealed by a six-fold oath.
Each meadow and each sheaf
Strong, smartly turned and clever –

Exhibit IV

People's wonder! Living good! May this life be large.
Revolve, the axle-happiness of many.

Six times I keep in mind his mighty way,
The laggard witness of this labour, struggle and mowth,
His passage through the taiga, Lenin's great October,
Down to the consummation of the oath.
The hills of human heads recede, and I grow small,
Until I am no longer to be seen,
But in the tender books and children's games
I shall rise up to greet the rising sun.
There is no truer truth than the warrior's sincerity:
For honour and for love, for valour and for steel
There is a fine name for the reader's lips –
We heard it and partook in time with him.

V

May 1934 – May 1938
Two sets of prison photographs of Osip Mandelstam, taken four years apart.

VI

December 1938
Note on time of death issued at Vtoraya Rechka transit camp:

> *Note*
> Prisoner Mendelshtam
> was in treatment
> since 26/XII died
> 27/XII at 12:30
> upon examination of the corpse
> it was discovered that on
> the left arm on the lower
> third of the upper arm
> there is a birthmark
> 27/XII, 1938
> [*illegible signature*]

PROLOGUE

Biography Between Contradictions

> what quality went to form a Man of Achievement especially in Literature & which Shakespeare posessed so enormously – I mean *Negative Capability*, that is when man is capable of being in uncertainties, Mysteries, doubts, without any irritable reaching after fact & reason.
>
> John Keats

As with Osip Mandelstam's biography, so too with his posthumous reputation, one thing is by now well-understood: the whole figure, the man and the poet, is a study in contradictions. And yet, no scholarly or critical study has attended to the nature of these contradictions a such; they perplex us yet elude scrutiny; and for as long as they continue to evade us, much about Mandelstam is destined to be misapprehended despite the sheer quantity of scholarship. This is true, for instance, of an early poem, written in 1909, Mandelstam's year as a philosophy student at Heidelberg University, and uncollected in *Kamen*, the collection drawing on poems of the surrounding period. This poem is generally assumed to be a 'love lyric', as it is in Pavel Nerler's Russian-language documentary study, *Osip Mandelstam in Heidelberg* – but what are the grounds for this categorization? The poem – a meditation in four stanzas – opens by invoking the 'cold' sound of lyres, and concludes with two lines that clasp a puzzling image:

И пальцы тонкие дрожат,
К таким же, как они, прижаты.

*I pal'tsy tonkiye drozhat,
K takim zhe, kak oni, prizhaty.*

'And slender fingers tremble', we might translate these lines, 'Pressed against their own counterparts'. Or, perhaps, 'Pressed against others that are just like them'. The 'love lyric' interpretation takes this trembling as indicative of the bashfulness and exhilaration of unexpected closeness. Yet the gesture described in these lines is very difficult to picture if we assume that these trembling fingers are 'pressed against' the fingers of *another person* – another person, no less, whose fingers happen to be *exactly the same* as the protagonist's, as the final line assures us that they are. To insist on this reading is to attribute careless phrasing to Mandelstam himself, for failing to say what we might expect him to mean. The alternative is to admit that he might be saying something unexpected. Evidence for such a reading is supplied by Nerler himself, with the valuable quotation of a passage concerning Mandelstam's art history professor, Henry Thode. At the time of the poem's composition, Mandelstam attended Thode's course on sixteenth-century Venetian painters and another course on the foundations of art history. Thode himself is described by another student from Mandelstam's cohort, Fyodor Stepun:

> In Moscow, this elegant and sophisticated man, whose clean-shaven face was softly lit by a pair of sad eyes, would have been taken for an actor rather than a scholar. He looked especially colourful in his toque and gown at formal university events. . . . Each year he gave, in a packed auditorium, a cycle of public lectures that attracted, like the concerts of Nikisch, not only the whole city but even listeners from the neighbouring towns. The lecturer's beautiful pale hands were often joined prayerfully, palm to palm. His long fingers touched to his lips. Like all Romantics, Thode would speak a great deal and very well about the ineffable and the mystery of silence.

This casts entirely new lighting on the perplexing lines about the fingers. Stepun writes: 'The lecturer's beautiful pale hands were often joined prayerfully, palm to palm. His long fingers touched to his lips.' Mandelstam, already attuned, largely during his earlier Paris year, to the powerful rhetorical implications of the Gothic, sat in the same lecture hall, witnessed the same symmetrical gesture, 'palm to palm' and fingertip to fingertip, fingers 'pressed against their counterparts', and saw in them the same elastic tension that he had witnessed in the 'tremendous ribs' of Notre Dame and of which he would write in the poem of 1912. In Mandelstam's eyes, Thode's gesture flourished into an emblem of the Gothic: the arch, the basis of the Gothic edifice, whose glory is the architectonic employment of opposed forces.

If we accept this reading of the final lines, the rest of the poem, too, becomes intelligible. Its 'cold' and ethereal musical opening invokes the Heraclitean significance of a lyre – a symbol of the harmony of opposites. At the centre of the poem is an elision, from ashes sealed in 'urns' to wine aging in 'amphorae'. Both figures are suggestive of something sealed from us as the past is sealed and yet present to us, aging – and getting better with age. To the figures of *ashes sealed in an urn* and *wine sealed in a jug*, Mandelstam will add, some years later, when writing on the literary tradition in his essay 'On the Interlocutor', the cognate idea of a *message sealed in a bottle* – and this corroborates the sense that, like the message in a bottle, the ashes and the wine are representations of a certain maturing tradition that cannot be altered by us (it is sealed) but that beckons, standing ready to influence us. It is being in the presence of the European intellectual and philosophical tradition that has Mandelstam transfixed, during his first and, as it would turn out, his only autumn at Heidelberg. This is what the poem witnesses. The proximity within it of sealed vessels and professorial fingers poised in a Gothic arch suggests a realization about a tension inherent in the tradition of European thought: the tension between (on the one hand) animistic enchantment with the sensuous world and (on the other hand) the stringency of critical inquiry whose main vehicle is scepticism, of whose neo-Kantian strain Heidelberg was an important centre at the time. The supposed 'love lyric' proves to be a poem in which Mandelstam feels himself, finds himself profoundly a European – as to be a European is, above all, to be in the grip of the central contradiction from which the entire edifice of European civilization arises, to be spellbound by the music of the lyre which is the Heraclitean *harmonia*, the productive aspect of opposition.

Emil Lask, one of the two significant neo-Kantians who taught philosophy at Heidelberg during Mandelstam's year there as a philosophy student, characterized the fundamental problem of history and historical scholarship as the '*Irrationalitätsproblem*'. In Frederick Beiser's scholarly encapsulation, what Lask meant was that

> the individual, the subject matter of history, is 'irrational' in the sense that it cannot be fully analyzed, described by concepts, or explained by general laws. Since the

individual is indivisible, unique and infinitely rich, it acts as a surd, eluding complete analysis, adequate description or exhaustive explanation. We can *subsume* particulars under universals, i.e. we can make true statements about them; but the problem is that we cannot *derive* their determinate content from universals, i.e. it eludes complete conceptualization. Hence the individual is radically *contingent* for our understanding, which is limited to purely abstract concepts or general laws. Borrowing a term from the later Fichte, Lask gives a special name to this contingency: the *hiatus irrationalis*.

This does not amount to radical scepticism about science, not even social sciences, barring the conceptual muddles that compound a problem that cannot be eliminated by eliminating conceptual muddles. What Lask's philosophical position represents is prophylaxis against mistaking models (which are here referred to as 'universals') for complete accounts, against forgetting that what makes models serviceable to science is their economy, and therefore incompleteness, relative to the phenomena they represent: what makes a good model is a high ratio of predictive accuracy to descriptive complexity, and this ratio is improved by omitting those features of the phenomenon which happen to be irrelevant in the analysis. In the study of particulars, which is the domain of history, singled out by Lask for that reason among the disciplines, all accounts that claim exhaustiveness or forfeit a disclosure of their tacit assumptions and limitations of knowledge are compromised in principle. What Mandelstam's philosophy mentor warns against is, among other things, the kind of forgetfulness of the nature of historianship exemplified by the note on the flap of *Stolen Air*, a volume of Christian Wiman's versions of Mandelstam issued in 2012 by the very respectable Ecco. The poet is introduced, presumably for the benefit of those readers who need an introduction, and who are immediately misled:

> Political nonconformist Osip Mandelstam's opposition to Stalin's totalitarian government made him a target of the communist state. The public recitation of his 1933 poem known in English as 'The Stalin Epigram' led to his arrest, exile, and eventual imprisonment in a Siberian transit camp, where he died, presumably in 1938. Mandelstam's work – much of it written under extreme duress – is an extraordinary testament to the enduring power of art in the face of oppression and terror.

The trouble here is not with solecisms like 'imprisonment in a transit camp' but with the description of Mandelstam's particular case entirely by means of conceptions – 'universals' – and clichés, figures of speech which impose a tidy relational and causal scheme on a singularly complex biography, while signalling none of that complexity to the reader and instead creating an impression that nothing beyond the habitual reflexes of judgement is needed to apprehend the plot involving a 'political nonconformist' (the 'good' side, of course) in 'opposition' to 'totalitarian government' ('bad', needless to say). 'Target', 'extreme duress' (as against what other kind?), 'extraordinary testament', 'enduring power', 'oppression and terror': what are these clichés if not an invitation to relax, an assurance that economizing on thought will not result in some unexpected loss? But one is always free to decline the false assurance and the invitation, or to be prompted, by that very assurance, to scrutinize its soundness – in the light, for instance, of the absurdity of the supposition that a free person should primarily be characterized by a compulsive struggle against unfreedom, that he should be crucified upon his opposition to oppression. (It would seem that the only reliable indicator of freedom in a person would be his, or her, capacity to behave unpredictably, which then could not ensue in the deterministic and clockwork-like succession of being 'targeted', arrested, exiled and imprisoned – death, of course, remaining, as of press time, the one reliable *end* to all behaviour. At the same time, it is predictability that we prize in other people – valuing in them the recognition of the social ties and bonds and of the social contract that limits our freedoms in every practical direction. Freedom, too, is a conception rarely conformed to by any actual state of affairs; and yet, conceptions like 'freedom' supply the building blocks of slogans and ideologies.) Similarly, we discern freedom of thought in a person who surprises us, by virtue of being in touch with her or his inner irrational wellspring – irrational not in the sense of being contrary to reason, but in eluding full explicit grasp, for reasons that preoccupy several branches of philosophy. A partial analogy for Lask's sense of the 'irrational', which is being provisionally adopted here, is the case of irrational numbers, which cannot be explicitly denoted and must simply be rounded to a specified degree of precision in applied calculations. The relation of the individual to the irrational – to that which resists expression yet constitutes the only *bona fide* object of expression – is central in the case of an artist, whose 'voice' – the individual's distinctive manner of answering the artistic vocation, 'calling' being another notion historically associated with voice – is fully dependent on the irreducible richness of a highly particular consciousness to which none but the individual her- or himself has access and which, by the specificity of its nature, cannot be practically apprehended by conceptual means or in cliché-ridden language, with consequences for literary theory and literary journalism alike.

It could be protested that book jackets and publicity texts are not intended for such close scrutiny, yet it is fair to expect that an introduction should contain, at minimum, true facts. Facts being less ambiguous than judgements, how do the anonymous annotators of *Stolen Air* dispose with such information? The book's rear flap informs the reader that Mandelstam 'was born and raised in St. Petersburg', unwittingly reiterating one of the falsifications that compromised the first posthumous edition of Mandelstam's poems, published in 1973 with Alexander Dymshitz's factitious preface. Even this error as to Mandelstam's birthplace (which was, after all, Warsaw) might not have been worth pointing out if not for the indication of the poet's place of *death*, which the same publicity text specifies blithely as the 'Gulag Archipelago', apparently in blissful unawareness that no such 'archipelago' is to be found on the map. The compounded effect is of indifference to the facts of biography, of carelessness strikingly at odds with the tones of utmost moral gravity permeating these passages. Given this degree of attention to facts, how true, then, are the judgements offered in this brief introduction? Specifically, was Mandelstam really a *nonconformist*? Was he *opposed* to Stalin's government? Was he a 'target' of the communist state? Not one considered answer to these questions turns out to be an uncomplicated 'Yes'. It is believed in writing these pages that precisely complications and qualifications attendant upon answering questions such as these can get us progressively closer to understanding the reasons for which Mandelstam's better readers recognise in him a poet of genius.

Boris Kuzin, a close friend of Mandelstam's and a *bona fide* nonconformist (he was a Lamarckian biologist at a time when a crude variety of Darwinism came to be enthroned as orthodoxy), wrote of Mandelstam with unmistakable affection and equally unmistakable superiority:

He was particularly tempted, evidently, to be converted to the official ideology, to make peace with all the horrors it concealed and to join the ranks of active champions of the Great Ideas and of the Beautiful Socialist Future. But in these delusions he did not have the certainty of a fanatic. Anyone who became friendly and intimate with him knew how uncompromising he was in anything that concerned art and morality. I have no doubt that, should we have diverged sharply in one of those areas, our friendship would have become impossible. Whenever he was in for the next round of his orthodox chirping – which would provoke me to tempests of indignation – he would not mount a polemic, would not defend his positions heatedly, but only pleaded with me to agree: 'Come, Boris Sergeyevich, it really is good, isn't it?' And a day or two later: 'Could I really have said that? Nonsense, dog's ravings!'

Sometimes, then, Mandelstam was a 'nonconformist' (the prophylactic quotation marks cordoning off, provisionally, the complexities of defining nonconformity), and sometimes he wasn't. Kuzin's bemusement is rooted in a certain set of principles. Kuzin was a man of principles and intelligence, but he was not prepared to see in Mandelstam's oscillations a commitment to a higher-order principle – namely, the requirement of speculative impartiality with regard to ideas, including ideas about social order.

What substantiates this intuition is the neo-Kantian element into which Mandelstam was plunged during his year of intensive philosophical study at Heidelberg, under the tutelage of the neo-Kantians Wilhelm Windelband and Emil Lask (continuing his philosophical studies later, in St. Petersburg, under Ivan Lapshin). Windelband's intellectual temperament is noted by Frederick Beiser:

> Any expositor of Windelband's philosophy faces special difficulties. Not the least of these is Windelband's frequent changes in position. His thinking was intentionally experimental, leading him to propose and explore ideas which he would later abandon or retract.

This profligacy is seen as valuable: we understand that philosophical creativity is concerned primarily with generating conceptual possibilia, and that to insist on 'commitment', as against a detached and provisional attitude, would be inimical to such speculative fecundity. (Commitment may arise spontaneously in the course of philosophical speculation; what cannot, should not happen is that such a commitment be legislated, expected.) What could be, then, the grounds for repudiating the same kind of speculative attitude in a poet?

It happens to be the case that Russian poets in particular have been collectively held up as the culture's moral compass in the political 'here and now', the fixedness of a 'compass' trailing further metaphors, as exemplified by the following passage from Darra Goldstein's monograph on *Nikolai Zabolotsky*:

> The lives of Russian poets are like the lives of saints, legendary but unenviable. Too many gifted voices have been silenced; too many altered through censorship, criticism, and imprisonment. Faced with this historical injustice, scholars have set out to resurrect work which might otherwise have been lost, and now a number of poets have a broader readership than they enjoyed in their lifetimes. Some have been hailed as martyrs, others cast as prophets.

The appeal to the world of faith – of saints, martyrs and prophets – has been the standard rhetoric of 'witness literature' commemorating chiefly the twentieth-century European experience, and in a way that was most flatteringly advantageous, at the time of its emergence in the English-speaking countries, to those countries' ideologies in opposition to the Soviet threat in the Cold War. Russian poetry itself – its finest and most revered poet, Alexander Pushkin – supplied the precedent for bringing poets, prophets, the word of God, individual liberty and resistance to autocracy in potent rhetorical alignment. Dimitri Obolensky's *Penguin Book of Russian Verse*, published in 1962, contained a prose translation of Pushkin's mysterious poem 'The Prophet':

> Tormented by spiritual thirst I dragged myself through a sombre desert. And a six-winged seraph appeared to me at the crossing of the ways. He touched my eyes with fingers as light as a dream: and my prophetic eyes opened like those of a frightened eagle. He touched my ears and they were filled with noise and ringing: and I heard the shuddering of heavens, and the flight of the angels in the heights, and the movement of the beasts of the sea under its waters, and the sound of the vine growing in the valley. He bent down to my mouth and tore out my tongue, sinful, deceitful, and given to idle talk; and with his right hand steeped in blood he inserted the forked tongue of a serpent into my benumbed mouth. He clove my breast with a sword, and plucked out my quivering heart, and thrust a coal of live fire into my gaping breast. Like a corpse I lay in the desert. And the voice of God called out to me:

'Arise, O prophet, see and hear, be filled with My will, go forth over land and sea, and set the hearts of men on fire with your Word.'

The 'prophet' whose experience is dramatized by the poem is given direct knowledge of things in themselves: not only of 'the shuddering of heavens' and 'the flight of the angels in the heights', but also of 'the movement of the beasts of the sea', 'the sound of the vine growing'. This unmediated knowledge is the prophet's source of absolute certainty and conviction; as a fantasy of escape from uncertainty and doubt, an escape felt to be necessary for poetic speech, it is deeply consonant with Mandelstam's own insistence that 'poetry is a deep knowledge of being in the right'. Yet Mandelstam's words come from no other place than his essay 'On the Interlocutor' – an essay fervently defending the principle of attentive respect for other minds as a prerequisite for poetry, where 'being in the right' is stringently balanced by an eager, fraternal alertness to one's respondent, to the prospect of the 'not-I' revealing some other, wholly unforeseen because wholly individual, wholly other way of 'being in the right'. It is on the grounds of Balmont's 'forfeiture' of the respondent that Mandelstam rejects his poetry, on whose scales 'the side of the "I" has decisively and unjustly outweighed the side of the "not-I", which has proven to be too light'. This allusion to Fichte's *Foundations of the Science of Knowledge*, where the interplay of the 'I' and the 'not-I' supplies the leitmotif of epistemic anxiety, alerts us once again to Mandelstam's own vigilance about the matter of knowing others through oneself and oneself through others.

If adopted as part of one's intellectual repertoire, scepticism concerning knowledge of things in themselves, which the neo-Kantians inherited from Kant's Critical philosophy, would generally temper one's readiness to defend a fixedly dogmatic position on questions of value. At Heidelberg, Windelband channelled the distinction between truth and validity introduced by his teacher, Herman Lotze, stressing thereby the value of entertaining ideas irrespective of their correspondence to the realm of the actual. In his *Logik*, writes Beiser, Lotze

> made a simple but seminal distinction between the realms of existence and truth. Whether or not a proposition is true or false, he argued, is completely independent

of whether it corresponds to something that exists. This discovery of a realm of validity or truth independent of existence – 'the most wonderful fact in the world', Lotze called it – proved intoxicating for a later generation.

While the 'Copernican revolution' inhibited one's confidence with regard to knowledge, the introduction of validity as a logically independent realm opened up previously unimagined vistas, paving the way for the development of competing theories of truth in the twentieth century, in some ways broadening the spectrum of operating definitions, in some ways limiting the domain of the properly knowable:

> The doctrine of validity of practical reason defines validity or value in terms of practical attitudes. Truth and validity is that to which we ought to give our assent; it is therefore an ought, a norm. But the idea of an ought or norm has ethical connotations, Lask argues, that strictly speaking do not belong in the realm of truth. Truth is fundamentally concerned with our theoretical attitudes, with what we know or must accept to be true. Norms or obligations, however, have an ethical connotation, because they are directed toward the will or our voluntary attitudes. Norms therefore hold for the practical realm, which concerns what we do, the realm of action.

Emil Lask had been a teacher of lasting importance to Mandelstam, and his death at the Galician front in 1915, months short of turning forty, appears to be linked with two poems of 1932. Pavel Nerler makes a similar conjecture in the *Mandelstam Encyclopedia* ('there are grounds for supposing that Lask's figure and his fate are reflected in the "Verses to German Prosody"'), yet admits to not possessing sufficient evidence to affirm Mandelstam's knowledge of Lask's fate in the war. Yet even without establishing the exact means by which Mandelstam might have learned of Lask's fate, the pertinent poems, 'To German Prosody' and 'Christian Kleist' (dedicated to Ewald Christian von Kleist, a poet and cavalry officer who died at the age of forty-four, while serving Frederick the Great), bring up reminiscences of Heidelberg. Rowan and ivy, mentioned in the poems of 1932, make their previous appearance in two poems of 1909 (uncollected in *Kamen* and *Tristia* but following one another in succession in the *Juvenilia* section of Alexander Mets's three-volume collected edition, with the lines 'When rowan in the spring develops / The leaves whose fate is to be dead' and 'The verdant ivy by the window'. It is striking, too, how consonant the two poems of 1932 are with the upright sense of obligation that led Lask to enlist, in spite of the fact that, as a professor, he would have been categorized as 'indispensable on the home front' and was not therefore obligated to volunteer. This biographical detail – together with Lask's substantial prophylactic efforts against relativism – underscores that the elaboration of accounts of truth and validity need not entail any lapse into moral relativism, nor do they rob us of a positive portrait of Mandelstam as a principled 'nonconformist'. The originality and independence of his thought (independence even of the approval of close friends like Kuzin, whose intellect Mandelstam respected and trusted) make him a nonconformist of a higher order.

At the same time, not exactly cutting it politically as a nonconformist does not automatically make one a *conformist*, and Boris Kuzin himself wrote (in defence of Mandelstam's conduct under interrogation in 1934). His clipped aphorism – 'not to be a hero is not the same thing as to be a scoundrel' – cautions against derisions that sometimes tempt journalists near the difficult cruxes of the poet's biography, like his testimony to the secret police about the identities of the friends to whom he had recited 'The Stalin Epigram'. (And recite it he did – though not publicly, as suggested by the publicity text of *Stolen Air*, but very much privately, secretly. These and other biographical details run against the grain of opportunistic 'late praise' – to foreshadow Geoffrey Hill's substantial criticisms of the attendant rhetoric). The facts of Mandelstam's biography, no less than his poems, urge caution and restraint with regard to our valuations. This does not mean that we should simply desist with our attempts at understanding and settle for the existing 'myth of Mandelstam the antagonist of Stalin and his regime', to which Mikhail Gasparov objected in *Mandelstam: Civic Poems of 1937*.

> This myth is tidy and vivid, but it oversimplifies the actuality. In 1933 Mandelstam wrote an epigram on Stalin, for which he did die in the end. Mandelstam also wrote, in 1937, an ode in honour of Stalin, which did not save him. A historian must be able to explain how these two works, two ways of thinking could coexist and succeed one another in Mandelstam's consciousness. The myth, on the other hand, only requires that one of these modes be proclaimed 'authentic' and another 'inauthentic' and therefore negligible. And, of course, to a contemporary of ours there can be no doubt that the 'authentic' Mandelstam is the Mandelstam of the epigram, and not of the ode.

This is partly a misunderstanding of the historian's role, since, if honest, she or he might have to admit to being quite unable 'to explain how these two works, two ways of thinking could coexist and succeed one another in Mandelstam's consciousness'. We may speculate, and shall attempt to do so responsibly. Still, what is fair to expect of a literary historian is a countenancing of the baffling facts of Mandelstam's political inconsistency (or apparent inconsistency) – a countenancing accompanied by a capacity for humane and imaginative reflection on the meaning of these perplexing facts. At eighty-two lines, the 'Ode' cannot be negligible to any consideration of Mandelstam's political persuasions, and yet, in venturing an assessment of the 'Ode' as part and parcel of all that we value in Mandelstam, we enter into a territory of considerable discord. The tradition of bracketing the 'Ode' as an aberration, extraneous to the proper body of Mandelstam's poetry, ascends to Nadezhda Mandelstam, who 'was by no means a passive shadow of her husband', writes Gasparov (responding implicitly to the rhetoric of the memoirist's posthumous reputation). *Au contraire*, she was

> an independent and very talented belletrist who wrote a book denouncing the Soviet totalitarian regime and its ideology. In this book, she deployed the fate and the words of her husband as the means of argumentation. When she was faced with facts contradicting her conception – first and foremost, with the 'Ode' – she represented them not exactly as false, but as the poet's coercion upon himself, and she had a gift for describing Mandelstam's heroic self-flagellation very convincingly.

From dissident literature, this line of interpretation penetrated into literary scholarship. While avoiding any unnecessary finger-pointing, Gasparov's 1996 study objected to assertions similar to Sergey Averintsev's, who had opined six years earlier:

> It is entirely obvious that Mandelstam – no matter how contradictory his perhaps by then not always 'sane' thoughts – had to do considerable violence to himself in his work on the 'Ode'.

It is, in fact, far from *obvious* how to come to grips with this slippery statement, qualified as it is by 'perhaps' and 'not always' and 'no matter', and hedged with equivocating quotation marks over 'sane'; the effect of all this is to coerce ascent where no sound evidence is presented, while the only alternative to 'self-coercion' is, supposedly, that the poet was not – perhaps – always – entirely – 'sane', whatever that means. Eight years later, Averintsev would write that poets like Pushkin and Mandelstam 'must be accepted – not without bewilderment, but compliantly – at once, in full measure, and on their own terms' – yet this statement was not accompanied by any revision of his prior opinion of the 'Ode'. The poem remained too bewildering, too inconvenient for a certain kind of liberal intolerance. It is against this inability to give due consideration to a poem representing a foreign viewpoint that Gasparov presses, pointing out a much more generously tolerant disposition in Mandelstam himself, who 'called himself an heir to the *raznochintsy* and never put himself in opposition to the people'. 'The heritage of the *raznochintsy*', Gasparov explains, referring to the mixed-estate political force that fomented reform and revolution in the nineteenth century, 'did not permit Mandelstam to think that everyone was out of step, whilst he alone wasn't'. Quite just, this observation, and generalizable, too, on the grounds of what it means to be a sane individual in the context of family and society in W. R. D. Fairbairn's psychoanalytic intuition:

> it is better to be a sinner in a world ruled by God than to live in a world ruled by the Devil. A sinner in a world ruled by God may be bad; but there is always a certain sense of security to be derived from the fact that the world around is good – 'God's in his heaven – All's right with the world!'; and in any case there is always a hope of redemption. In a world ruled by the Devil the individual may escape the badness of being a sinner; but he is bad because the world around him is bad. Further, he can have no sense of security and no hope of redemption. The only prospect is one of death and destruction.

Every person who finds himself radically at odds with the majority of his peers must confront the question of who is in the right – himself *or* everyone else. Apart from the intuitive sense that the majority would weigh more in the balance, Fairbairn's statement of the dilemma makes it clear that any substantial dissent from the accepted norm threatens the individual's sense of belonging and security within the social system. In Fairbairn's pragmatic analysis, to realize that one is actually right, but surrounded by people who are in the wrong, because either mad or bad, would result in irredeemable hopelessness, since one generally cannot change the entire society to suit oneself; on the other hand, should one imagine oneself in the wrong in a society that is generally alright, this would allow for the possibility of making amends. Given this immense pressure to surrender one's difference of opinion, maintaining a position of cardinal dissent requires extraordinary conviction and fortitude. Apart from its disadvantages, this inequality of individual and collective serves the benign purpose of maintaining social coherence, where an individual's sanity is defined as congruence with the social group. The young Mandelstam's essay 'On the Interlocutor' conveys a similar view of the Self's relations with Others as a balance with a tendency to correct towards sanity. 'Tell me', he writes,

> what makes on you the most sinister impression of madness when you encounter a madman? The dilated pupils – because they do not see, are not directed at anything in particular, appear empty. The mad speech – because a madman does not acknowledge you and your existence, does not want to recognise it, is absolutely uninterested in you. We are afraid in the madman chiefly of that terrible, absolute indifference that he shows us. There is nothing more frightening to a human being than another human who is completely indifferent to him. There is profound meaning in the cultural pretences, in the politeness with which we underscore our interest towards one another every single minute.

This position of alert interest in other minds and concern with social coherence as intimately related to art, its meaning and value, is curiously at one with what the Soviet dissident Andrey Sinyavsky declared in his 1985 essay 'Dissidence as a Personal Experience':

> all real literature in modern history is, as a rule, a deviation from the rules of 'good taste'. It is the nature of literature to be heretical (in the broad sense) in relation to the prevailing view of things. Every writer is a heretical element within the society of people who think alike or, in any case, in concert. Every writer is a pariah, a bastard, a not completely legitimate person on earth. For he thinks and writes against the majority opinion, or, at the very least, against established style and direction of literature.

Mandelstam is at one with Sinyavsky in differing from him, as the two writer's positions are deviations from a shared platform of concern for the writer's social context, concern for the relation of literature to 'the prevailing view of things', for the degree to which it coheres or not with the existing body of thought and feeling realized through language – the body that T. S. Eliot called the tradition. In the context of the tradition that obtains, the signal characteristic of any original contribution is, for Sinyavsky, its deviation from its precedents, its otherness in relation to what has come before. The etymological meaning of *inakomysliye*, the Russian noun used by Sinyavsky and translated here as 'heresy', is *otherthink*. What I have translated as 'heresy' has been historically rendered as 'nonconformity'. The same noun could be pertinently rendered as 'dissent', particularly in the context of Sinyavsky's seminal dissent at the centre of the Soviet dissident movement. What all these renditions imply is difference arrived at as if by splitting from a prior position that is being modified or abandoned: as the words 'orthodoxy' and 'heterodoxy' share a root (the Greek *doxa* approximately equivalent to 'opinion'), so do the bodies of thought these words represent, and it would not be just to consign all heterodoxy to the business of *opposing* whatever orthodox position it may stem from. *Emancipation* is a no less plausible *raison d'être* for dissent, and may consist partly in liberation from the imperative to oppose, that is, to be defined (as a dependent variable is defined) by that which one seeks to resist. Sinyavsky himself resisted being characterized as an 'anti-Soviet' writer, denying such allegations in court during the Sinyavsky-Daniel process of 1965–66 and insisting, with good cause, that his writing was characterized not by *opposition to* but by *independence from* the official ideology. Nevertheless, it is this sense of reaction against the pressures mounted by the official ideology and institutions that predominates in Sinyavsky's and his contemporaries' accounts of literature's aims. Having traversed the Iron Curtain, this weary sensibility was eagerly embraced in England and especially in America, against a political backdrop defined by the opposition of the superpowers, so that poetry newly translated from the Russian (as well as Polish and other languages of the Soviet Block) was welcomed in the role of an unheralded political ally.

Although this sense of literary priorities was partly reflected in and partly engendered by the writings of Nadezhda Mandelstam, a key witness of her husband's plight under Stalin, Mandelstam's own critical writings testify to a wholly different worldview. In a letter to Tynyanov, Mandelstam wrote:

> It has been a quarter of a century of my looming before Russian poetry; but soon my poems will merge with and dissolve in it, changing something in its structure and contents.

Here Mandelstam, once a listener to Bergson's lectures at the Collège de France and familiar, then, with the Bergsonian conception of the inherence of the past in the present, shares a viewpoint with another of Bergson's students, T. S. Eliot, who wrote in 1919, in 'Tradition and the Individual Talent', of the inherence of the past in the present (a Bergsonian notion) with respect to the literary tradition:

> The existing monuments form an ideal order among themselves, which is modified by the introduction of the new (the really new) work of art among them. The existing order is complete before the new work arrives; for order to persist after the supervention of novelty, the *whole* existing order must be, if ever so slightly, altered; and so the relations, proportions, values of each work of art toward the whole are readjusted; and this is conformity between the old and the new. Whoever has approved this idea of order, of the form of European, of English literature will not find it preposterous that the past should be altered by the present as much as the present is directed by the past. And the poet who is aware of this will be aware of great difficulties and responsibilities.

As to the novelty of the individual artist, Eliot's understanding of what constitutes 'the really new' is markedly different from Sinyavsky's, since for Eliot a new writer no more writes 'against established style and direction of literature' than a tributary runs against the river it joins, merges with, and dissolves in.

> We dwell with satisfaction upon the poet's difference from his predecessors, especially his immediate predecessors; we endeavour to find something that can be isolated in order to be enjoyed. Whereas if we approach a poet without this prejudice we shall often find that not only the best, but the most individual parts of his work may be those in which the dead poets, his ancestors, assert their immortality most vigorously. And I do not mean the impressionable period of adolescence, but the period of full maturity.

What is this 'tradition', which Eliot cautions us not to confuse with *traditionalism*?

> It involves, in the first place, the historical sense, which we may call nearly indispensable to anyone who would continue to be a poet beyond his twenty-fifth year;

and the historical sense involves a perception, not only of the pastness of the past, but of its presence; the historical sense compels a man to write not merely with his own generation in his bones, but with a feeling that the whole of the literature of Europe from Homer and within it the whole of literature of his own country has a simultaneous existence and composes a simultaneous order. This historical sense, which is a sense of the timeless as well as of the temporal and of the timeless and the temporal together, is what makes a writer traditional. And it is at the same time what makes a writer most acutely conscious of his place in time, of his own contemporaneity.

Bergson compared temporal development to the movement of the tape between the spools on a tape recorder, the tape shifting from the bobbin labelled 'the future' to the one labelled 'the past' whilst its total length remains constant. In adopting and adapting a Bergsonian view of time, Eliot echoes Mandelstam's sense of his place in 'the whole of literature of his own country': 'my poems will merge with and dissolve in it, changing something in its structure and contents'. Bergson's mind, other minds and 'other minds' (in the literary-historic sense) are constantly present to Mandelstam. He concludes his note to Tynyanov: 'It would be easy not to answer me. To supply grounds for abstaining from a letter or a note would be impossible.' Here, again, a philosopher is implicitly invoked – it is Kant himself, his distinction of *quid facti?* and *quid juris?* discussed by Windelband in the Heidelberg lectures. The scepticism about knowledge, contrasting with validity of belief, which the distinction suggests, had become constitutive of Mandelstam's innermost principles, precluding 'any irritable reaching after fact & reason' and inviting a significant tempering of attachment to one's 'personal opinion' at the expense of all others.

Given all this – the shape of the dissenter's dilemma as observed by Fairbairn, the heritage of shared and diffused ferment in the minds of many that characterized the tradition of *raznochintsy*, pointed out by Gasparov, and Mandelstam's evident sense of respect for other minds witnessed by his reflections 'On the Interlocutor' and elsewhere – it is not all that surprising that Mandelstam's 'key poems of the final years' are 'poems of accepting Soviet actuality', perhaps not rationally but only on faith. 'At the beginning of this sequence', writes Gasparov, stand

> the programmatic 'Stanzas' of 1935 and adjacent poems; in the middle is the 'Ode'; in the end are adoring verses to 'Stalinka' E. Popova, wife to the actor Yakhontov.

Among these, there are powerful poems – such as the 'Ode', judged by J. Brodsky to be a work of genius; there are also weak ones, such as the poem to Popova; but to think all of them insincere and written in spite of oneself is simply impossible. The tragedy of Mandelstam's fate is not weakened by this but made all the more resonant: when a man is being killed by enemies, it is frightening, and all the more so when he is being killed by those whom he senses as friends. The sense of tragedy pervades these late, accepting poems of Mandelstam – because of it they are so complex and deep and so unlike the official Soviet poetry. But they never take the position of opposing it.

Yet in taking this position, Mikhail Gasparov found himself in the situation of a saint in a world ruled by the Devil, as a dissenting voice amidst the majority of 'Mandelstamologists' whose predominant disposition made it impossible for Gasparov to articulate his views fully in public. At a London conference, writes Andrew Kahn in his survey article, 'Canonical Mandelstam', Gasparov found himself demurring to the sense of impending scandal, by deferring a full statement of his views to the fullness of time. So the adherents of the myth of Mandelstam-the-silenced-dissenter silenced a dissenter in their own midst, without any embarrassment about the contradiction.

The consternation caused by Mandelstam's 'Ode' to Stalin is not without precedent. A century earlier, a similar sense of liberal alarum attended Nikolay Nekrasov's composition of an ode to Muravyov, the suppressor of the Polish rebellion who was subsequently made Poland's absolute dictator by the Czar, against a backdrop of nationalist feeling that spread through Russia, engendering Muravyov's astounding popularity. This startling defection of the staunchly progressive poet to the side of autocracy puzzled Korney Chukovsky, who attempted to solve the question of Nekrasov's motives in his 1922 essay, 'The Poet and the Hangman'. Chukovsky prefigures his analysis with an account of the atmosphere of patriotic excitement in the wake of the rebellion.

> The intervention of the European powers on the side of the Poles did much to further the development and reinforcement of that feeling. The hostility toward the European powers, which took firm footing in the philistine civil-service and military circles of the time, strengthened the so-called ultra-Russian party of the Moscow-Slavophile ilk, which included such people as Metropolitan Filaret, Pogodin, Tyutchev, Leontiev and Katkov. Toward the end of 1863 Muravyov became its idol. It saw in him a Russian *vityaz*, a Russian *bogatyr*, a fearless fighter for a unified autocratic Russia, a brilliant

advocate of the Russian national idea, the man who had made Poland a bulwark of the Russian principles of state, Russia's savior from the machinations of cunning Europe, which dreamed of exploiting the Polish rebellion for the humiliation of the Russian land. 'Muravyov is a fine chap!' wrote the Slavophile Pogodin in 1863. 'He's hanging and shooting them left and right. May God grant him health!'

But not just his party, all of Russia, with the exception of a small number of intellectual circles, hailed Muravyov as its savior. A 'patriotic syphilis', in Herzen's term, gradually seeped into all the juices and fibers of Russian society, and since precisely at this time the Moscow tavern vogue for after-dinner speeches, congratulatory telegrams and deputations was coming into being, Muravyov had no more begun his struggle with polonism when he was showered with such an enormous number of speeches, dispatches, addresses, deputations, prayer services, gala receptions, deafening shouts of hurrah, ringing of bells, bouquets, garlands, monograms, flags, plates, albums, congratulatory letters, ikons (especially ikons: without end, large and small, gold and silver), that in the end these daily homages became a necessity for him.

Nekrasov, too, was moved to present Muravyov with an ode at a highly publicized dinner. The liberal papers responded with indignation and ridicule, calling Nekrasov 'a liveried doorman', 'an after-dinner singer' and, finally, 'a hireling slave'. Herzen's feuilleton in *Kolokol* (*'The Bell'*) egged him on sarcastically: 'Bravo, Nekrasov, bravo! We must admit that we didn't expect this from you, but still you are aware of how intimately we know your biography and how much we could have expected. Bravo, Nekrasov, bravo!' Herzen found satisfaction in showing that the 'surprise performance' was not that surprising after all, given Nekrasov's reputation for 'duality'. Chukovsky illustrated anecdotally what this meant:

> Someone is walking down Nevsky, for example, and sees a carriage with nails protruding, points up, from the rear footboard. The purpose of the nails is to deter small boys from rides. Seeing the nails, the pedestrian recalls one of Nekrasov's poems:
>
> > Don't put in your carriage sharp nails
> > To pierce the small boys who jump on.
>
> And suddenly, glancing aside, he notices to his amazement that none other than Nekrasov himself is seated in the carriage with the nails and that the carriage is Nekrasov's own, which means that Nekrasov on the one hand pounded nails into his floorboard, while on the other humanely expressing his sympathy for the children who might become impaled on them.

Nekrasov's duplicity, wrote Chukovsky, 'is confirmed by a multitude of facts, and if one is disproved, dozens of others will crop up to take its place', culminating in the jarring dissonance: 'A poet – and at the same time a speculator. A poet – and at the same time a wheeler and dealer. In his poems a proletarian, but in reality a magnate. He advocates feats of heroism, but he himself appropriates other people's estates!' Yet Nekrasov's paean to Muravyov sealed his reputation as a traitor to the liberal-reformist cause; the general feeling was that 'it would have been less base of Nekrasov to build a gallows for us at his own cost'. Chukovsky recounted this opprobrium, concluding resolutely: 'This is such a gross betrayal of his convictions that it seems both incomprehensible and unpardonable.' And yet, this judgement was followed immediately by a reversal no less intriguing than Nekrasov's behaviour itself: 'But it is curious', wrote Chukovsky,

> this betrayal seems such a great crime only when we scrutinize it outside of the context of the public life of the time, artificially divorcing it from the totality of social and historical phenomena. On the other hand, if one relates the whole affair as it occurred then, without isolating Nekrasov from his epoch and his environment, he immediately appears justified, if not completely, then in part. Not a single prosecutor in all of Russian society would dare accuse him, for the Russian society of the time was just as guilty as he.

Chukovsky, astoundingly agile and politic in his own relations with his time, excuses Nekrasov on the grounds of conformity, viewed as a characteristic of a sane person, a person congruent with his own time and with the society of his contemporaries. Nevertheless, the effect of this *volte-face* is to abort the investigation and to dismiss the case opened so pointedly. This is no less baffling than Nekrasov's behaviour itself, yet one senses that Chukovsky's difficulty, in countenancing the very problem that interested him, has to do with the 'patriotic syphilis' and its relation to healthy, commonsensical conformity. Chukovsky's conflict with his time and with himself plays out on this study of Nekrasov just as it does in his diaries, in which, decade after decade, Chukovsky lives while his friends die.

> An all too familiar Russian picture: talent smothered and killed. Polezhaev, Nikolai Polevoy, Ryleev, Mikhail Mikhailov, Yesenin, Mandelstam, Stenich, Babel, Mirsky,

Tsvetaeva, Mitya Bronshtein, Kvitko, Bruno Yasensky – crushed by the same boot one and all.

Written five years after Stalin's death, these words still denote Stalin cautiously, almost superstitiously, by that singular 'boot'; in later years, the word 'system' will replace the euphemistic but personal 'boot', and again the unnamed and depersonalized 'system' shall be cast in opposition to its victims, individuals invoked by name only to be placed in a submissive relation to impersonal state power, as signalled by the passive voice – 'talent smothered and killed', 'crushed by the same boot one and all', 'the intelligentsia was hit particularly hard' – the killing 'system', on the other hand, appearing to be resolutely active, the only *bona fide* agent in the relationship between the state and its subjects, the latter reduced to the role of pure objects of power. The same rhetoric of one-sided power has, since Chukovsky's time, permeated the efforts to memorialize victims of Stalin's regime in the post-Soviet space. It is difficult to object to, the state having exercised truly inordinate power, but it precludes the responsible imagining of the individual experience of these 'victims' when construed as victims only, passive objects of power and no more.

Hence a certain imaginative helplessness amongst the interpreters of Mandelstam's relations with Soviet 'actuality', at the crux of which the Stalin 'Ode' is particularly resistant to being viewed as written by an 'innocent victim'. On the contrary, this poem is staunchly indicative of some kind of active and deliberate dialogue with power, yet this is the possibility that the rhetoric of innocent victimhood does not allow. Symptomatically, Sergey Averintsev was able to interpret the 'Ode' in terms of but two possibilities, attributing it either to Mandelstam's crumbling under pressure and losing his sanity and poetic integrity, or to his acquiescence to coercive necessity and writing against his own convictions. The possibility excluded from this dilemma is that of the poet's active, independent and responsible position with respect to the Soviet state, marked not by submission but by a generous readiness to entertain, in his conflict with the state, the viewpoint of the state itself, conceived as an opponent who must be treated fairly and respectfully, must be granted a proper hearing, must even be assisted by Mandelstam himself in articulating a defence of its authoritarian practices. The intimation from which this monograph proceeds is that, in Voronezh, Mandelstam resolved to look at his Soviet surroundings with the unprejudiced eyes of a European, a foreigner who is neither beholden nor *a priori* hostile to what he observes as he makes his way through the estranged reality of Soviet Russia, much as Dante made his way through the Inferno, marvelling at what he saw and attempting to enter the reasoning behind the torments he witnessed. One of the critical points advanced here is that, far from compromising Mandelstam's integrity, his capacity for disinterested and responsible imaginative engagement with Soviet ideas and ideals, even when at the mercy of the state, is part and parcel of what makes him a poet of capacious vision, philosophical significance and unmistakable genius. If Mikhail Gasparov's observation concerning Mandelstam's 'movement towards Soviet contemporaneity' were true, it would also be true that within it 'we find no self-compromising nor self-coercion'; 'what we find instead is the difficult and elaborate logic of poetic thought'.

This 'difficult and elaborate logic' and its antinomies – not only in 'poetic thought', but also in the language of biography and criticism – is the subject of the present study, a subject that must be explored in cognizance of the limitations of conceptual description in relation to the *hiatus irrationalis* (the chasm of private and inscrutable lived experience), yet by conceptual means nevertheless, since only concepts, understood as relational structures, supply us with a sense of the priority of some elements of experience over others where exhaustive evidence is unavailable. While analysis along conceptual key lines cannot be traded for full description, decisions can be made about the applicability of certain concepts, about which ones are better in a particular case, and which ones not so good. There are, of course, the reliably applicable universals, as noted by William Empson in a note to his poem 'Bacchus':

> The notion is that life involves maintaining oneself between contradictions that can't be solved by analysis, e.g. those of philosophy, which apply to all creatures, and the religious one about man being both animal and divine.

The present book can be said to be an essay both *on* and *in* the art of 'maintaining oneself between contradictions that can't be solved by analysis', the implicit belief being that to bring to light the central contradiction of a complex situation – the contradiction that curtails analysis – is to uncover something without which our understanding of that situation could not be complete, as our understanding of the human condition could not be complete without the recognition crystallized by Empson:

> Twixt devil and deep sea, man hacks his caves;
> Birth, death; one, many; what is true, and seems;
> Earth's vast hot iron, cold space's empty waves:
>
> King spider, walks the velvet roof of streams:
> Must bird and fish, must god and beast avoid:
> Dance, like nine angels on pinpoint extremes.

Similarly, our comprehension of Coleridge's madness is made more humanely embracing by Empson's conceptualization in '*The Ancient Mariner*': 'Psychologists tell me that they do not recognise the term "neurotic guilt", which I have long heard used as of a familiar reality'; and yet –

> There was nothing mad about Coleridge except a peculiarly severe conflict of this kind; he could not bear to rebuff the fundamental sympathies of his society and yet found that accepting the theology in which they were expressed, when he was beaten down to it, was a kind of suicide.

There was nothing mad about Mandelstam, one might echo, 'except a peculiarly severe conflict of this kind': the conflict between the 'I' and the 'not-I', between the One and the Many – a metaphysical conflict, one of 'those of philosophy, which apply to all creatures', the conflict conceptualized by Fairbairn in the words of his maxim: 'It is better to be a sinner in a world ruled by God than to live in a world ruled by the Devil.' It is better to believe that one is mad and wrong than to believe oneself right and sane but surrounded on all sides by madness.

Perhaps fittingly to its theme intent on paradoxes, this book seeks to localize and concretize the real suffering evident in Mandelstam's plight under Stalin in order to remedy the overemphasis, in the critical estimation of his art, on 'suffering' in the generalized and sing-song sense in which 'suffering' becomes 'cant', to borrow a word from Geoffrey Hill. The end of revisiting a poet's biography is taken to be the 'diversion of interest from the poet to the poetry', in a way that 'would conduce to a juster estimation of actual poetry, good and bad', as T. S. Eliot wrote in 'Tradition and the Individual Talent', reflecting in the same essay:

> There are many people who appreciate the expression of sincere emotion in verse, and there is a smaller number of people who can appreciate technical excellence. But very few know when there is expression of *significant* emotion, emotion which has its life in the poem and not in the history of the poet. The emotion of art is impersonal.

To Eliot, the impersonality of high art was a result of arduous sublimation very much dependent on the raw material of the poet's inward experience, on lived biography. This sets up a perhaps curious notion of literary biography – that in itself being a study of fragility and frailty – as an inroad to the impersonal and the artistically enduring. The goal, then, is to show that Mandelstam is a better poet than we had thought, for better reasons than we had previously imagined.

In 1978, Henry Gifford, a sensitive appreciator of the Russian poets who were then being discovered by the West, expressed both curiosity and reservation about Anna Akhmatova's comparison of Mandelstam with Keats, writing in his essay 'Mandelstam Whole':

> Anna Akhmatova once said that Mandelstam reminded her 'almost physiologically' of Keats. She must have been referring to his sensibility, which is rich and alert in a Keatsian way. There are other parallels. He too 'touched the beautiful mythology of Greece' without dulling its brightness. He also resembles Keats in a sure knowledge of his own powers, and in the generosity and acumen with which he could assess the powers of others. Comparisons like this are never more than approximate, and may mislead as much as they help. But Mandelstam, with his 'flint and iron', and his eager curiosity, and that quiet confidence in his own art and in the importance of poetry, stands as near to Keats as to any other English poet.

But perhaps an even more pertinent point of similarity between Mandelstam and Keats is the one given by Keats himself, in the letter that supplied the epigraph to this prologue. It lies in the quality by which Keats recognized 'a man of achievement': the capacity to remain 'in uncertainties, Mysteries, doubts, without any irritable reaching after fact & reason'. In this 'Negative Capability' we can recognise Mandelstam, too – and value anew his sceptical poetic gift.

CHAPTER I

'The Stalin Epigram' and the Liberty of Protest

> best if no light had shone
> on my creations! And just as your eloquence had been aided
> by serious arts, so an Art of another kind
> hurt me. But my life's well known to you – the author's
> own morals had no truck with these 'arts'
> Ovid, *Tristia*, Book I

The state of settled opinion, in the English letters, about Mandelstam and the significance of his epigram on Stalin, is reflected in the critical piece published in the *New York Review of Books* by José Manuel Prieto. We should thank Prieto for bringing together, in such compactly quotable form, so many errors of fact, interpretation and valuation that we can survey the whole territory of common half-truths by hovering over the briefest of passages:

> Curiously, the poem's two final lines did not satisfy Mandelstam at all. It is astonishing that a fact as remote from politics as the verbal perfection of these final lines could occupy his mind during the suicidal sessions during which he recited the poem aloud, but people remember him saying: 'I should get rid of these lines, they're no good. They sound like Tsvetaeva to me.' But there was no time for that, and the lines remained in the minds of those who heard the poem. Many years later when Vitaly Shentalinsky discovered the manuscript of the 'Epigram Against Stalin' in the KGB archives, he found no variation at all from the samizdat version that had circulated across the USSR. The poem had etched itself faithfully in the memories of those who heard it recited in the distant year of 1934.

Prieto (his translator, of course, choosing the exact words) is 'astonished' that Mandelstam should concern himself with poetry above politics. The supposition that his motives *should* be primarily political is crudely incognizant of the disinterestedness of literature, which is fundamentally at odds with politics as based always, and normatively, in interest and representation. To expect that Mandelstam's poetry, even his overtly political poetry, should be harnessed into political ends, is to put the cart before – or above – the horse. What one does feel astonished by is the mention of what Prieto calls 'suicidal sessions', implicitly attributing to Mandelstam a kind of dementedly determined suicidality that reflects none of Mandelstam's real tragedy, and which Prieto does not take any trouble to explain. Prieto does not seem to understand that in attributing to Mandelstam this suicidality he attributes to him a murderousness, and with respect to his closest intimates no less, for to disseminate the poem was to implicate every witness in the crime of complicity. There were, as we shall see, no such 'sessions', no such deliberate self-destruction and destruction of others. There was hesitation, and impulsiveness. And there was time – time enough even for more poetry before Mandelstam's arrest in May 1934. There were variants in the poem, and divergences between the text recorded in Mandelstam's interrogation protocols and what had been published in the early editions, prior to their discovery – but not in 'KGB archives', as Prieto imagines, since the KGB was but one of the Soviet secret-police structures, albeit the only one commonly known in the West.

What would be, then, a truer narrative concerning 'The Stalin Epigram' and its coming into being? The tragedy of Mandelstam's impulsively suicidal composition was that it erupted as a response to insistent provocations from the outside. It would be wrong to think of this poem as a staunch and principled expression of protest by a comfortable man. It should be understood as an expression of the self-respect and liberty of a person faced with oppression, but when we say that Mandelstam was 'faced with oppression', we mean a concrete situation – that he was pinned to the wall by his oppressive circumstances – namely, joblessness and *de facto* homelessness – before he came out with the poem. The paradox of 'The Stalin Epigram' is that, as much as a manifestation of liberty and personal principle, the poem was also a forced measure, which accrued a personal cost that Mandelstam, a sane person, never would have invited upon himself voluntarily – costs that should not be chalked up to the kind of infantile extremism which Prieto seems so happy to attribute to Mandelstam.

To understand the meaning and the *raison d'être* of 'The Stalin Epigram', we need to engage with its impulse and its impulsivity. The argument is simply that *impulse is not irrational*, even though it might be incalculable. Impulsiveness arises when circumstances and available knowledge will not 'compute' – will not indicate a calculable, reasonable, 'rational' course of action; yet impulse itself should not be construed as counter-rational. A blind act, a shot in the dark: this is believed here to be the nature of Mandelstam's 'epigram', yet to substantiate this intuition is to follow a circuitous path, beginning with the implications of the poem's genre attribution.

Disputations about the genre to which 'The Stalin Epigram' might be attributable are prone to devolve into the intractable. What *is*, after all, an epigram? What is the *definition* of an 'epigram'? What is the definition of 'definition'? Is there a difference between *being* something and being *definable as* something? Was 'The Stalin Epigram' indeed an epigram, and if not, how or why did it acquire the title by which we frequently refer to the poem that received no title from Mandelstam himself? Genre definitions spring up, as do definitions of schools and movements, inductively, on the basis of perceived family resemblances. When setting out, for instance, to describe the nature of the Gothic, John Ruskin observed:

> The principal difficulty in doing this arises from the fact that every building of the Gothic period differs in some important respect from every other; and many include features which, if they occurred in other buildings, would not be considered Gothic at all; so that all we have to reason upon is merely . . . a greater or less degree of *Gothicness* in each building we examine.

> We have, then, the Gothic character submitted to our analysis, just as the rough material is submitted to that of the chemist, entangled with many other foreign substances, itself perhaps in no place pure, or ever to be obtained or seen in purity for more than an instant; but nevertheless a thing of definite and separate nature, however inextricable or confused in appearance. Now observe: the chemist defines his material by two separate kinds of character; one external, its crystalline form, hardness, lustre, etc.; the other internal, the proportions and nature of its constituent atoms. Exactly in the same manner, we shall find that Gothic architecture has external forms and internal elements. . . . And unless both the elements and the forms are there, we have no right to call the style Gothic. It is not enough that it has the Form, if it have not also the power and life. It is not enough that it has the Power, if it have not the form. We must therefore inquire into each of these characters successively;

and determine first, what is the Mental Expression, and secondly, what the Material Form of Gothic architecture, properly so called.

The historic examples that supply the grounds for a genre definition necessarily display characteristics that range past the bounds that the definition outlines on the basis of the most central and persistently observable traits. In other words, a genre definition will always be narrower than the genre itself, whose actual variety is enriched by the more peripheral examples that, whilst exhibiting some the key markers of the given genre, nevertheless show that the contours of the genre phenomenon are not sharp and hermetic but instead dissolve into the neighbouring genre territory. The definition is more liable to be excessively constricting when it unduly stresses the formal aspects of the phenomenon in question, at the expense of what Ruskin calls 'Mental Expression'. As it happens, in the learned analyses of 'The Stalin Epigram' that attempt to determine whether the poem could be attributed to the epigrammatic genre, the predominant focus has been on the formal characteristics of the poem, not on the question of the disposition it represents and whether that disposition could be said to be sufficiently epigrammatic in character. It appears best, then, to reopen the question of the poem's genre, and of the meaning of such a genre attribution, by considering not the poem's formal features but its 'Mental Expression' – that is, the character of the poem's animating impulse.

From this inwardly-oriented point of view, we might venture: 'An epigram is a brief poem written to provoke its subject.' This aspect of provocation, of deliberately causing unease (and not only, or not even primarily, to the poem's subject), appears to be the main, though rarely articulated reason, for Mandelstam's sixteen lines about Stalin having been permanently associated with the notion of an epigram and with their conventional title in English – in spite of scholarly protestations against this genre attribution. One sense that cannot be eliminated from the cluster of senses of 'epigram' is that an epigram comes into existence to provoke its subject, often by means of portraying what the subject himself has done to provoke *it* – this portrayal and satirical commentary being a form of objecting to a violation, of some degree, *against* the author of the epigram, a violation that supplies the spontaneous impulse whose force puts in question the writer's freedom in writing an epigram, similarly to the way in which, in societies where duels were the norm, one wasn't free *not* to challenge one's offender to a duel, and therefore the one who challenged was in actuality submitting to the tacit prior challenge implicit in the offensive behaviour necessitating the rescue of his honour.

To provoke is to exercise a measure of power. The consequences of a satire on Stalin were readily foreseeable. To provoke Stalin (a thing that just wasn't done) was to invite him to arrest and execute, through the mediation of the penal apparatus whose ways and processes were familiar to all in all their obscurity, the known and the unknown reinforcing the compound effect of terror, which Mandelstam named openly in the opening lines of his epigram on Stalin. And yet, to invite the wrath of the regime was to escape the very same mechanisms of terror, and to trigger the penal process was to exercise reversely directed control over a system in which control was supposed to be strictly one-way. To look ahead to the result of Mandelstam's provocation is to notice Stalin's resistance to being simply goaded into doing what he was expected to do: declining to execute the poet, he issued a paradoxical injunction – 'Isolate but preserve' – and the struggle continued. The small 'but' of Stalin's two-part order is an acknowledgment of the contradiction between 'isolating' any living entity and 'preserving' its life, for nothing can live in isolation. The word 'preserve', however, has a sinister tinge of abstracting what is being preserved from what once lived, the way animals can be 'preserved' by taxidermy and pressed flowers kept in an herbarium.

The advantage of this inward and functional approach to what constitutes an epigram is that it links this specific genre with motives supplied by biography – and in the detective line of work, motives are essential. While the formal boundaries of the genre are porous, the technical matter of genre attribution, if settled on formal grounds, would be unlikely to solve the psychological question of motive attendant upon the suicidal provocation. On the other hand, if we view 'The Stalin Epigram' primarily as such – as a suicidal provocation – we immediately gain recourse to instances of incisive analysis, such as Byron's, in *The Giaour*:

> The Mind, that broods o'er guilty woes,
>   Is like the Scorpion girt by fire;

> In circle narrowing it glows,
> The flames around their captive close,
> Till inly searched by thousand throes,
>   And maddening in her ire,
> One sad and sole relief she knows –
> The sting she nourished for her foes,
> Whose venom never yet was vain,
> Gives but one pang, and cures all pain,
> And darts into her desperate brain:
> So do the dark in soul expire,
> Or live like Scorpion girt by fire;
> So writhes the mind Remorse hath riven,
> Unfit for earth, undoomed for heaven,
> Darkness above, despair beneath,
> Around it flame, within it death!

Here is, then, a certain kind of success and self-affirmation: the suicidal success very much attributable to an epigram composed when 'girt by fire', put in untenable circumstances, at odds with one's surroundings and their demands. The presence of guilt ('The Mind, that broods o'er guilty woes') is fundamental to the ambivalence inherent in a genre so well-suited to self-incrimination, to heightening the conflict that occasions the epigram in the first place, and, by attacking its subject (a subject with lethal means at his disposal), courting retaliation against the author. It is, in other words, one of the inherent potentialities of the genre to respond to injury with an insult that supplies the pretext for a symbolic duel. That the European culture of the duel, with the ever-present possibility of a duel challenge, would not have had the effect of instilling a climate of wariness suggests that the insult supplying the motive for a challenge was in itself a covert challenge, a provocation. Along the same lines, the epigram that courts imminent wrath ameliorates thereby another sentiment to which Byron points as concomitant in the scorpion's progress towards suicide – the 'Remorse' that would otherwise partake in the deadlock against the 'ire', amounting to the paralysis of 'neurotic guilt', a condition in which Empson discerned a process, apropos Coleridge:

> Psychologists tell me that they do not recognise the term 'neurotic guilt', which I have long heard used as of a familiar reality. For example, Dylan Thomas, with the dead earnestness which so often came as a surprise, told me it was curious he was such

a martyr to attacks of neurotic guilt, as he led such an innocent life, but he found the only way to handle them was to hide in the country for a week or two, stopping drinking altogether, speaking to nobody, and so on. His meaning in using this term was clear; he felt struck down by guilt though by his own principles he had done no wrong; and it was easy to reflect that he had done wrong by the principles of the hostess of Fern Hill, his peasant aunt. A psychologist (as I understand) finds this trivial because it does not involve the mechanisms of the deep Unconscious, and indeed it is more like 'split personality' – one moral code goes on dragging against another. But it is the most prominent cause of mental upset among present-day educated people, and I think psychologists belittle it because they dislike admitting that there can be genuine rational disagreement about a moral question. There was nothing mad about Coleridge except a peculiarly severe conflict of this kind; he could not bear to rebuff the fundamental sympathies of his society and yet found that accepting the theology in which they were expressed, when he was beaten down to it, was a kind of suicide.

One way of escaping 'a kind of suicide' – a moral suicide, to which Mandelstam was 'beaten down' by the relentless scapegoating in the press, together with other pressures that compounded the sense of diminishment – was to commit an act that, while probably suicidal, would cause, nevertheless, considerable trouble to one's tormentors. Baratynsky's lines of the invincible epigram, the 'betaloned flyer' that cannot be stopped, waiting only for the right victim to cruelly sink its claws into his eyes, doubtlessly presented the genre to Mandelstam as the weapon of choice in his looming duel – a duel into which he was being forced.

The feature that makes the 'The Stalin Epigram' such a dubious exemplar of the epigram genre (and it is repeatedly argued, with reason, that the 'Epigram' is not at all an epigram) is its inaugural pronoun 'we' (the Russian *'my'*), which announces that the poem is about to speak not solely of a private predicament but *for the many*, and therefore with a gravity not usually associated with epigrams. In the context of the monolithic collectivism of Soviet art and of the enforced unanimity of all public expression, the significance of such an opening cannot be overestimated, as the poem runs entirely against the grain of the supposed concord amongst the Soviet *many*. Line by line, over the course of its sixteen lines, the poem proceeds to alienate itself from proletarian art as such, committing irreversibly to radical protest exceeding all standards of 'counter-revolutionary activity' attributed to the 'class enemy', with the consequences readily understandable to anyone who might have become acquainted with the text, as indeed a number of people soon were. While the opening of the poem inspires just qualifications of genre attribution, if not an outright disqualification of the poem as a specimen of the epigram genre, it is its ending, of a purely *ad hominem* nature, giddy with its childlike primitivism, that makes the most convincing bid for membership in the genre:

> Every death is as sweet as a berry,
> The Ossetian chest mighty and broad.

After reciting the poem to Emma Gerstein, a young friend of the Mandelstams, the poet exclaimed: 'No, this is a bad ending! It's got something Tsvetayevan about it. I am canceling it. It'll hold up fine without it.' He read the poem again, ending with the line that translates: 'One gets hit in the brow, one in the groin, one in the eyebrow, one in the eye!' (The sequence of words in these lines as remembered by Gerstein differs from the standard text, and the text that Mandelstam would produce for his interrogator, when under OGPU arrest, includes those final two lines.) Yet without the 'berry' (or 'raspberry', to follow the Russian original, '*malina*'), without that 'broad chest', 'The Stalin Epigram' would be even more loosely tethered to its purported genre than it already is. Endings have been of salience in the history of the epigrams. The *OED* leads with the definition of an epigram as 'a short poem leading up to and ending in a witty or ingenious turn of thought'. The Second Edition supplements the idea with a point taken from Topsell (*Serpents*, 1653): 'Some learned Writers .. have compared a Scorpion to an Epigram .. because as the sting of the Scorpion lyeth in the tayl, so the force and vertue of an Epigram is in the conclusion.' On the other hand, Geoffrey Grigson, the great collector of epigrams and editor of *The Faber Book of Epigrams and Epitaphs* (1977), objected to the narrowing of the genre's bounds along the lines of what the scorpion figure might suggest, insisting on a much greater variety among the instances of the genre:

> Sir Thomas Browne (who liked epigrams and epitaphs) wrote down in his commonplace book that the bones from the charnel house of St. Paul's – more than a

thousand cartloads of them – were transported to Finsbury Fields, 'and there layd in a moorish place, with so much soyle to cover them as raysed the ground for three windmills, which have since been built there'.

It was a proper subject, he thought, for an epigram: 'To make an epigramme or a few verses . . . of a windmill upon a mount of bones.'

There you have one idea of what an epigram should be: sententious and pointed – grinding food for the living on the bones of the dead – and unexpected, yet applicable to our general experience.

Epigrams no doubt made Sir Thomas Browne think of the Roman epigrammatist Martial. All educated men of Browne's century (or the 16th century, or the 18th, or the 19th) were familiar with Martial's epigrams, witty, hard, brutal, and indecently brutal, many of them. They all knew that an epigram wasn't necessarily short, though it inclined that way. Martial had sometimes written two lines, sometimes twenty. They would have known that poems of a different character were also epigrams, tender and light poems from the *Greek Anthology*. They would have expected both kinds from an English (or French or Italian) poet of any consequence. If Sir Thomas Browne had picked up *Hesperides* by his contemporary Robert Herrick, which came out only ten years before his *Urne-Buriall*, he would have found both derivatives from Martial (if rather crude and blunt in an unsuccessful way) and the derivatives from the gentler and subtler Greek epigrams; a mixture of what one Elizabethan writer (William Camden), in defining epigrams, described as 'short and sweete poems, framed to praise or dispraise'.

And so, not *just* 'dispraise'. 'Point, it can be claimed', goes on Grigson,

is what distinguishes and unites epigrams –

Epigrams must be curt, nor seem
Tail-pieces of a poet's dream. . .

To be curt is to be pointed, 'to the point'; and since poetry should always be to the point, as far as possible without superfluousness, that really is to say that a good epigram has simply to be a good poem.

Such is the necessary condition, but is it a sufficient one? Points, after all, of which the first requirement is to be clear (crystal-clear, loud and clear), are, crystal-clearly, not all there is to poetry. But in the instance of 'The Stalin Epigram', the point simply cannot be missed. The 'tail' of the poem, what it was intended to entail or trail in, in the form of subsequent events, reached long past its final lines. There is no better emblem for the poem's enfolding of the extra-poetic events and contexts than Byron's figure of the suicidal scorpion.

Mandelstam's epigram, as his most celebrated poem is usually referred to in English, was not a thing born suddenly whole, like Venus from the sea or like Athena from Zeus's head. Its abrupt emergence was prepared by a long and painful gestation witnessed by nearly all of Mandelstam's poems, prose and letters since the turn of 1930. It could not have been otherwise, for the poem's coming into being unleashed a cascade of irreversible consequences – a sequence spanning arrest, interrogations, an exile sentence and, most intimately, the irretrievable loss of Mandelstam's sense of security in his world. Recited to this and that acquaintance, sometimes deliberately, sometimes impulsively, but always mischievously, as if tempting fate, after a while the poem could not be contained and began to dart, sparrow-like, about Moscow. Not only was Mandelstam in no doubt whatsoever about its destructive potential, he revelled in it. Emma Gerstein, an early witness to the epigram, remembered being instructed to keep it an absolute secret: 'I'm warning you: not a soul! If this gets where it may, I'll be...' Gerstein's ellipsis signals a pause: for a moment, Mandelstam froze, contemplating the outcome before completing his thought, in Gerstein's capital letters: 'EXECUTED!' 'And, lifting his head with greater-than-usual pride, he returned to pacing about the room, rising up on his toes with every pivot.'

As body language, this 'rising up' to his full stature reads like Mandelstam's reaction against the indignities that blighted his existence during the opening of the 1930s, as his professional life and practical circumstances became increasingly and ominously untenable and as his writings filled with expressions of proportionate rancour and protest. Nevertheless, despite this continuous crescendo of anxiety and despair, the appearance of the 'Kremlin highlander' in the November satire of 1933 is quite unheralded by any prior utterance by Mandelstam, in poetry or in prose. This fact prevents any plausible reading of the poem as an expression of consistent, principled dissent against Stalin's government, and the feeling of the poem in regard to Stalin himself cannot be properly described as civic or public in nature – instead, the epigram rings with strikingly *ad hominem* rancour and resentment – 'his fingers are fat like worms', 'the broad chest of an Ossetian' – reinforcing the impression that the poem's object was, to borrow a phrase from Daniil Kharms, 'to light up trouble round oneself' – in other words, to provoke his subject very much personally, and thereby to break out of the untenable situation that Mandelstam could find no other way of resolving.

From Bergson, whose Parisian lectures he had attended as a young man, Mandelstam had inherited a sense of the centrality of an energetic impulse for the work of art it animates, contrasting such works with 'readymade things', the products of insipid scribbling, which is what Mandelstam in the 1930s was increasingly referring to, and disavowing, as 'writing'. Such transfer of 'conscientious, purple ink' from the inkwell to the page, he believed, makes no difference in the sphere of art. Impulse, on the other hand, is neither predetermined nor calculable, born within the feeling consciousness, its *hiatus irrationalis*, fertilized by all that enters it from without. Emil Lask's formulation of the indeterminate contents of the consciousness accounts for the mystery that imbues literary art as a manifestation of free will – conceived as an impulse emerging from the depths of the personality, in response to the fecundating impressions from without. It is because of the irreducible question of personality as the irrational mediator, between what is objectively given and the impulse that emerges in response, that the shape of that living impulse only becomes known as it manifests, and cannot be determined in advance, like the product of a syllogism. This realization was dear to Mandelstam, with the consequent respect for impulsiveness that he never attempted to suppress or conceal by rationalizing his actions. The futile endeavour to give 'Count Tolstoy' (Aleksey Tolstoy, nicknamed thus by the members of *FOSP*) a slap on the face; the invitation to Lev Gumilyov, 'let's do something *nasty*'; the much earlier, sudden, fateful decisiveness in coming to Kiev to marry Nadya Khazina: these and many other biographical instances become transparent and intelligible in the light of the principle of respect for the irrational impulse. Why, then, attempt to explain a poem as ambiguous and bewildering as 'The Stalin Epigram' as if it were a product of some 'conscientious, purple' syllogism: 'If

Stalin be a monster; If a writer's purpose be to speak truth to power; If I am a writer; *Then*...' Such an explanation, in actuality, makes 'The Stalin Epigram' appear not at all like the supreme act of freedom and courage it is purported to be, but like an action that might have been performed by a computer programmed with appropriate inputs. To restore to it the supreme independence of an impulse, born of conditions some of which are known and some of which cannot be known, would be to return the poem to the state of tremulous ambiguity which is undoubtedly its native element and therefore the starting place of analysis.

Among the first things one might notice about the so-called 'Stalin Epigram' is that its author did not supply it with a title; the title indeed *could not* have been anything as overt as 'The Stalin Epigram', because its effect depends partly on the reader's own recognition of the leader in the features itemized by the caricature. Given the transparency of the hint, however, the indirection seems puzzling, a profligate gesture; but this redundancy communicates the atmosphere of fear in which one dare mention even the obvious, and perhaps a certain Judaic reverence implicit in abstaining from taking the dreaded name in vain:

> We live without sensing the country beneath our feet,
> Our voices die down at ten paces away,
> And wherever there's even a half-conversation,
> The Kremlin highlander will be remembered.

This, like any other translation, is an attempt to secure specific gains by making corresponding concessions. The feeling of the first line depends on a phrase familiar to every Russian child raised on fairy tales where, at the appearance of Baba Yaga or some similar villain, the child in the story, say, Alyonushka, runs in such terror that she 'does not sense the ground beneath her feet'. That 'ground' in this unmistakably familiar figure has been replaced with 'country' signals that the relevant context is the civic one, and that the nature of the fear felt in the opening line is itself political. The appearance of 'ten paces' in line two is continuous with the sense of flight we glean in the preceding line. What heightens the effect of the opening two lines – the effect of the poem committing itself to every word of its text – is the anapaestic metre determined, in the accentual-syllabic conditions of Russian verse, by the stresses falling on the final syllable in each three-syllable cluster, every decisive fall of a stress prepared by two syllables felt to do the work of thinking twice before speaking (on the count *three*). To pay attention to the sound of the Russian lines is also to notice that every word, apart from service words like the prepositions '*pod*' and '*za*', is accented within the anapaestic stress pattern – in other words, that the line is entirely unmodulated, the stresses fall evenly, mimicking the steady advancement of a solemn march:

*My zhi-**vyom**,* | *pod so-**bo**-* | *-yu ne **chu**-* | *-ya stra-**ny**,*
Na-shi re- | *-chi za **de**-* | *-syat' sha-**gov*** | *ne slysh-**ny**,*

Because Russian words have, as a rule, only one stress, a word of six syllables or more will modulate a line written in anapaest, as it would create a triplet in which no syllable were stressed. Modulation, in actuality, is an omnipresent device in Russian versification, accounting for subtle effects across poetry; against this background of modulation as a norm, the unmodulated line stands as one modal possibility, such that each word is given emphasis, with the effect of great deliberation. One exception to this observation is the opening pronoun '*my*' (the Russian second-person plural), the unstressed 'we' that emerges from its de-emphasized position as if from the shadows, with the impression of great intimacy and sincerity indicative of what we can expect from the rest of the poem. When the metre changes, in lines three and four, by dropping the two final syllables of each concluding triplet, those dropped syllables are replaced with dramatically expectant pauses that might have been marked each by two strikes of timpani:

*A gde **khva**-* | *-tit na **pol**-* | *-raz-go-**vor**-* | *-tsa,* (Tam-tam!)
*Tam pri-**pom**-* | *-nyat krem-**lyov**-* | *-sko-vo **gor**-* | *-tsa.* (Tam-tam!)

The poem is at one with what it describes: it barely gets to the end of the first quatrain before it inevitably brings up the one it fears, justly, to name. The effect is of Stalin's omnipresence in the minds of the collective 'we' and of his being at the same time unmentionable, and in the poem it is unclear whether Stalin is 'remembered' in the sense of being mentioned or in the opposite sense of stifling the conversation. This might appear to contradict the facts, as the name 'Stalin' was then blasting from newspaper front pages and loudspeakers everywhere, yet the metallic pseudonym (translatable as 'of steel') had replaced 'Jugashvili', a murkier, more mysterious Georgian variation on the Ossetian name 'Dzugaty' (from Ossetian '*dzug*' – 'herd') punning on the ancient-Georgian word '*juga*', signifying 'steel'. To this layer of Stalin's personality the poem alludes briefly, declining to use the leader's official name and thereby indicating that it is about to say something rather unofficial about the man himself. As it steps over this threshold, we sense that all bets are off. The immediately following lines reward our suspense in full measure, as, upon the drum-beat, who should burst onto the stage but a circus strongman –

> His thick fingers are fat as worms,
> And his words sure as kettlebells.

This opens a sequence of couplets that itemize the grotesque and odious features of Stalin, in a manner which Christopher Ricks's remarks on Robert Lowell's 'Caligula' illuminate because of the two poems' salient affinities.

> The poem interrogates the conjunction of the body politic and the body personal, incarnating a conviction that the imperial psychopathology is at one with an immitigable revulsion from the emperor's own person. . . . Each couplet is a plank, firmly in position in order to build a platform which is to be at once highly personal and extendedly political. . . . The ugliness of Caligula's body is being remorselessly itemized. Behind the sequential hatred is the loving convention which itemized the beauties of the loved one's person.

Among the *ad hominem* attributions in 'The Stalin Epigram', the reference to the Russian *pood* weights is perhaps the most opaque, and has misled translators into aligning its meaning with some notion of measure and precision ('his words like measures of weight' – W. S. Merwin with Clarence Brown), when in actuality a forty-pound cannonball equipped with a handle (the better to be gripped by thick fingers, greased prior to the exercise) was the standard prop of circus strongmen. That Stalin lifts his Russian words the way a strongman lifts kettlebells (each such achievement met by a crash of cymbals, cheered by awed applause) is a murderous caricature of the leader's laboured command of Russian, and simultaneously of his grotesque strength, at once horrifying and laughable. And yet, the word 'sure' ('*verny*') in these lines might have been instead rendered as 'right' or 'true'. Stalin's words are bewilderingly unambiguous – mysteriously unequivocal, which, from the point of view of a poet as deeply attuned to the antinomies of language as Mandelstam, could only be felt as an anomaly verging on the supernatural – or on a kind of 'monstrous infantilism'. Caricature depends on irony, a sentiment crucially different, and more complex, than sarcasm, for irony acknowledges value and simultaneously deprecates. This may explain the meaning of the 'Ossetian chest', 'mighty and broad', that makes this caricature of Stalin such a picture of rude health, especially when contrasted with a line from a significantly later poem: 'I grew up sickly and turned out feeble' ('*Ya ros bol'nym i stal tschedushnym*'). The caricature is not all at Stalin's expense. In attributing to its subject apparently infinite strength, the epigram expressly *agrees* with all the official hyperbolic praise of Stalin at that time, while asking the unexpected questions: what would it be like if a leader really *did* have infinite strength? and would it be such a good thing all around? This is a patent *reductio ad absurdum*, yet what the epigram probes are not Stalin's own words but the rhetoric *about* him – a rhetoric perpetuated by the society at large, the 'we' of the opening line who then appear not solely as victims but as a political body charged with a degree of responsibility. When the epigram goes on to contrast Stalin himself with his henchmen, it is not *he* but *they* who appear contemptible:

> Surrounded by the rabble of thin-necked chiefs,
> He toys with half-men's favours,
> And they yowl, whistle, and moan –
> He alone prods and probes and points.

By the lurid disproportion of the central figure's overdevelopment to the bantam stature of his lackeys, the poem shows: it is the indignity of those in his power that condemns Stalin, whose grotesquely hypertrophied strength takes the form of perverse playfulness. What is observed in passing, without overemphasis, is that power reaches its apotheosis when it ceases to be accountable and, instead of justifying itself rationally, begins to indulge in 'play' – that is, in the unaccountable arbitrariness which is the hallmark of tyranny. This arbitrariness shows in the way in which everyone gets struck by Stalin's decrees: 'in the groin, in the brow, in the eye and the eyebrow'. Robert Lowell, one of the early translators of Mandelstam (his versions were published in 1965), was fully attuned to the menacing connotations of play: 'He plays with them' ('his thin-necked, drained advisors'); 'They make touching and funny animal sounds. He alone talks Russian.' Although, like others, his translation misses the significance of the kettlebells for Stalin's Russian (Lowell himself relied on Olga Carlisle's Russian trots), this toying is all that Lowell needs to get the right idea. Like Mandelstam in the later years, Lowell, too, compared himself with a tyrant, contemplated as the poet's namesake. Lowell, once nicknamed 'Cal' (a moniker invoking at once Caliban and Caligula), conceived his namesake in *For the Union Dead* (1964) as 'the rusty Roman medal where I see / my lowest depths of possibility'. In *History* (1973), the theme returns: 'you wish the Romans had a single neck' – the better to be wrung, all at once, 'with your strangler's twist' (a phrase from the 1964 version of 'Caligula'). Continuities of feeling, between Mandelstam and Lowell, abound on both sides of the contrast between the tyrant and his 'drained advisors' (Mandelstam: 'his thick fingers are fat as worms'; Lowell: 'your hand no hand could hold'), and the contrast itself defines the root problem: 'yours the lawlessness of something simple that has lost its law' (this diagnosis is so durable that it is retained by Lowell through both versions of the poem, separated by nearly a decade). Lowell's poem 'Stalin' (1976) articulates the situation, again, as that of a malignant overgrowth of power resulting from a lack – a lack of some limiting principle.

> Stalin? What shot him clawing up the tree of power –
> millions plowed under with the crops they grew,
> his intimates dying like a spider-bridegroom?
> The large stomach could only chew success.

But next to this flaw, the presence of the diminished and doomed 'intimates' acknowledges a different insight: that unbridled power is an emanation of the behaviours of the 'thin-necked chiefs' and 'spider-bridegrooms' who find it irresistible, fertilize it and perpetuate it at the cost even of their own lives. For this reason, the thriving villain is but one side of the 'Roman medal' representing a syndrome in the society as a whole, where those who live in fear supply the substrate for the tyranny. The artistic impossibility of portraying a tyrant apart from those who are tyrannically governed is indicative of a complicated moral situation: the responsibility for tyranny cannot rest solely on the tyrant himself, as it is in the nature of his cult to be upheld by the masses. The ground precedes the figure drawn against it. Mandelstam's poem portrays the grotesque deformity of an entire society, where the distribution of power makes a circus monster of the leader and a freak-show of his followers. That arenas and circuses appear in both Mandelstam and in Lowell is suggestive both of the political function of 'bread and circuses' and of the give-and-take of celebrity (a solo act, usually) and the mass of onlookers; and yet,

> Animals
> ripened for your arenas suffered less
> than you when slaughtered – yours the lawlessness
> of something simple that has lost its law,

then relishing an execution as if it were a simple 'berry' (in the concluding line of 'The Stalin Epigram'). Consequently, the 'we' that is invoked in the first line of Mandelstam's poem is not simply a 'we' of innocent victims; as odious as Stalin might appear, the entirety of the poem and of the circus drawn within it and encompassing both the leader and the multitude of those governed by him, appears to be asking the question, 'what have *we* done – to have produced *him*?' and, more broadly, 'what is the true nature of the relation that binds us – and him?' Speech-acts and word-magic figure importantly in each quatrain of Mandelstam's satire: in the first quatrain, it is the paradoxically oblique invocation of the unnamable; in the second, it is the weight of Stalin's word that contrasts implicitly with the weight of words in the stone-masonry of the poetic edifice, a long-standing figure of Mandelstam's imagination; in the third, Stalin's speech is contrasted with the mewling and yowling of his diminished and humiliated courtiers; in the fourth and final one, Stalin's decrees are likened to horseshoes with which the giant playfully knocks down his subjects, one by one. Corruption of power is therefore inseparable from, and fully expressed in the corrupted uses of speech that Mandelstam invokes to portray the malaise of his society (emulating Dante, who aligned distortions of character with specific habits of speech, and who was on Mandelstam's mind during much of 1933). The final couplet of the poem signals its closing with the closing of the Ossetian's mouth, which had been, throughout the poem, expelling words like monstrous metallic ammunition. Now, at the end of the poem, it takes something *in* – a person, we are made to understand, delicate, mashable, pleasing and small like a 'berry'. The primal cannibalistic feeling here sends us right back to the world of fairy tale. It is the feeling that supplied the poem's point of entry – that, however one might can caricature a fairy-tale villain (Baba Yaga, Koschey the Deathless, or the mysterious mountain man whose real name cannot be spoken aloud), one cannot do away with an irreducible, grim respect for the monstrous, a respect perhaps due to its pre-linguistic resistance to words and analysis, as fear itself appeals not to our reason but to our knees, making them tremulous and soft, and to our feet, making us lose the sense of the ground underneath.

All of this, together with the flourishing of Mandelstam's irony into Lowell's 'pity the monsters', indicates that Mandelstam's satire is, on the one hand, something much richer than a 'lampoon', as it has sometimes been called (notably by Mandelstam's interrogator, Nikolay Shivarov, after the poet's arrest in 1934), and, on the other hand, that, in being a provocation, it had the quality of touch, which is unlike all the other senses in being always reciprocal: one cannot touch something without being touched by it (as against seeing without being seen, hearing without being heard, and so on). In having been affected by Stalin's personality, the poem's provocation seeks to reciprocate, to touch Stalin back, and to invite being 'touched' by Stalin – a lethal reciprocity, as we can divine from the grotesque strength attributed to this Goliath, and as we know from Mandelstam's biography. The danger, then, was not only evident to Mandelstam himself but constituted an integral part in the mechanism of the poem's coming into being, out of a crisis of decision that issued in a cry: '*Così gridai colla faccia levata*'. Dante's line might have been Mandelstam's epigraph, not to the *Conversation About Dante*, but to 'The Stalin Epigram'.

The half-decade of Mandelstam's life that preceded the poem's emergence supplied enough trouble to drive a man out of his mind. Although Stalin played no direct role in these travails, this was the time when the Soviet leader was furthering an agenda of atomizing the society by means of systematic dismantling of all associations bound by class, professional ties, familial attachment, or any other unity of interests and values. There may be no better elucidation of that feeling of instability at one's feet that opens 'The Stalin Epigram' than Hannah Arendt's insight: by 1930, the evisceration of the Soviets and other community-based organizations of autonomous self-governance spelled the unprecedented situation in which the citizenry was forced to realize that 'their lives and the lives of their families depended not upon their fellow-citizens but exclusively on the whims of the government which they faced in complete loneliness without any help whatsoever from the group to which they happened to belong.' It was this repressive atmosphere that 'The Stalin Epigram' responded to, but it is doubtful that this would have happened if specific events did not unfold against that backdrop. Meticulous studies have been made of this exhausting period of Mandelstam's life, a period that nevertheless opens with a picture of the healthy, 'well-nourished' Mandelstams (as one acquaintance described them in a 1928 diary), just back from a seaside vacation in Sukhum. That perception would contrast with impressions of Mandelstam as he entered a period of relentless troubles as the year matured. It is principally on the basis of Alexander Mets's valuable *Chronicle* of Mandelstam's life and letters that the drama of the next five years can be envisioned.

For Mandelstam, the year 1928 was marked by a number of new publications: a collection of *Poems*, another volume of his critical essays, his experimental prose work, *The Egyptian Stamp* (in the May issue of *Zvezda*), and finally the publication, by Land and Factory ('*Zemlya i fabrika*' or 'ZiF'), a state publishing house, of what English copyright law would see as Mandelstam's original translation of Charles de Coster's 1867 novel, *La Légende et les aventures héroïques, joyeuses, et glorieuses d'Ulenspiegel et de Lamme Goedzak au pays de Flandres et ailleurs*. Yet, in the context of Soviet publishing practices, when the book was issued with a title page crediting Mandelstam as the translator, this was immediately perceived, by Mandelstam himself and by others, as an unfortunate misattribution. Mandelstam's specific commission had been to amalgamate two existing translations, Vasiliy Karyakin's and Arkadiy Gornfeld's, cross-checking one translation against the other and further revising the amalgamation to achieve a new and improved text; this type of revising was classified in the industry as editorial work, and it was the publisher's oversight not to have credited the two translators whose texts had supplied the basis for Mandelstam's revisions and refinements. (Although Pavel Nerler considers the attribution of the text to Mandelstam as the translator an 'unpardonable mistake', this stems from a basic misunderstanding of literary translation that discounts the significance of revisions and only accepts the first transposition from the original to be translation as such. On this view, translators like Robert Lowell and any number of others who worked with trots instead of the original would not be considered translators at all, though it is unclear what their role would then be.) A year later, when the '*Ulenspiegel* affair', instead of being resolved, continued to rage, involving by then a whole class of new translations reliant on prior, unacknowledged or under-acknowledged work, *Zvezda* ('*The Star*') published the scholarly opinion of A. V. Fyodorov, who recognized the difficulties associated with the accepted methods of amalgamation and revision. 'In revising an old translation', he wrote, 'especially in the case of a canonical work, the editorial task becomes complicated: different methods of transmission may come into conflict, or else an unprincipled and compromised fusion of different manners of translation and different speech-systems may occur.'

> Instances of complete creative revision are rare. One such case is De Coster's *Ulenspiegel* published by ZiF, in O. Mandelstam's refashioning. Here, we see the amalgamation of two previously published translations of this novel, a selection of the more felicitous variants, a verification of one translation against the other, and finally, the original's distinctiveness has been, truly, found (or perhaps divined) through the word-thicket of two translations. The brilliant results achieved by Mandelstam are, of course, not accidental in the context of Mandelstam's own work – him being a first-magnitude artist and the author of excellent translations – and only from the viewpoint of editorial criticism can this success appear to be random, in being excessively individual.

In other words, where 'there is no method but to be very intelligent', success may appear, misleadingly, to be a product of sheer luck. Still, more than one expert asked to comment on Mandelstam's 'plagiarism' at the time concluded, on deliberation, that his was an original translation, arrived at by means of careful integration of two available texts functioning as trots. Yet these testimonies were not enough, and the scandal took on a life of its own.

As soon as Mandelstam became aware of the error, he took it upon himself to notify the 'unsuspecting Gornfeld', declaring himself fully responsible for his fees 'against the entirety of my literary earnings'. Gornfeld's reaction to this honourable gesture is evidenced by a letter penned in October:

> *Ulenspiegel* has been published, translated apparently by O. Mandelstam (the poet), while in actuality it has been stolen from me and another translator. Mandelstam is a talented but immoral person, a scholar, a swine, a petty thief – he is bombarding me with telegrams pleading for mercy (I could put him in the defendant's booth), but I remain, for the time being, severe.

Gornfeld's maliciousness had little to do with any practical harm caused by the editorial mistake, and in the subsequent months it became clear that he had benefited from Mandelstam's interest in his translation and from the ensuing scandal:

> Poor devil – his shenanigans have helped me a great deal: I have sold *Ulenspiegel*, which will be published in the spring, the money will come in a trickle, but it is still a decent assistance. And had this fool translated properly, I would have never again placed that translation!

Yet by the time this was recognized, Gornfeld's sharp feuilleton had been printed in *Krasnaya Gazeta* ('*The Red Newspaper*'), pushing Mandelstam into the public spotlight in a way that tainted his reputation regardless of the facts of the matter.

In order to defend himself, Mandelstam had to argue that his case was representative of the generally accepted process in Soviet publishing, when new translations were produced in mass quantities, by means of revising existing versions and with permissions often acquired late and back-dated, the entire process having the character of contempt for the labour of both translators and editors and resulting in dubious texts unfit to be called literature. These practices became the subject of 'Streams of Hackwork', a feuilleton dictated to Emma Gerstein in March of 1929, in the aftermath of ZiF's cancellation of Mandelstam's publishing contracts for new translations of Mayne Reid – a colossal financial blow that contributed to the exasperated tone of the piece, published in April in *Izvestiya* ('*News*'). Following the publication, on April 16, Mandelstam was appointed a member of a special commission for regulating the practice of translation, and by April 19 he had compiled a list of books translated and published by methods analogous to those employed in *Ulenspiegel*. Meanwhile, an exchange of insults on the pages of *Vechernyaya Moskva* ('*Evening Moscow*') the previous December had prompted Gornfeld to forward his last word on the subject (which the paper declined the publish) to the Writer's Union (*Vserossiyskiy Soyuz Pisateley*), thus embroiling the professional organization in the scandal. The escalating momentum of the affair received another impulse on May 7, with the publication, in *Literaturnaya Gazeta* ('*The Literary Paper*'), of Zaslavsky's infamous feuilleton 'On Modest Plagiarism and Unbridled Hackwork', a striking specimen of a new genre, which, as noted by Pavel Nerler, would be carefully cultivated by *The Literary Paper* throughout the 1930s. The new genre was that of an exposé that would surprise its victim by a public dressing-down whilst exhorting the readers to join the paper in righteous indignation and to mete out swift 'justice' upon the subject of the profile. Zaslavsky's involvement in the sparring between Mandelstam and Gornfeld was, as he himself confessed in a letter to Gornfeld, accidental:

> *The Literary Paper* asked me to write a feuilleton, the topic seemed to me suitable, the editorial staff (those of its members who had spoken with me) endorsed this topic, and I could not have foreseen that so much noise would arise because of it.

This fundamental indifference made it that much easier for him to write without scruple: 'Let us grab him by the scruff of his neck, this poisoner of literary wells', cried the article, inciting the subjection of Mandelstam (the translator of *Ulenspiegel*) to the severe justice of Mandelstam (the author of 'Streams of Hackwork'). Fallacious at it was, the loop invented by Zaslavsky was not easy to escape, as it now showed Mandelstam to be an individual exponent of the flawed practices he himself condemned.

Yet no less striking than the irresponsible malice of this casuistry was its political savvy. Nothing could have been more in line with the party strategy of the moment than to invert Mandelstam's claim about his work being an individual case within a larger phenomenon and to isolate the individual, heaping blame on the victim, singled out amidst his frightened peers (who were, meanwhile, glad to remain in the shadows) and cut off from sources of solidarity and support, in an act of ritual scapegoating. The opening of 1930s was, after all, the time of 'repeated purges which invariably precede actual group liquidation'. Stalin tested the idea of purging social groups and community organizations as a way of extinguishing all solidarity among their members under the threat of guilt by association. It would soon be understood that anyone who showed support to the victim of a public show-trial would be next in line for his (or her) own round of tarring and feathering. The mechanism was extraordinarily effective in eroding the social relations from which an individual in a healthy society derives strength and security. Under these conditions, in Hannah Arendt's analysis,

> it is obvious that the most elementary caution demands that one avoid all intimate contacts, if possible – not in order to prevent discovery of one's secret thoughts, but rather to eliminate, in the almost certain case of future trouble, all persons who might have not only an ordinary cheap interest in your denunciation but an irresistible need to bring about your ruin simply because they are in danger of their own lives.

It was this irresistible atomization of the Russian society that speaks from the opening lines of 'The Stalin Epigram'. The poem's insight, gleaned from his own show-trial in the Moscow press, cost Mandelstam dearly. The unprecedented character of this prosecution in print was clear to him, as evidenced by his open letter to the Federation of Soviet Writers ('*FOSP*'), penned early in 1930, in which he declared,

> in the face of the Federation of Soviet Writers, that it has tainted itself by a most abominable persecution of a writer, having used for its purpose unprecedented means, resorting to deceit and swindling, suppressing facts, fabricating documents, turning to the services of false witnesses, covering up for its functionaries with shameful cowardice, using its authority to hush up debaucheries in publishing, and finally answering

a writer's attempt, the first in USSR's history, to intervene in the publishing business, with a dramatization of a scandalous criminal process.

'The gravest accusations', he went on, 'are leveled at a person publicly, in print, without preliminary investigation, in the form of a feuilleton full of sleight-of-hand', with 'all but the respondent' figuring as 'full-fledged prosecutors' and with the end result of 'an insinuating verdict' full of contradictions and equivocations – shifting, magic-lantern-like, between plagiarism and hackwork.

> If one could collect everything that I have written to you in the past months, it would make up a whole book – a mortifying book, shameful to all of us. You have entered a chapter into the history of Soviet literature, a chapter that emits the rank smell of death and decomposition.

The futility of this protest was conditioned by the fact that insinuation, deceit, fabrication and all the sleight-of-hand named and condemned in this letter would, from that time on, constitute the standard toolkit of the persecutions organized by Stalin and his cabinet, in a system of governance where blame would strike now this individual and now another ('in the groin, in the brow, in the eye, in the eyebrow'), to keep all the rest cowed. And even though, on May 13, 1929, *The Literary Paper* had run a letter of support for Mandelstam signed by fifteen Moscow writers, including Olesha, Pasternak and Zoschenko (the letter that would soon be seconded by a telegram from Leningrad, with additional signatures), at the end of the month Pasternak would write privately to Tsvetayeva with a mixture of sympathy, antipathy and perplexity at Mandelstam's lack of political tact in the situation:

> In mid-winter he had the stupidity and the misfortune to present in a 'social cross-section' the matter synonymous with the area where he misbehaved, or, I would like to think, only got burned through no fault of his own. He published in *Izvestiya* a feuilleton about translation practices in USSR, brilliantly written and, in my opinion, deeply disagreeable. In it, he exposed as a flaw in the process the practice of assigning translations (how can I put it more concisely) to those people to whom only I myself would assign them – those in need, people who know languages but are not literary professionals. This actually struck somewhat against my own continuous efforts and my sympathies. I like ordinary people, I myself am an ordinary person. Now

> a genuinely unworthy hounding has been unleashed against him, and, as always in our midst, under a false pretext.
>
> He, meanwhile, is astonishing. It is true, one should get inside his shoes, but I can only envy his certainty of being in the right. No, I look at it as something unexpectedly alien. Objectively, he has done nothing that could even remotely justify the injuries inflicted on him. At the same time, he himself is increasing and multiplying them by the total absence of that which could save him and what I am constantly appealing to. According to him and his wife, I am a philistine, and we nearly fell out after one particular conversation.

In this way, Mandelstam was becoming increasingly isolated even from his most helpful and sensitive supporters. At the same time, it appears that he was correct in judging the deliberate role of *The Literary Paper* in instigating the show-trial under the guise of impartial reporting. On May 14, 1929, he wrote to *FOSP*'s executive bureau concerning the paper's continued involvement in the conflict and its attempts to steer the events by appointing a conflict commission, 'whose decision will be published in one of the nearest issues of our paper'.

> I dispute the right of the editors of *The Literary Paper* to continue shaping the 'process' instigated with its support by Zaslavsky. From the very beginning, the editorial office of *The Literary Paper* behaved like an interested party. A feuilleton, *extremely sharp in tone and wording*, of Zaslavsky's was printed with no verification and no editorial remarks whatsoever. Meanwhile, the editors found it necessary to accompany my letter and the letter of a group of writers with the equivocation: 'the editors leave it to the responsibility of the authors of these letters what sharpness of tone and phrasing have been permitted therein'.

Mandelstam discerned the paper's 'solidarization' with Zaslavsky and could therefore predict its editorial policies in the future. His dark expectations would soon be justified.

On June 2, 1929, *Komsolmolskaya Pravda* ('*Komsomol Truth*') published a piece under the title 'The Incident is Over', suggesting a conclusion to the 'Mandelstam affair'. Two days later, Zaslavsky reported to Gornfeld: 'I have written a sharp answer to *Koms Pravda*, which, probably, will not be published.' The same day, he and Kanatchikov, his editor, summoned a meeting of the *FOSP* conflict committee, continuing their efforts to sway the outcome of the debate in the press. On the other side of the divide, two weeks later, *Komsomolskaya Pravda* published an unsigned statement with the headline 'Mandelstam Has Created a New Work of Literature'. Meanwhile, according to the judicial expertise connected with Karyakin's court case, it had been established that 'Mandelstam's work constitutes not re-typing but an independent revision of every phrase of the old text, as a result of which, as concluded by the expert witnesses, a new literary work has been created'. But when Luknitsky, an acquaintance friendly to Mandelstam, visited him the same day, it appeared to be too late for concessions: Mandelstam, he recorded in his diary,

> is in a terrible state, hates everyone around, is dreadfully embittered, without a kopek of money and with no opportunity to get any, starving in the literal sense of the word. He lives (separately from N. Y.) at the Tsekubu dormitory, does not pay rent, his debt is increasing, and if not today then tomorrow he will be evicted. He is overgrown with stubble, nervous, irascible and irritable. Cannot talk of anything but this whole story. Considers all writers his enemies. Proclaims that he has forever left literature, will never write another line, and has torn up all his publishing contracts.

On June 27, Vygodsky corroborated this description with a record of what could be heard in Moscow: 'Mandelstam declared that he is not a Russian writer, that he won't write anymore, that he means to get a job.' According to Vygodsky, Mandelstam

> telephoned Zaslavsky and said approximately the following: I stand here with two witnesses who can hear what I'm saying. In front of them, I state that you are a scoundrel.

The person who appears to have had the right sense of what to do was Nikolay Bukharin. His sympathetic opinion was that Mandelstam should be decisively, physically extricated from the brawl. To this end, in mid-June he wrote to Sahak Ter-Gabrielyan, the Armenian party official, about the possibility of arranging academic work for Mandelstam in Armenia. Yet the sinecure, which had been so close to realization and might have changed the course of Mandelstam's life, indeed might have saved it, was not to be. On his arrival Mandelstam was met with the incomprehension of the local party personnel who had not been in any way informed of the teaching post prepared for him under Bukharin's and Ter-Gabrielyan's protection; by the time clarifications from above came, the disappointed Mandelstams had already left in a huff. Having endured an exceptionally alarming ordeal in the preceding year, Mandelstam was becoming increasingly prone to perceiving hostility in the merest hint of unwelcome or disrespect. This reactive readiness to go into a frenzy at the slightest provocation was only advantageous to his persecutors, whose business was going terribly well. Meanwhile, the evidence of the process up to this point is rich enough to enable us to step back from the succession of events that would continue to unfold (very soon, Zaslavsky would publish his new attack, 'Beetles and Black Slaves', in *Pravda*) – and to analyse the situation.

The first unignorable element of the situation was Mandelstam's very real dependence on the writing and publishing establishment, not only for income (it was, after all, Mandelstam's very livelihood, not merely his *amour-propre* that Ionov's cancellation of translation contracts had struck against) but even for his right to housing, for all the events of this narrative unfolded against a crisis of homelessness that the Mandelstams had been enduring, week by week and month by month, as they stayed by turns with Mandelstam's brothers Alexander and Yevgeniy, with Nadezhda's brother, Yevgeniy Khazin, with Emma Gerstein (in the very first winter after their acquaintance in 1928), occasionally escaping to a sanatorium, and often living apart, with different relatives, because there wasn't room for them to live together. The various hopes for a room here or a flat there presented themselves only to be frustrated – but these hopes always appeared through the professional channels, which underscores the real danger that befell anyone who, like Mandelstam, suddenly found himself a target of a campaign designed to make him a pariah, to single out and alienate a member of a profession, stripping him of the rights implicit in professional association. (As a point of fact, when Mandelstam left the Federation of Soviet Writers in justified protest against its silent collusion with Zaslavsky's campaign, it did not take long for some politically alert insider to petition for Mandelstam's removal from the waitlist for professional writers' housing.)

The second feature of Mandelstam's position in the *Ulenspiegel* affair is that the situation offered no clues as to how to escape it. Zaslavsky's original feuilleton, couched in shifty, 'magic-lantern' rhetoric, was impossible to deflect because it stated nothing specific, instead insinuating, taunting and inciting the readers to imaginary, metaphorical wrath without specifying the concrete forms appropriate for the 'justice' it demanded or any limits thereon. By taking issue with the attack on the basis of the flawed publishing practices of the time, Mandelstam the accused became a whistleblower, alienating himself from the publishers who were the very source of his livelihood. To take sole responsibility for the incident might have been more politic, if only one was willing to sacrifice outright one's own sense of justice and, second, if one only knew *what* exactly he needed to confess under the circumstances: revising the preexisting translations instead of translating from scratch? – but this had been precisely his commission; taking credit for the translation? – but he had never done so. It is evident that any admission of guilt was only possible if the 'defendant' (the role in which Mandelstam, to his indignation, was thrust, and not by legal means but through a duplicitous publicity campaign) embroiled himself in a web of lies and half-truths that would later supply further evidence to benefit the prosecution. *The Literary Paper*'s smear campaign was exemplary in its inescapability – a successful assassination.

To sum up the contours of this situation, it presents itself as an impossible dilemma (since either to defend oneself or to accept guilt would amount to self-incrimination); this unresolvable dilemma is set in the context of the utter necessity of a resolution (because one's livelihood is tied intimately to the professional relations attacked by the feuilleton's insinuations that one does not belong in the community of Soviet writers). The fact that one depends on one's standing in the professional community translates into an imperative to *do something* to preserve this belonging. At the same time, the mere presence of the possibility of choice (as in any dilemma) does not mean that any of the available courses of action are tenable. In Mandelstam's case, it appears that the choices with which he was presented amounted to nothing more than a selection of roads to damnation. The formal lineaments of the situation, to think of it as a logical problem of decision, amount to a double deadlock: the deadlock of contradictory injunctions imposed by the situation, and the deadlock of necessity to act, against the futility of action under the conditions of the first deadlock. Gregory Bateson, who spent years of his productive life in the sciences studying the ramifications of this kind of situation, formalized it under the term 'double bind'. He observed that its effects on the victim's behaviour can manifest in either utter dejection and paralysis or, on the contrary, in erratic displays of profligate inventiveness – put in one word, in creativity. Under this aspect, what followed – the profligate creativity of a man unable to defend himself – appears richer and more tragically ambiguous than we might have thought.

Bateson's intuition was that, where we encounter behaviour that cannot be rationalized in terms of the outcome it would achieve for the subject, the cause of this may be that the subject has been forced to operate under the conditions of the double bind. Under such conditions, the subject is unable to see any avenue for achieving a positive result (as decisions are modelled in the rational choice theory), and yet it is part of the structure of the double bind that it compels the person to respond to the situation in some way. In some cases, such pressure was observed to instigate paralysis and catatonic states, a product of the deadlock of injunctions portrayed to such effect by Kipling in 'Riki-tikki-tavi': 'Keep very still, all you three. If you move, I strike, and if you do not move, I strike.' In other instances, the subject was observed bidding on a course of action whose outcome could not be predicted at all, depriving the action of observable 'rational' motivation. An early example comes from Bateson's 'Towards a Theory of Schizophrenia' (1956):

> A young man who had fairly well recovered from an acute schizophrenic episode was visited in the hospital by his mother. He was glad to see her and impulsively put his arm around her shoulders, whereupon she stiffened. He withdrew his arm and she asked, 'Don't you love me any more?' He then blushed, and she said, 'Dear, you must not be so easily embarrassed and afraid of your feelings.' The patient was able to stay with her only a few minutes more and following her departure he assaulted a orderly and was put in the tubs.

In the situation of 'intense dependency and training' instantiated by the child-mother relationship – in other words, given the mother's power advantage over her son, which prevents him from commenting freely on her behaviour while she comments, not only freely but also negatively, on his, he has a dog's chance of unravelling the diabolical knot that played out in seconds of real communication time. The mother's repeated repudiation of the son's gestures and reactions (his arm on her shoulder, withdrawing his arm, blushing), coupled with negative attributions (the unspoken disgust of nonverbal rejection, followed by the suggestion that he doesn't love her (as he, it is implicit, *should*), and finally the attribution of an immature ('Dear') and laughable fear of his own feelings) bypasses the son's defences, instantly filling him with self-loathing and destabilizing the behaviour of this previously 'fairly well recovered' man. In the words of R. D. Laing, who was interested in similar behavioural patterns in the family context,

> the victim is caught in a tangle of paradoxical injunctions, or of attributions having the force of injunctions, in which he cannot do the right thing.
>
> One person conveys to the other that he should do something, and at the same time conveys on another level that he should not, or that he should do something else incompatible with it. The situation is sealed off for the 'victim' by a further injunction forbidding him or her to get out of the situation, or to dissolve it by commenting on it.

It is important to the structure of the double bind that the contradictory messages intercepted by the victim have the form of commands, be those explicit or implied: the contradiction may take the form of a simultaneous injunction to 'move to the left' and 'move to the right', or 'move' and 'stand still', or 'confess your guilt' and 'defend yourself', or 'forget and forgive'. The characteristic effect of a double bind is of 'at once paralyzing you and tearing you apart'; when such contradictory injunctions are issued from a position of power (which prohibits critical remarks 'from below'), the victim will eventually experience 'trouble in identifying and interpreting those signals which should tell the individual what sort of a message a message is.' In a nutshell, a double bind is a 'traumatic situation which involves a metacommunicative tangle'; yet, the presence of contradictory injunctions alone does not 'exhaust the rhetorical situation', as Laing himself would have put it. The power disparity between the subject and the source of 'feedback' – meaning, the entity whose responses are for whatever reason of crucial importance to the subject, as in the case of authority with real power over the subject's life – accounts for what, to Bateson, was an essential element of the structure: the subject's inability to comment on the situation and his subsequent incapacity to resist the attributions forced upon him. About the situation just described and the erratic behaviour it provoked, Bateson wrote: 'this result could have been avoided if the young man had been able to say, "Mother, it is obvious that you become uncomfortable when I put my arm around you, and that you have difficulty accepting a gesture of affection from me."' (Something more direct, though less printable, might have been yet more effective in warding off the trauma.) One way or another, 'the schizophrenic patient doesn't have this possibility open to him. His intense dependency and training prevents him from commenting upon his mother's communicative behaviour, though she comments on his and forces him to accept and to attempt to deal with the complicated sequence.' The upshot is that, within the framework of the double bind, the seemingly irrational behaviour that followed the mother's visit finds a rational explanation in view of the statements, most of them indirect, made by the mother during her brief appearance.

The formal statement of what constitutes a double bind is expressed in these three criteria:

(1) When the individual is involved in an intense relationship; that is, a relationship in which he feels it is vitally important that he discriminate accurately what sort of message is being communicated so that he may respond appropriately.
(2) And, the individual is caught in a situation in which the other person in the relationship is expressing two orders of message and one of these denies the other.
(3) And, the individual is unable to comment on the messages being expressed to correct his discrimination of what order of message to respond to, *i.e.* he cannot make a metacommunicative statement.

This model presupposes primarily the context of intimate relationships, such as the parent-child relationship, from which one would have a very difficult time emancipating oneself completely, due to the 'training' retained from the dependency of the early ears and the habit of unconditional trust in the parents necessitated by the intolerable insecurities that would plague the person in the absence of such a trust. (No more concise statement of that problem than Fairbairn's: 'it is better to be a sinner in a world ruled by God than to live in a world ruled by the Devil' – and this spells a pressure to believe the more soothing alternative.) But the description does not rule out relationships that are 'intense' for reasons other than familial intimacy, and the 'person' who figures as the source of feedback in the double-bind situation may not be an actual person but a group, an organization, a community: what is important is the presence of an acutely felt necessity to 'discriminate accurately what sort of message is being communicated', so that one could 'respond appropriately'; 'severe pain and maladjustment can be induced by putting a mammal in the wrong regarding its rules for making sense of an important relationship with another mammal' – *or a group*, when the lineaments of the situation, notably the subject's dependent position, are otherwise preserved. On the other hand, Bateson realized, 'if this pathology can be warded off or resisted, the total experience may promote *creativity*.'

This benign potential of the double bind is not distinguished, in principle, from the negative symptomatology it may engender, as humour, art, poetry, etc., belong to the same range of behaviours as assaulting an orderly, when viewed under the aspect of what they have in common. What holds true for all these behaviours is that they cannot be interpreted as expressly motivated by a predictable outcome; their motive is a bid for escape from the equally undesirable alternative outcomes foreseeable under the constraints of the situation. In the same vein, one cannot reverse-engineer Mandelstam's composition of *The Fourth Prose* in terms of practical motives in structuring his relationship with the community of writers. He began dictating (not *writing*) this new work in December 1929 – the process of dictation in principled agreement with the work's paradoxical disavowal of writing as such:

> I have no manuscripts, no notebooks, no archive. I have no handwriting, because I never write. I alone in the whole of Russia do my work from voice, while all around me the mangy curs are writing away.

This repudiation of writing as an instrument of prosecutors ('mangy curs' being a necessarily approximate rendering of *'gustopsovaya svoloch'* suggestive of a mob of ferocious dogs) signals something ominous: that Zaslavsky's attacks, in proceeding from a writer, albeit a third-rate writer, succeeded in creating a rift between Mandelstam and the writing community, in spite of the solidarity shown by many writers in the course of the scandal's unfolding. These attacks were also delivered against a backdrop of a progressively consolidating ideological assessment of Mandelstam, as evidenced by the reviews published between 1928 and 1933. These reviews have been traced and assembled by Alexander Mets in his *Chronicle* and can be summarized as follows.

When, in October 1928, a journalist named Postupalsky read his manuscript of a review characterizing Mandelstam as a 'brilliant and principally bourgeois poet' whose poetry has 'museum character', Polonsky, the editor of the journals *Revolyutsiya i Pechat'* (*'Revolution and Print'*) and *Novyj Mir* (*'The New World'*), declined to publish the piece, admonishing Postupalsky: 'One better not trouble Mandelstam nowadays, your article could cause him harm.' (In January 1929, Postupalsky would write to Polonsky, insisting that the article meant a lot to him and that he would like to see it published.) Given Polonsky's circumspect approach to reviews, one can read darker intentions into the editorial policies of publications that ran reviews like the one that appeared in *Na Literaturnom Postu* (*'The Literary Post'*), in response to Mandelstam's book of critical essays, *On Poetry*: 'The book is of signal value, in spite of its philosophic uselessness. It is signal as an attempt (conscious or not – I cannot judge) to break the continuous chain of the monistic Marxist worldview.' This was an accusation of heresy and sacrilege, just as another review, published in the same journal the following February, in which Anatoly Tarasenkov accused Mandelstam of 'perverting' Lenin's phrase 'the tutor of revolution' and denounced the book as 'a clot of bitterness about the vanishing of the past'. Published the same month, Tynyanov's *Archaists and Innovators* did Mandelstam the dubious favour of aligning him with 'older theorists' and ascribing to him a sensibility that stressed 'harmony' over 'melody':

> Mandelstam is solving one of the most difficult problems of poetic language. Among older theorists, the difficult notion of 'harmony' had already gained currency – 'harmony presupposes the fullness of sound, in accordance with the scope of thought', and, as if anticipating our own times, these older theorists warn against conflating 'harmony' with 'melody'.

In the atmosphere of 'out with the old, in with the new', this was as *unhelpful* as anything could be, but still not as ominous as Gorbachyov's assessment, in a book-length survey of contemporary Russian literature published in June, 1929: in it, Mandelstam's poetry was likened to 'a sophisticated "dish" suitable for the enjoyment of bookworms and philologists', archaic and reminiscent of the eighteenth-century high style. Gorbachyov was, incidentally, quite aware of what such opinions could cost to their object, and he relished the 'comedy' of the despair among people left behind by the train of history:

> Considering the art of Pasternak and Mandelstam of the most recent period (he read a mass of new poems at the Capella), I think that it would be good for someone to write an article about the liquidation of the bourgeoisie as a class – and, as a consequence, of the fitful efforts of bourgeois poets to refashion themselves, to tear themselves away from their sinking ship; about their convulsions, curses, funny and tragic attempts to keep up with the new life – and to compare these tragicomic knights of the past with others, who attempt to survive like parasitic plants upon a foreign tree, engaging in not unsuccessful mimicry and in slipping in enemy ideas under a benign guise (the topic of objective sabotage in poetry and prose).

Just what it meant to be pronounced a thing of the past in a country breathlessly and rapturously enthralled with the communist future is evident from another menacing review, signed by a certain 'Olkhovsky', which ran the same month in *Print and Revolution*: 'Certain individual representatives of the class vanquished by the proletariat must sense, if not realize consciously, that their class is doomed. It is on this despondency that Mandelstam's muse feeds.' Pronouncements concerning the 'vanquished' and 'doomed' classes were, of course, the currency of Stalinist propaganda that manufactured such judgements overnight and without due process, framed them as final and thereby transformed them into self-fulfilling prophecies: everybody knew that a 'doomed' class was, well, doomed from now on. This is why, when A. Manfred's review ran, that August, in *Kniga i Revolyutsiya* ('Book and Revolution'), the constructive programme that it proposed for Mandelstam, inviting him to choose whether to remain a thing of the past or to reform, was a dilemma in form only, and substantively represented an ultimatum. By the opening of the 1930s, the party line with regard to Mandelstam had been understood by all politically savvy writers (no writer feeling sufficiently secure as to afford a lack of such savvy). And so, Tarsis, of *Contemporary Russian Writers*, 'hesitated' to 'recommend' Mandelstam to 'any but the most sophisticated readers', 'a severely restricted circle' of 'highly qualified' appreciators. If this denial of contemporary relevance was disguised as praise (dubious as it might be), the reviewer of Tarsis himself, Mazurin, referred to Mandelstam with unabashed hostility – as an 'antiquarian rarity'. Shklovsky's attribution to Mandelstam of a crippling Kantian self-consciousness, in his review of *The Journey to Armenia*, did not help the poet any more than Selivanovsky's 'comradely criticism' in *The Literary Paper* of November 1932: 'Pasternak, Antokolsky and the old men, Mandelstam and Andrey Bely, need our help, and, first and foremost, by means of systematic comradely criticism.' Such perversely patronizing offers of help from the youngsters – the masters of the new world – came with a very clear implication of what the fate of the 'old men' should be in the event of non-compliance. The following winter showed that it was actually too late to heed any such prophylactic, comradely ideological advice: an article on Mandelstam in the newly published volume of the *Literary Encyclopedia* supplied arguments pointing to 'the bourgeois and counterrevolutionary character of acmeism, the school of aggressive bourgeois art on the eve of the proletarian revolution'. From here onward, the recommended prophylaxis would be *against* Mandelstam as an ideological threat:

> Here lies the dreadful danger for contemporary poetry, the danger of falling into the chasm of Mandelstam's system – all the more dangerous because, outwardly, this system appears to be a product of exceptionally high culture.

This review, penned by Nikolay Kovarsky, in *The Literary Contemporary* (*'Literaturnyy Sovremennik'*) inaugurated the New Year 1933. In March, it was followed by Goffenscheffer's internal review of the volume of Mandelstam's critical prose, projected by Gosizdat: 'Mandelstam's essays are the quintessence of the refined ideology of the liberal Russian bourgeoisie';

> To reissue them at present (even with a critical introduction) would be a large-scale political misstep. No nods to the necessity of treating carefully the old intelligentsia that stands today on the Soviet platform can justify this republication, as it would not only constitute a political mistake on the part of the publisher, but also a disservice to Mandelstam himself.

Finally, *Pravda* – the oracle of party policy in all matters – decisively consigned Mandelstam to the realm of shadows, with Rosenthal's review, 'Shadows of Old Petersburg': 'Mandelstam's images smell of an old, stale, imperial chauvinist who, lavishing praises on Armenia, praises its exoticism, its enslaved past, for Mandelstam has not written a line about its present.' With boundless bile, the review went on about the 'boundless bile of the man who does not understand proletarian literature'. 'The old Petersburg poet O. Mandelstam has missed the abundantly blossoming Armenia that joyfully builds socialism.' All this made it rather plain that 'O. Mandelstam' himself would not be missed, if he were to go missing from the literary scene. Having appeared, black on white, in *Pravda*, the writing might as well have been on the wall; nothing could better foretell the future of a writer than being consigned, decidedly and unapologetically, to the past.

In this situation, from which there was no clear defence, where attacks were pouring on him in the form of words on paper, Mandelstam invented a distinction between his literary existence and everybody else's – a distinction that condemns all 'writing' as the activity of snarling opportunists, brazen, treacherous, cowardly 'curs':

> I have no manuscripts, no notebooks, no archive. I have no handwriting, because I never write. I alone in the whole of Russia do my work from voice, while all around me the mangy curs are writing away.

The pages of Mandelstam's collected works flicker with canines in these years, and it is in this period that his poem 'Wolfhound' emerges, with the line '*Mne na plechi kidayetsya vek-volkodav*' ('This wolfhound age throws itself upon my shoulders') – the line that shares the grave and decided anapaestic metre (two syllables on the upswing before each fall of the stress) with the opening lines of the Stalin epigram. In both instances, anapaest mediates considered and ripened statements about the dark state of things, confessions about the inescapably menacing character of one's times, the three-syllable *volkodav* ('wolfhound') itself arriving like a final judgement at the end of a line. The word is capable of carrying the richness and the weight of such a judgement: its history imbues it, and its neighbours, the various dog nouns, with a considerable complexity of sentiment. The word 'dog', after all, is one that has made its way through

'The Stalin Epigram' and the Liberty of Protest 81

European literature, cycling through a variety of phases tinged with a 'period feeling', as William Empson observed in *The Structure of Complex Words*. Because the use of images and figures traverses linguistic divides, because Mandelstam was an avid reader of Dante, in Italian, because the dog's ancient presence alongside humans accounts for the development of complexes of feeling about the animal in all European languages – for all these reasons, we might well pause our excavations when we come upon a dog artifact in Mandelstam. There are many to wonder at.

> Now I look with bitterness over my past life. A dog's jubilee was my reward. What kind of example of respect for a worker's personhood and his labor do you, writers, set for the rest of our country? The trouble isn't that you've broken my life in two but that you've managed not to have even noticed it.

This appears to have been a draft letter addressed to the remaining *FOSP* members at the time of Mandelstam's termination of his membership at the opening of 1930. 'A dog's jubilee' is hot with incandescent indignation: here, Mandelstam *himself* is imagined as a dog – a dog who, after a long life of service, is 'honoured' by being thrown out of the house. This letter, of course, neighbours various references to the *hounding* (*'travlya'*) of Mandelstam over the course of the preceding year, the 'hounding' invoked not only by Mandelstam himself but being in the air, as witnessed, for example, by Pasternak's letter to Tsvetayeva. When this 'hounding' finds its way into the 'Wolfhound' (not a title but the shorthand reference to the untitled poem written in 1931), we read:

> This wolfhound age throws itself upon my shoulders,
> But I am no wolf by blood:
> Rather, stuff me away, like a hat in the sleeve
> Of a smothering Siberian fur coat.

The closing figure of the quatrain is dual in presenting two opposite possibilities of escape from the mortal pursuit: one is enclosure (what could be more snug than a hat in a sleeve, a foetal, prenatal comfort within a dark, warm, furry tube – a maternal environment), the other is release into the open steppes of Siberia, the legendary place of exile for many a Russian *persona ingrata*, envisioned not as a place of confinement, but as a space of release. In this way, the poem plays with the possibilities of *in*clusion and *ex*clusion, the advantages and the disadvantages of being inside (and an 'insider') or outside, with the attendant connotations of outsiderism. To be safely enclosed, while the danger is kept outside is a kind of imprisonment, in some ways preferable to, in others worse than being sent out into the open, expelled, exiled. Belonging and non-belonging is the central dilemma considered in the poem, which, through its successive rich images, attempts to answer the question: 'what kind of a dog am I, in relation to this age of dogs?' Another canine, after all, will appear in connection with the third emblem of liberation, produced in a later quatrain: it will be the 'blue' arctic fox, in its 'primordial' beauty, envisioned shining in the night sky – well out of reach of all the violent, temporal goings-on down below, the workings of the 'wolfhound age'. Yet it is the negation in the second line – 'I am no wolf by blood' – that may cover the greatest imaginative distance, as its allusion reaches all the way to Dante, his poetic solidarity (not 'writerly' solidarity, in Mandelstam's mind – he would attribute to Dante and the world of Dante's metaphors, in the same period, the same method of composition, embodied and rooted in breath and walking, that he had proclaimed for himself). To be a wolf 'by blood' is, of course, to be born of wolf. In his essay 'Dante's Dog', Alberto Manguel has pointed out that Dante's sense of the word *'cani'* – the epithet Dante attached repeatedly to the wrathful, the 'angry, greedy, savage, mad, cruel' inhabitants of Hell – is enriched by a concomitant sense derived from Brunetto Latini's *Livre du Trésor*, where dogs are depicted as animals who love humans more than does any other animal in the world, and only dogs born from the union of bitches and wolves are, on Latini's view, wicked. Coming from Mandelstam, an enthusiast of Dante and a superb observer of the referential capacities of words, 'I am no wolf *by blood*' appears to suggest a vision along these lines: 'Everyone is some kind of a dog in this age of hunting with hounds – either a hound, a wolf, a polar fox, or an inert pelt; given the choice, I prefer not to be a vicious half-blood; yet the question remains, how to survive.' The first of these three statements mirrors the English sentiment of two centuries before:

> I am his highness's dog at Kew;
> Pray tell me, sir, whose dog are you?

Alexander Pope engraved this epigram on the collar of a puppy given to Frederick, Prince of Wales, for the bemusement of anyone who would stoop to read the dog's collar. The English 'dog', it turns out, has all the markings of that 'vague, rich, intimate' way in which Mandelstam uses his dog words to discharge complex emotions, and the history of 'dog', constructed by Empson in 'The English Dog', matters in judging just how much work that single noun gets done in the fabric of a poem or a prose text – because words like '*arch, rogue, fool, honest, dog* and so forth', Empson's 'complex words', are the ones in which 'a man tends finally to make up his mind, in a practical question of human relations', and he does so 'much more in terms of these vague rich intimate words than in the clear words of his official language'.

> The word plays an unusual trick in first getting its hearty feeling in one or two special phrases, which seem already to depend upon a feeling about dogs denied in other uses of the word. Before the Restoration the dog of metaphor, by and large, is snarling, sycophant, an underdog, loose in sex and attracted by filth, cruel if it dare; 'love me, love my dog' means 'love the meanest thing about me'. There is the Biblical dog, a pariah, living on crumbs and Jezebel as they drop ('a dog's chance' – he is dependent on human society and yet friendless in it); also the dog-faced Thersites of Homer, a mean and envious mocker (staying in the manger, barking at the moon). Shylock is eminently a dog of this sort and often called so; a man so placed can hardly be expected not to pervert justice, though this is a warning for you, not an excuse for him. It is not clear how far this feeling would apply to actual dogs; they do not get the full weight of it, but the change in a stock proverb seems to show that the earlier feeling was that they deserve pity as being normally (yet therefore rightly) ill-treated. 'As good a deed as to help a dog over a stile', 1546, an act of supererogatory and unconventional mercy; whereas the version of 1638, 'help a lame dog over a stile', puts in the adjective to make an otherwise natural action pathetic, and is a direct metaphor for helping a man. It is clear anyway that very mixed feelings are there to be drawn upon.

The fecundity of complex words is derived from the layered accumulations of 'period feeling'; the resulting ambiguity makes them highly suitable for conveying ambivalence, and therefore for 'making up one's mind'. The presence of complex words, then, is the close reader's cue to the intensity of ferment that prepares a difficult decision, and all the documents of this period in Mandelstam's life corroborate this intuition.

In the aftermath of leaving the Federation of Soviet Writers (opting, provisionally, for the 'outside' in the dilemma of safety, which nevertheless would not be put to rest), he refused to shake hands with any of *FOSP*'s remaining members. A few of the professional writers appeared to understand and to feel chastened. Far from dying down, the scandal continued to enlarge, leading to the formation of a special committee for investigating what Mandelstam now referred to as his very own 'Dreyfus affair'. In a letter to Nadezhda of February 24, 1930, he described hours of depositions. 'Summoned before the committee', he began;

> Four hours of questioning or, rather, my own uninterrupted talking. I was extremely displeased with myself. In the morning: 'You have given us many valuable points, don't worry, don't try to accomplish the impossible. We are not going to procrastinate with this case.' Now, the investigation has been subdivided into sectors. Each investigator works with me separately. I have been summoned along the line of *FOSP*. A three-hour interrogation. The investigator is a woman, an old party member and an editor at *The Young Guard*. She dragged out of me the formal points of the accusation. Like a dentist, extracted seventeen of them. She was not happy. Enjoined me to get organized at home and send additional points in writing by post. Done. (Berezner blurted out during the meeting: 'Keep in mind, the feuilleton had been *commissioned*.') A four-hour interrogation on the third, along the line of ZiF. Method: answers on the spot, in writing and strictly in accordance with the questions. Colossal patience.

'Curious', he added, 'I hadn't brought the papers with me; they sent me home, and waited until I came back (one quick flight by taxi)'. The committee's 'colossal patience' was mobilized to the very important end of getting all the evidence *in writing*. But what would be its subsequent use, or uses? The situation was disturbingly opaque. The deliberate extraction of written testimony appeared to pursue some such purpose as isolating the testimony from its source so as to incriminate the latter. The letter to Nadezhda of March 13, 1930, teems with foreboding, confusion and the diffuse general sense of alarm:

> Dearest Nadinka! I am completely lost. I am having a very hard time. Nadik, I should have been with you all this time. You are my strong one, my poor little one, my sweet birdy. I kiss your sweet brow, my little old one, my young one, my beloved. You are working, you are doing something, you are wondrous. Nadik, little one! I want to come to you in Kiev. I will not forgive myself for leaving you all alone in February. That I did not overtake you, that I did not come right away towards your voice on the telephone – and did not write, almost nothing at all, the whole time. How you wander, dearest one, up and down our room, all that is dear and eternal is there with

> you. To hold on, to hold on to this precious, this immortal thing, till the last breath. Not to part with it, not for anything in the world. Dearest one, it's hard, I always feel it's hard but now I cannot even find the words to describe it. They've confounded me, they keep me like a prisoner, no light is coming in. I keep wishing to brush off the lies – and cannot, keep trying to wash off the dirt – and that, too, is impossible.

'Need I tell you', he goes on, 'what a madness, what a savage dull nightmare it is, all and every bit of it'. Now, the details. 'Tormented me with the investigation, summoned five times. Three different people. Long intervals: three to four hours.' This, too, engendered bewilderment: 'What do they want from me? Again, I am being toyed with.' In a game of cat-and-mouse, only the cat can be said to be 'playing', with ease and control; the feeling of 'being toyed with', on the contrary, has a suffocating character of powerlessness that desperately needs a cure. Polonsky's diary the following September recorded how the events continued to fray Mandelstam:

> Mandelstam called on me. He looks old, bald, gray, unshaven. Destitute, hungry, threadbare. Agitated, as always, neurasthenically winds up in conversation, jumps up as if stung, gesticulates furiously, with tragic howls. Unusually self-assured, speaks of himself as a singular, or, at any rate, extraordinary phenomenon. That he doesn't get published he understands not as a failure of his poetry to meet the demands of the time. He explains this with a myriad reasons: the triumph of mediocrity and hackwork, his own persecution, etc. Demands to be published, demands money, insistently, peskily, hinting at the possibility of a tragic outcome. Of course, one senses a tragedy in him: a man of huge poetic powers, of great culture – he is alien to our time and has nothing to give it. He lives in his own world – partly of the past, of refined aesthete's emotions, deeply individualistic and narrow though deep – but in no aspect do they coincide with the spirit of our time, with its character and moods prevalent in the journals. This is why he, with his classical but cold verses, is an outsider. And certainly, the patina of decadence upon them is great. What to do with him? Filthy, threadbare, ready to have a fit at any moment, suspecting everyone of the wish to humiliate and insult him – he has something like a mania – it is hard to meet and talk with him. Even more so because it is difficult to help him. I gave him an advance – something like six hundred roubles – against the prose.

We can let go here of the thread of events that would only continue to escalate, the circumstances becoming more dire and the tone of Mandelstam's protestations becoming more desperate, and fast-forward closer to the day when the cure decidedly appears to have been found. In July 1933, an internal report was submitted by an OGPU agent:

> Some days ago, O. MANDELSTAM has returned from Crimea. His mood is luridly coloured in anti-Soviet tones. He is agitated, sharp in his remarks and judgements, obviously intolerant of other views. He has isolated himself sharply from his neighbours, even keeps his windows shut with curtains drawn. He is depressed by the scenes of hunger he witnessed in Crimea, and by his own literary misfortunes.

'MANDELSTAM', the report continued, 'plans to write again to Comrade STALIN'. What swayed Mandelstam from writing *to* Stalin, in the direction of writing *against* him? Could it have been Zelinsky's attack of September 5, in *Literary Leningrad*? 'In the poems of Mandelstam and Pasternak, we hear the voices of the receding and vanquished powers.' 'In all such instances', he clarified for the insufficiently alert, 'we hear the voice of a class enemy'.

In September 1933, Lydia Ginzburg listened to *Conversation about Dante* at Akhmatova's. Her keen insight would be confirmed by the later events:

> Mandelstam has the reputation of a madman and really does appear to be mad among people who are used to hiding and camouflaging their impulses. For him, perhaps, there is no distance between an impulse and an action – the distance that constitutes the essence of the European way of life.

The impulse was waiting only for a form to be realized in, and that form may have presented itself on October 18, when Mandelstam's friend Mark Talov called on the poet, noting later in his records:

> He astonished me with the news that has long ceased to be such a thing. It turns out that a month or a month-and-a-half ago, *Pravda* ran an article in which he, Mandelstam, was pilloried as a 'class enemy'. Together with him, Klychkov, Klyuyev, Akhmatova and one more Leningrad poet were classed as 'class enemies'. The Mandelstams are in a new flat, their own, of two rooms with an entryway and a kitchen. Osip Emilyevich has erected his library shelves quite primitively: bricks stacked on either side are overlaid with a board, on top of it – more bricks, then another board – in this manner he has set up several rows of books. The other walls are bare. He has no money even for necessary furniture. I let him have a look at my epigram on A. M. Efros. I asked O. E. whether he had ever written epigrams. 'Never.' Then we recalled Baratynsky's brilliant 'Laughing Epigram'.

Baratynsky's poem, published in 1827 under the title 'Epigram', was a brief, six-line praise of the genre depicted as a betaloned flying creature

'The Stalin Epigram' and the Liberty of Protest

on the lookout for the first passing 'freak' and swift to sink her claws into his eyes – the rhyme pattern of the little poem, *aaBccB*, dramatizing the expectant delay after the end of the three-line introduction tied off with the first masculine ending, with the two feminine endings of lines four and five (the epigram circling around in search of a victim), before the poem pounces, clinching the masculine rhyme in its final line. This curious vision of an epigram as a poem alive and energized before its subject is found, prowling restlessly, waiting to strike, could not have left the already sensitized Mandelstam inert, and his conversation with Talov cannot be ignored as a signal element in the prehistory of the poem that would appear a month later.

The following November would be the first time in years when Mandelstam could be witnessed in excellent spirits: the record is Boris Kuzin's, who recalls the fateful morning when the poet came to him alone, 'looking very agitated but cheerful'.

> I understood that he had written something new that needed to be shared right away. This new thing turned out to be a poem about Stalin. I was astonished by it and no words were necessary to show it. After a pause of sheer shock I asked O. E. whether he had read it to anyone else. 'Not a soul. You are the first. Well, of course, Nadenka, too.' I implored O. E., in the fullest sense of the word, to promise me that N. Ya. and myself would remain the only ones to know about these verses. He responded with happy and satisfied laughter, but finally O. E. did promise me not to read the poem to anyone else. After he left, I thought immediately that it would be inconceivable at least for N. Ya.'s brother, Evg. Yak., and for Anna Andr. not to learn about the poem as soon as they saw O. E. And Klychkov? No, he would not keep his promise. Too strong was the need for 'A Reader! An Adviser! A Physician!' Literally two or three days later, with the sweetest smile, as if he had just eaten a piece of marvelous cake, O. E. stated to me: 'Read the verses (it was obvious which verses they were) to Boris Leonidovich.' My heart sank. Of course, B. L. Pasternak was beyond any suspicion (as were Akhmatova and Klychkov), but he (just as O. E.) was always surrounded by people that I would only speak to with the greatest circumspection. Above all, it became clear to me that over the preceding days O. E. had read the terrible poem to more than a few of his acquaintances. The end of that story could be predicted with absolute certainty. The only surprise is that it took a year for the poem to reach its destination.

Such was the price at which Mandelstam was able to regain his sense of agency – the exorbitant price paid for moral survival under the conditions of a public persecution. Survival, and not suicide, as has often been asserted, was the object of 'The Stalin Epigram', and the self-destructive dimension of the poem arose from a need to stave off a moral death, a total collapse of personal agency inherent in the paralysis pressed upon the poet by his circumstances. Self-affirmation through self-destruction and free speech under duress: these contradictions must be grasped in order to get a handle on the poem so often placed right at the centre of Mandelstam's *oeuvre* and right at the heart of his significance. In celebrating the poem by which Mandelstam asserted his free personhood, we should not forget to what degree 'The Stalin Epigram' was composed under duress, coerced from the poet in the course of relentless hounding: *Così gridai colla faccia levata.*

CHAPTER 2

A Moulten Falcon

Poetry as Consolation and Dialectic

> Since the created mind, possessing but limited actuality, exists in the other but in otherness, it follows that a difference is preserved between all who venture their conjectures, and, certainly, different persons' different conjectures are but steps towards a single yet unknowable truth, even though they be incommensurate with one another, and, however close one person might be to another, he will never understand that other completely.
> Nicholas of Cusa, *On Conjectures*

The impulsive aspect of 'The Stalin Epigram' is brought into further relief by that towards which Mandelstam turned once the impulse had been spent. Having committed the irretrievable and imminently consequential acts of not only composing the 'Epigram', but also of making it known – not exactly publicly, but also not in a securely private way – and having turned away from the literary establishment that betrayed him, Mandelstam still needed an interlocutor. He found one in Petrarch, whose verses – sonnets 301, 311, 164 and 319 of *Il Canzoniere* – he translated as 1933 drew to a wintry close. (One liberating function of literature is to expand our choice of friends, so that we need not be imprisoned in our own time and place, nor limited in our choice of company.) If a reader, discovering an affinity with a poet of the past, may feel her or himself honoured as that poet's 'providential interlocutor' (as Mandelstam had felt himself to be in relation to Baratynsky, when writing 'On the Interlocutor'), then a poet-translator's relation to the poet behind the original can, too, be seen under the same aspect, exhibiting a still-greater degree of involvement, reciprocity and commitment. This view of translation as a species of dialogue, unfolding across time and space, augments the creative agency of the translator, as the translation itself becomes at once a testament that the earlier poet has been heard and understood, and, at same time, a subtle commentary upon the original, embodying the poet-translator's own sensibility and perspective. Free versions that would be seen as poems inspired by, yet distinct from the original under a more literalist conception of translation, can figure as *bona fide* translations under this view of translation as an interpretive art balancing self-effacement with distinctive authorial presence. As this is the view being espoused here, Mandelstam's versions of Petrarch are freely referred to as 'translations', without further qualification. That each version is anchored in a specific Italian sonnet and maintains a coherent set of formal correspondences to its predecessor is felt to be sufficient.

Despite the close proximity of Mandelstam's Petrarchan sonnets to the time of the epigram's emergence, the author is not aware of a study that seeks to consider them in the light of this tragic proximity and the gravity with which it imbues these graceful versions. Superficial conjecture attributes the sonnets' inspiration to the memory of Olga Vaksel, who had shot herself in Stockholm in 1932. Lada Panova, for instance, furthers this interpretation of the sonnets, particularly the Sonnet 311, whose 'most plausible addressee', she claims, was Olga Vaksel. What Panova declines to recognise is the distance between demonstrating (quite plausibly) that the news of Vaksel's death must indeed constitute one filament in the complex tapestry of this cycle – and stating outright that the cycle, or a part of it, should be thought of as *addressed* to that one particular woman.

Meanwhile, it is true that the entire cycle of four sonnets is coloured by a mood of loss and transience. Yet it is also undeniable that some irrevocable transformation has taken place within the narrator's psyche, and the sobbing quality of Petrarch's feminine line-endings supply an expressive vehicle for the mood. The impression is of translations that were as much a consoling distraction from current troubles as a meditation upon them, chiefly upon the irreversible step that had just been taken by Mandelstam and that was now awaiting its consequences – an event of cardinal importance, comparable to a death, and offering thereby a sympathetic link to Petrarch's experience of death and grief. Together, the four sonnets constitute a sequence with its own internal development, bearing upon various facets of the new setting within which Mandelstam finds himself in the wake

A Moulten Falcon

of composing the 'Epigram', and concluding with a kind of after-glance upon the aftermath – upon what (or, rather, who) might be left, or preserved at the end of the destructive transformation of the world: a woman moving in a crowd, a vision of a billowing storm of undulating pleats (a visual idea irresistibly reminiscent of another Italian connection – the billowing and clinging finery of Botticelli's *Primavera*).

It is in the synthetic nature of a poem to be a confluence of influences, to be, in other words, open to the infusion of any material capable of contributing to its rich unity. In the context of the previous discussion of the biographical events of 1928–33 and of the persistence of the double bind as the form assumed by the various social pressures experienced by Mandelstam during those years, it is impossible not to be struck by the opening image of the first sonnet in this sequence, 'Valle che de' lamenti miei se' piena', for it opens with a vision of 'the little river, swollen with salty tears' – swollen *because* it is pressed or squeezed *between* its opposite banks; although the birds could speak of this moment, and the sentient beasts witness, the fish, who are properly caught between these twin pressures, are silent. The landscape, seen as if through time, at once as it were in the past and as it appears in the present, is remarked as unchanged, unlike the felt constitution of the poet: the latter is like a granite slab, granular (the rock being composed largely of quartz, feldspar and mica) in such a way that everything that is trapped within it is constitutive of it. Earlier drafts of the translation made the psychological parallel rather transparent, though it comes to be less direct in the final version: 'sorrow's grains are embedded in the former nest of pleasure',

> Where I seek the traces of beauty and honour
> That disappeared, like a moulten falcon,
> Leaving its body in an earthen bed.

The 'falcon' ('*sokol*') that replaces, quite surprisingly, ''l mio bene' of Petrarch, arrives in these lines straight from *The Lay of Igor's Campaign*, a twelfth-century (and therefore temporally commensurate with Petrarch's sonnets) account containing the famous lines of the older prince Svyatoslav's rebuke to Igor and Vsevolod for not having acted upon his will and advice: 'It is no wonder for an old man to be as young again. When a falcon is moulten many times over, he whips the other birds up high, will let no one offend against his nest.' To 'moult many times over' is a measure of advanced age in a falcon, and that is why Svyatoslav, the patriarch of this narrative, likens himself to such a bird. In Mandelstam's version of Petrarch, it is the disappearance of the falcon that indicates his high flight: 'Sometimes a falcon soars so high that he can barely be seen, and only as a dark speck in the sky', writes Lydia Sokolova in a very fine essay devoted to the meaning of Svyatoslav's invocation of a moulten falcon, and it is when the falcon is out of *human* sight that the bird itself can enjoy the proverbial 'bird's-eye view', with all the acuity of the privileged sense sympathetically divined in the avian species by Comte de Buffon, in the 'Discourse on the Nature of Birds' (1770):

> the sight is in birds vastly more perfect, and embraces a wider range. A sparrow-hawk, while he hovers in the air, espies a lark sitting on a clod, though at twenty times the distance at which a man or dog could perceive it. A kit which soars to so amazing a height as totally to vanish from our sight, yet distinguishes the small lizards, field-mice, birds, &c. and from this lofty station he selects what he destines to be victims of his rapine. But this prodigious extent of vision is accompanied likewise with an equal accuracy and clearness;

> Our bird's-eye views, of which the accurate execution is so tedious and so difficult, give very imperfect notions of the relative inequality of the surfaces which they represent. But birds can chuse their proper stations, can successively traverse the field in all directions, and with one glance comprehend the whole.

This capacity to see the landscape whole, to resolve the apparent local contradictions through panoramic comprehension, is also implied in the figure of the falcon of several moults, wise and practised because of his age. Yet neither this, nor the reference to advancing age exhausts the richness of Mandelstam's two-line simile, since the soaring of his aged 'moulten falcon', which in the context of the hunt precedes a lightning-fast downward stoop, an attack, is at the same time a death, a Petrarchan figure of a soul ascending to the heavens, abandoning the body 'in an earthen bed'. The naturalness with which the merging of these figures – of the ascending falcon, and the ascending soul who has shed 'la sua bella

A Moulten Falcon

spoglia' – is attained can be appreciated in the presence of myths such as those mentioned in Georgiy Dementyev's monograph on gyrfalcons, published in 1951 and cited by Sokolova, which points out the existence among eighth-century Oghuz Turks of legends concerning dead warriors – believed to have turned, in death, into falcons. However, this also does not exhaust the richness of Mandelstam's 'moulten falcon', which is further amplified by the particulars of tending to moulting falcons: in some traditions, they were given a rest from hunting, as a moulting bird's powers were thought to be compromised. The sense that the moulting falcon is ailing in a certain way is evident from Dahl's dictionary, where the noun for 'moult', '*myto*', appears in a single entry with its relative, '*myt*', translated as 'strangles' – *Coryza contagiosa equorum*, or equine distemper. Although particular to horses, this sense nevertheless inflects the bundle of meanings represented by the entry as a lexical totality, and the inflection implies a limited and weakened status, of injury, and even of shame and discredit. The falcon's recovery after a moult, amplified by the significance of the moult as a sign of maturation, signals a joyful and at the same time dangerous transformation into a raptor fully capable of the martial behaviour proper to its species. Although in Russian falconry usage only the female is referred to as a proper 'falcon' ('*sokol*'), the males being much smaller and lighter and signified by the noun '*cheglik*', these technicalities were probably omitted from the literary descriptions of the falcon that remained after the fading of falconry from the arena of ordinary life in the eighteenth century. The sensibility of the sonnet, then, is predominantly masculine.

As we shall see in the translation of Sonnet 319, which concludes the sequence, it is the poet who is seen as having crossed the mortal divide, leaving behind the world and life as they once had been known to him. Among the things left behind, a woman, who appears to be very much a living one, or else, an ideal image informed, quite possibly, but more than one historic or even artistic prototype:

> And, furrowing my brow, I now wonder,
> How well she looks, and with what crowd mingles,
> And how the storm of gathers swirls around her.

And even Sonnet 311, which Panova makes the centre of her case for 're-addressing' the sequence to Olga Vaksel, contains lines indicative of at least an undertow of ambiguity – which, if it is there, it can only be profitable to notice, since it is ambiguity, in the varied Empsonian sense, that makes good poetry good and great poetry great. For this reason, even if news of Vaksel's death had reached Mandelstam by the winter of 1933, it would be wrong to ignore the literal meaning of the lines

> He sings farewell, alone from now on –
> To me, to me!

and to insist on reading them *solely* as an inversion, an internalization of another's death (as one would have to, in order to make the case for exchanging a variable – 'some loss' – for an unambiguous constant – 'Olga Vaksel'). The more probable interpretation is that a complex of impulses was involved in the wish to translate these sonnets – a complex possibly including the reaction to the news of Vaksel's death, but inevitably coloured, and strongly, by the very ominous events of Mandelstam's own life, by the recent composition of a poem felt by Mandelstam himself to be a watershed, one that split his life into what it had been before 'The Stalin Epigram' and the nebulous afterlife that awaited him in its wake. Even Mandelstam's prototype, Sonnet 311, opens with an ambiguous object of loss:

> Quel rosignol, che sí soave piagne,
> forse suoi figli, o sua cara consorte

Mandelstam's translation passed through a draft opening with the words 'How the nightingale glories in his unhappiness', before settling on a wording that translates:

> How the bereaved nightingale proclaims
> His feathered kin within the deep-blue night,
> Over the hills or down in the valley,
> Melting the silence of the countryside

The molten quality of the space around the bird who commands and transforms it, *melts* it with his liquid trills, is continuous with the feeling about the falcon in the preceding sonnet where the bird energizes the entire open space he pierces as he prepares to stoop. Here, the 'bereft nightingale' *melts* the silence of the countryside, where the air, the hills and the valley below appear *molten* as a result, this being both an indication of the profound transformation within the landscape penetrated by the nightingale's song, and also emblematic of the psychological transformation within the person pierced by the same sorrowful trills at his own point of vulnerability, the ear. It must be agreed that, of the four sonnets in the sequence, this one does come closest to suggesting that the arrival of some news effects the transformation described in the poem. It is useless to render the next line, which opens the second stanza, according to the 'meaning' of the Russian words, since here their true primary meaning is the onomastic one, the sound of '*schekochet*', suggestive of a snapping trill, taking precedence over 'tickling', though that latter direct translation of the verb does bespeak a certain persistent and intrusive action of the nightingale's song on the ear, corroborated by '*muravit*' (rhyming with '*buravit*', 'drills', which is, in English, felicitously close to 'trills') – a verb, and a perfectly natural-sounding neologism, derived from '*murava*', a folk noun for vibrantly green and silky grass ('*trava-murava*'). But Mandesltam's verb, '*muravit*', is an invention that binds the penetrating action of these veins within the molten mass of rock at the moment of formation with the verb '*murovat*' – the Russian analogue of Italian '*murare*', 'to encase in a wall'. Mandelstam's '*muravit*' is brilliantly suggestive of the double-sidedness of what it is to be trapped within an unyielding solid mass, since to be perishing helplessly, slowly and painfully within a wall (like a condemned person) is also, potentially, to penetrate, driven by great pressure against the resistant element that yields and becomes a material record of the struggle that transformed it. Having compared himself, in the previous sonnet, to granite, whose graininess comes partly from the grains of sorrow embedded in and constitutive of it (and therefore impossible to remove and eliminate, unlike a foreign body that is isolated and then excreted by an organism), here the poet imagines himself being pierced, through the entry-point of the ear, by the nightingale's lament, the new figure elaborating the same configuration of forces: even the 'molten silence' of the countryside bespeaks some process of transformation effected by the penetrating sense of grief.

Sonnet 164 marks a new stage in the dramatic progression of the cycle:

> When the earth falls asleep and the heat dies down,
> And when a swan-like calm lies on the souls of beasts,
> Night makes her rounds, with her burning yarn,
> The mighty waters rocked by zephyrs on the seas,
>
> I sense, burn, yearn and cry – yet she doesn't hear

It seems naïve to think that a poet's imagination should be so compartmentalized as to 'dedicate' even the most straightforward 'love lyric' to a single fixedly specific person (and great love poems are never *merely* love poems, since what invariably accounts for their interest is the unexpected inflection of the central theme with ideas that surprise us by their appearance in that context). The synthetic nature of the poetic imagination suggests that all such portrayals, no matter how concentrated on a particular subject, must draw on varied tributaries from the spheres of life and art, and must not be imagined as outlined by hermetically sharp contours. There is, for these reasons, no possible way of demonstrating that Maria Petrovykh, a significant presence in Mandelstam's emotional life at this very time, could not have supplied some of the qualities of the erotically charged *donna* appearing in these sonnets:

> She whose nearness is invincibly the same,
> Alert, all night, all night, and all of her
> Of that far-away happiness is breathing.
>
> Though one the source, the water is confounded –
> Half-hard, half-sweet – could it be
> That my self-same beloved is two-faced?
>
> Each day a thousand times, to my own wonder,
> I must indeed extinguished be
> And then revive, just as startlingly.

In rendering Petrarch's 'mille volte il dí moro et mille nasco', Mandelstam's last line turns sharply towards Batyushkov's last known poem, which foreshadowed the nearing of the end of life with a clarity that might temper our uncritical trust in the late 'insanity', attributed to Batyushkov by his contemporaries and echoed by writers to this day.

> Wisely created am I, be my witness:
> Now I can sneeze, now I can yawn,
> I wake to fall asleep again,
> And sleep forever to awaken.

Sonnet 319 concludes this sequence, and itself concludes with the queries that revive the feeling of the living concreteness of the woman who is seen moving beautifully in the wavering drapery of her garments:

> And, furrowing my brow, I now wonder,
> How well she looks, and with what crowd mingles,
> And how the storm of gathers swirls around her.

The 'storm of gathers' reads irresistibly as a visual allusion to Botticelli's *Primavera*, and the connection is perhaps something more than one reader's fleeting fancy, as E. H. Gombrich, too, in *Symbolic Images*, drew a literary connection between the *Primavera* and the text of Apuleius' *Golden Ass*:

> nothing but a flimsy silken garment veiled the lovely maiden. A prying wind now lovingly and lasciviously blew it aside so that the flower of her youth was revealed to the sight, now with a wanton breath made it cling to her, the more graphically to outline the voluptuous forms of her limbs.

The garment, played with by the wanton breeze, reveals and conceals at once, or, more paradoxically, reveals both in concealing and in revealing, the concealing function of the garment inverted in such a way that the maiden appears to have been clothed only to be seen *as if* nude. The interplay of this passage and the composition of the *Primavera* is reflected in Mandelstam's spring-themed composition, which might well describe the subgroup of three figures on the right of Botticelli's painting:

> She strides but slightly overtaking
> Her sprightly friend and a youth a year younger than herself.

Olga Sedakova points out the figural composition implied in these verses:

I shall note another moment, little-known in Russian love lyrics, in Mandelstam's contemplation of gait. 'She' proceeds not on her own, but involuntarily contrasting with a walking group, which, too, is evidently beautiful – both her 'brisk friend' and 'a youth a year younger than herself'. This is a characteristically Italian technique (as well as that of classical poetry, where we constantly encounter rings of singing girls, groups surrounding a heroine). In *La Vita Nuova*, Beatrice is always accompanied: by friends, and once, by Donna Primavera, who not so much overtakes her as, rather, precedes her. Primavera (Spring, whose real name is Giovanna), the beloved of another poet, Dante's friend, walks before Beatrice like (in Dante's immodest comparison) John the Baptist before Christ.

Could it be a mere coincidence that Apuleius's account of Venus, who, Gombrich tells us, is leading this three-figure procession, is so continuous with Mandelstam's conveyance of Natasha Shtempel's 'sweetly uneven gait'?

> Venus placide commoversi cunctatinque lente vestigio ... et sensim annutante capite coepit incedere, mollique tibiarum sono delicatis respondere gestibus ....

> Venus began placidly to move with a hesitating slow step... and slightly inclining her head, she responded with delicate movements to the voluptuous sound of the flute ....

What does this Italianate connection, between the Petrarchan sonnets of 1934 and the love poems of 1937, tell us about Mandelstam? A modest claim seems to be justified: that the range of feeling in the poems is no narrower than the range of cultural reference, and that, given the subtleties of sensibility imbued in the artistic conventions of every epoch, each evocation of period art opens up gates, within the Modernist tradition, onto ways, codes, palettes and languages of feeling that cannot be understood reductively.

This lengthy objection to binding Mandelstam's Petrarchan versions to the figure of Olga Vaksel has a parallel in Irina Surat's careful and imaginative study of the so-called 'Verses to Natalia Shtempel' as the diptych (presented by Mandelstam to his subject in 1935) is sometimes referred to by editors of Mandelstam. Even though the history of the verses' composition is securely tied to specific episodes in Mandelstam's friendship with Shtempel, Surat cautions against a naïve reading of the two stanzas, or the two poems, as inspired entirely and solely by 'Natasha'.

> Let us not unambiguously tie the verses about a 'clear conjecture' to the person of Natalia Shtempel and to the episodes related by her. Strictly speaking, the editorial title of the 'Verses to N. Shtempel' is incorrect: the poem is not addressed to Natalia Yevgenyevna. The heroine of the first stanza is denoted by a third-person pronoun – 'she walks', 'she is drawn', and in the second part she dissolves among certain 'women' of a special vocation. The 'clear conjecture' is connected to her unusual, 'unevenly sweet gait', but the meaning of the 'conjecture' exceeds the bounds of one person's destiny.

And so do the sources of the poem's imagery, and the influences of which the poem is a confluence, naturally reach beyond the events of the day or two that conjured into existence what Olga Sedakova calls 'mesmerizingly harmonious, slow, undulating verses the likes of which would never occur again in late Mandelstam', verses that open with a portrait of Natalia Shtempel:

> Dipping against her will down to the empty earth,
> In her sweetly uneven gait, she walks
> Slightly ahead of her sprightly friend
> And a youth younger by a year than her.
>
> She is impelled by that constraining freedom
> Of an inspired defect . . .

'What once was gait, shall be unreachable', the second stanza concludes, having opened with a declaration of Mandelstam's rediscovery of Petrarch's discovery: the suitability of the feminine line endings, drifting off with unstressed syllables as if carrying off sighs and cries, for conveying sorrow:

> Some women are akin to humid earth,
> Their every step a resounding lament,
> And their calling is to attend to the resurrected
> And be the first to greet the newly dead.

The Russian *'rydan'ye'* does not have a sufficiently analogous English counterpart, as nouns for various kinds of cry acquire a disparaging tint when the crying becomes unrestrained, whole-bodied, so to speak, but to *rydat'* in Russian is to do just that, to cry in a whole-bodied manner, the crying involving breath, voice, shudders and copious tears. When '*rydan'e*' falls into the rhyme pattern of a *canzone*, it does precisely what the end-word of each line does in the Italian – shudder, sob, drift off – to initiate a new cycle of shuddering and sobbing in the next line.

Natalia Shtempel described scrupulously the circumstances leading to the poem's composition – the apparently trivial events that began with a walk (which turned into an impromptu 'wine tasting' around the town's numerous but uniformly uninviting cellars) and concluded with Mandelstam's words: 'When I die, send this to the Pushkin House as my last will and testament.'

> Not long before our 'journey' around the wine cellars, I called on Osip Emilyevich and said that I had an errand that required stopping to see my friend and coworker, Tusya. Osip Emilyevich decided to come with me. On the way back he asked: 'Tusya does not see in one eye?' I replied that I did not know, and that I had never spoken with her about that, but perhaps, she doesn't, after all. 'Yes', said Osip Emilyevich, 'people with a physical flaw do not like to talk about it'. I objected, saying that I never noticed that, and that I talk without difficulty about my own lameness. 'Goodness, but you have a beautiful gait, I cannot imagine you otherwise!' exclaimed Osip Emilyevich hotly.
>
> The following day, after a nighttime walk, I called on Mandelstam... He was serious and focused. 'I composed verses yesterday', he said. He read them. I remained silent. 'What is this?' I did not understand the question and sat in silence still. 'These are love lyrics', he replied for me. 'This is the best thing that I have ever written.' And he handed me the paper.

The self-evident biographical moment when the poem is born proves to be but the soil, within which the trunk of the poem is firmly rooted. Even more surprisingly, the poem flourishes the way it does (as we shall see, with the aid of Olga Sedakova and her careful study) because its Russian trunk is grafted, close to the ground, with exquisite limbs chosen freely from an unlimited range of cultural reference – chosen in such a way that we can recognise their form. 'What is this?' inquires Sedakova, asking us the same question that Mandelstam posed to Shtempel, and answering it for us:

> A diptych, two independent poems, one following the other... or could these be two stanzas of a single poem? The question of the independence of each part is connected... with the rhyme structure of each stanza, a complex 11-line stanza with

A Moulten Falcon

feminine line endings. This kind of stanza has no parallel in Russian poetry. Yet, against the backdrop of old Italian poetry, we recognise it immediately as a stanza of a *canzone* – one that repeats a complex rhyme pattern in each part, is composed of fairly independent stanzas ('rooms', in the original meaning). We move from stanza to stanza as from one room to another. This 'enfilade' structure of thought is typical of old ('classical') Italian poetry and of its source, Provençal troubadour lyrics. ... And with the recognition of Mandelstam's stanzas as stanzas of a *canzone* their Italian theme opens up before me.

'I am convinced', Sedakova continues, 'and hope to convince you',

> that the proper context of this poem is Tuscan poetry, Dante and Petrarch. ... Here, I shall permit myself a general observation: usually, Russian verses are considered in the context of Russian poetry. The scholar and critic never leave this sphere, looking for echoes and allusions in the corpus of Russian verse. In many instances, this is entirely justified, as the poets themselves inhabit the sphere of poetry in their mother tongue. But in some cases, this does not suffice. This applies to Pushkin, and to Mandelstam. To them (though, of course, not to them alone) foreign poetry was alive in the same measure as the Russian verse. We might remember that once Mandelstam said to someone, pointing at a volume of Dante, his *Divine Comedy*: 'This is what matters!' That was the main event of his life.

The critic, one might add, is also justified in leaving the sphere of native allusions when the poetry itself concerns ideas. This is pressingly the case with Mandelstam, a philosophically informed and disciplined poet (whose stanza, notes Sedakova, is a vessel – and 'not for sound, but for thought'). As the universals of philosophy tend to be perennial, illuminating connections may arrive in the form of 'ideas that occurred elsewhere', in the words of William Empson (who noted a 'Buddhist' sensibility in none other than England's Andrew Marvell). Meanwhile, Sedakova's formal observation concerning the rhyme pattern of a *canzone* leads to a series of insights concerning the poem's sensibility, its genuine range of reference and, in the end, a reflection upon the biographical dimension of the poem and what it intimates about Mandelstam's relation to Natalia Shtempel.

> In the Italian key, we can better understand the meaning of the *gait*, the main subject of these stanzas. ... I do not remember ... any other Russian love lyrics depicting a walking woman. What does she usually do in our verse? She sits, stands, *appears* ... But

in Provençal and Italian poetry, the gait of the beloved is very important. How does one depict a beautiful lady? Walking. In the way she walks, in her gait, in her step lies the power that immediately affects the narrator. In Dante's *Vita Nuova*, *three* poems are dedicated to Beatrice's gait, and what is effected by it! She walks – and all that is bad, all that is wicked in a person, dies. And all that is good and virtuous awakens and reaches towards her. At the site of her, as she walks, people forget all that is base, and forgive. Old poetry does not like description ... it conveys everything through the effect upon the people who witness her walking. Dante notes in Beatrice's steps a confluence of imperiousness and meekness; she proceeds regally, and humbly. ... The gait initiates a series of the beautiful lady's wondrous qualities: her gait is followed by her gaze (not by her eyes, but her gaze ...). The gait, then the gaze, then her smile, and then – her speech. ... Dante calls all these 'the balconies of the soul'. The human soul (especially the soul of a lady) comes out of its chambers, revealing itself on the balconies of the gait, gaze, smile, and speech.

Like Irina Surat, Sedakova, too, points out that her own commentaries 'are not concrete "sources" of Mandelstam's images'. 'They are, rather, that Italian sea from which this poetry arises, like Aphrodite from the "lilac clay" of her "native sea".' And here, too, the content of the lines so beautifully limned meets with the formal considerations that have been mentioned, and fruitfully interpreted, by Sedakova, yet can be coaxed into yielding yet more, if we turn to Mandelstam's own *Conversation About Dante*, to the significant parallel between the human gait and poetic metre. 'One must point out some elements of Dante's rhythms', Mandelstam begins the polemic about the sense of movement in verse and its emergence from the rhythms of human walk:

> I am wondering in earnest, how many soles, how many calf-skin shoes, how many sandals had been worn out by Alighieri over the time of his poetic work as he traveled the goat-paths of Italy. The *Inferno* and especially the *Purgatorio* extol the human walk, the length and rhythm of the steps, the foot and its form. The step, conjoined with breath and infused with thought, is understood by Dante as the beginning of prosody. To signify walking, he employs a multitude of varied, enchanting phrases. Dante's philosophy and poetry are always moving, always on their feet. A stop is a variation of accumulated movement: a ledge for restful conversation is a product of alpine effort. A foot of verse – inhalation followed by exhalation – is a step. Each step is a conclusion, vigilant like a syllogism.

Here, 'a foot' (and its shape, homonymous with form) is doing double duty in Russian as it does in English, serving anatomy and prosody at once. 'The *Inferno* and especially the *Purgatorio* extol the human walk, the length and rhythm of the steps, the foot and its form.' This proves to be excitingly fruitful, because shifts of gravitational centre, resulting in change of position, can be seen in the relations between stressed and unstressed syllables patterning the metre of a poem, between two different words that constitute a rhyme, between thesis and antithesis in a dialectical progression, between such reasoning and poetry, between question and answer, between vectors whose sum is a hypotenuse of a triangle of which both vectors are *legs*. Walking is, essentially, a model of all conversation as interchange, as reflected in the language characterizing movement: among the adjectives that describe someone on the move – 'ambulatory', 'itinerant', 'peripatetic', 'perambulatory', 'roving', 'vagrant', 'migratory', 'nomadic', 'locomotive', 'automotive', 'self-moving', – 'rambling' and 'discursive' are two that we see more often characterizing *speech*, as against movement. If speech and bipedalism are key characteristics of humanity, to Mandelstam they are not discrete characteristics but manifestations of a deeply ingrained habit, pertinent not only to locomotion but to patterns of thought and their expression in language.

If Dante is to Mandelstam the standard for all poetry, it is not least because he is a pilgrim on foot, engaged, as Mandelstam sees it, in rhythmical argumentation where alternating impulses resemble a succession of theses and antitheses moving a dialogue forward, in the direction of a discovery. Mandelstam senses the primacy of physical facts in determining the turns taken by ideas. If in 'The Dawn of Acmeism' words acted as units exerting the forces whose interactions were then being considered, the *Conversation About Dante* considers a variety of other units under the aspect of opposition (to use the language of physics) or contradiction (to use the term of logic). To deploy the resulting theory in practice is to rise above 'writing' towards poetry that grounds reason, with dialectic as its fundamental pattern, in the physiological habit of walking. As Dante's imagination conversed with Virgil and was assisted, on the path of the *Commedia*'s creation, by Virgil's imagined presence, Mandelstam, too, converses with Bely about Dante, Bely's vigorous mind figuring as an athlete of dialectic in a tribute Mandelstam wrote shortly after Bely's death on January 8, 1934:

> An ice-skater, a first-born, thrown out by his time
> Under the frost-dust of declensions formed anew.

This is a crucial insight into the unity of the dialogue form, for essential to dialogue is propulsion towards new conclusions, generation of new figures in the language. Like a blade-runner whose forward thrust is a product of vectors subsuming opposite forces, Bely – 'Turquoise mentor, tormentor, ruler and fool!' – is someone whose mind synthesizes prolifically.

Ice-skating gives an emphatic expression to that which walking communicates as a metaphor of thought. Walking supplies the model for both poetic rhythm and dialectical reasoning that advances by a succession of mutually compensating propositions of the form 'yes, but …' – the sequence being the basic form of dialogue. Implicit in the form of the dialogue – the model of civilized discourse – is dissent; moreover, dissent is essential for the continuation of a sequence where new statements must contribute something that at once absorbs and acknowledges the preceding contributions but also modifies them according to the point of view being expressed. The model simply does not accommodate full, static agreement as it takes for granted the difference of perspective necessary between individuals and the contributions of time and flux that is time's tangible expression. Dissent, then, is not annihilation by contradiction or mere finger-pointing, but advancement by change proportionate to what is being absorbed and retained unchanged because found right, good, true and valuable.

An illustration of opposition and its result shows up in Krylov's fable 'The Swan, The Pike and The Crawfish' where the three creatures' efforts of pulling a loaded cart, each in a different direction, result in a dead standstill. Of course, it has been reasonably pointed out that the result imagined by Krylov could not be confirmed in a physical experiment, for if the swan were to pull the cart skyward while the pike pulled it towards the water and the crawfish 'scrambled backwards', the totality of the forces exerted upon the cart would not have been equal to zero. The cart will in all likelihood advance along the diagonal of a parallelogram constructed on the force vectors belonging to the pike and the crab, moving little by little somewhere towards the water. The point of language to be taken from this is that opposition should not be construed to mean what logical negation means; in other words, not one, but a variety of statements coming from various positions may oppose a proposition, each combination of possible antithesis with the original thesis moving the dialogue in a different direction. This redeems the idea that dialectic is an art with ample room for the play of taste and imagination.

By calling Bely an 'ice-skater', Mandelstam intimates the character of Bely's imagination as capable of advancing in this zigzag fashion under its own steam, by orchestrating mutually compensatory movement in the manner of a dialogue – independently. This, of course, suggests a point of cardinal dissent from monolithic proletarian ideology, enlisting language itself as an ally: the seven Russian declensions fan out under the blades of the imaginary skater, raising the lively frost-dust of words, joyously reminiscent of Pushkin's lines, rendered thus by Charles Johnston: 'his collar in its beaver braiding / glitters with hoar-frost all about'.

Strolling is a form of soliloquy praised in the Moscow poems for its potential for flourishing into conversation, real or entertained in imagination, like the company of 'tender Batyushkov', a 'carefree walker with his magic stick' 'sniffing a rose and singing of Daphne'. One can see why Batyushkov's company might be imagined with pleasure: he had been a poet of fine sensibility and a person of great charm and modesty. Born in the provincial Vologda, a town roughly halfway from Moscow to the White Sea delta, he learned Italian and became a champion of Italian poetry, taking up at one time a translation of Tasso's *La Gerusalemme Liberata*. Described as constitutionally fragile, Batyushkov showed exceptional energy and bravery in many battles during Napoleon's invasion, yet on his return to country life and civil service he crumbled under the weight of internal conflicts that we may not have sufficient evidence to understand. Towards the end of his life he was seen as a harmless lunatic, writing paradoxically circular verses: 'I wake to fall asleep again / And sleep forever to awaken.' Shakespearean, too, should we be reminded of Caliban:

> That if I then had wak'd after long sleepe,
> Will make me sleepe againe, and then in dreaming,
> The clouds methought would open, and shew riches
> Ready to drop upon me, that when I wak'd,
> I cri'de to dreame againe.

The lines dedicated to Batyushkov by Mandelstam are of carefree, pleasurable civility: they breathe the open air of *la passeggiata*, a custom of 'walking with high-minded, often philosophical, conversation', described by Mary Beard as one of the classical civilization's gifts to the West:

> Rome was not the first ancient culture to link thinking and walking (Aristotle's 'Peripatetic' School is named for exactly that: *peripatein*, 'walking around'). But the Romans gave rather more weight, and concentration, than the Greeks to the walking itself. You wouldn't have caught the stereotypical Roman absent-mindedly falling into a well, like the Greek sage Thales, while wandering about, lost in his own thoughts. And when, in the second century BC, a visiting academic from Pergamum slipped into a drain at Rome and broke his leg, that must have seemed a typically Greek kind of accident.

'How and why a person walked were crucial cultural indicators in ancient Rome: ways of walking divided barbarians from Romans, and good Romans from bad', Beard observes, explaining the encompassing importance of the gait to character. 'The key Latin word is *incessus*, which literally means "gait" or "how a person moves on their feet". It is now regularly translated as "bearing" or "demeanor"; but that removes all the sense of movement from it.' How consonant this is with Mandelstam's sense of the poetic form and of its unity with physical movement is evident from the *incessus* of the 1937 verses to Natasha Shtempel, carefully synchronized with the walk of the woman it praises in tones of utmost delicacy:

> Dipping against her will down to the empty earth,
> In her sweetly uneven gait, she walks

The metre of the first line (a modulated iamb, where the actually stressed syllables are emphasized, '*K pus-toi* | *zem-le* | *ne-vol'-* | *-no pri-* | *-pa-da-* | *-ya*') was employed, as we have seen (in various modulations), in Mandelstam's Petrarchan versions. That the verses to Natasha Shtempel echo the prosody of those translations (and also the rhythms of Dante's *Commedia*) has been noticed before. Lada Panova's article on Dante in the *Mandelstam Encyclopedia* is notable because of its claim to certain scholarly sophistication and authority in the encyclopaedic context. Panova's analysis of Mandelstam's recourse to the two Italian poets has the advantage of absolute clarity. Its disadvantage is the corresponding lack of subtlety: 'Having found himself in the situation of unrequited and therefore Platonic love, O. M. turned to D. and Petrarch, the unsurpassed authorities in the sphere of Platonic veneration of Beautiful Ladies.' We might dislike the castrative prudery of 'unrequited and *therefore* Platonic love'; if we do, the phrase should rouse our attention in time for what follows:

> The diptych is organized as a palimpsest, whose top layer is Mandelstam's love story with its main dramatic persona: Natalia Shtempel, walking in a spring landscape. Because the limping Natalia is no match for Beatrice and Laura, beauties without a single flaw, the lyrical plot is called to eliminate this contradiction. In it, the 'uneven gait' of the Platonic beloved at first strikes the observer with what E. A. Baratynsky once called an 'uncommon countenance', and then evens out as '*postup*'. With the elimination of this 'fault' Natalia joins the ranks of the Beautiful Ladies and, in this quality, prepares to make a worthy match for the poet who praised her, if not on earth, then in heaven.

This passage is insufficiently conscious of what it takes for granted: that Mandelstam's Voronezh friend is insignificant and unworthy of the poet's artistic attention, that the poet himself shares Panova's sentiment (though love's blindness compels him to grapple with the issue) and that the overcoming of this supposed 'problem' becomes the subject of the two poems that Panova sees in terms of an imagined struggle with Natasha Shtempel's inadequacy. 'Natalia is no match for Beatrice and Laura', Panova writes, incognizant of the evident impulse of the poem, born out of a recognition that *this* woman, with her temporal – 'animating', life-giving (as signalled even by her name, *Natalia*), and therefore also death-giving (for every life is pregnant with death) – identifying particulars (and nothing, we have seen, identifies a person as individually as does their *incessus*), is just the kind of material apparition from which countless ideals are born. Olga Sedakova, on the other hand, continues to interpret the poem's Italian connections, eliciting from them a true measure of feeling in the poem:

> I am certain that the word '*sladkaya*' ('sweet') – strange to the Russian language – from the first stanza... is actually a calque of the Italian '*dolce*'. Petrarch would have had 'dolce' here, and so would Dante. '*Dolce*' translates literally as 'sweet', 'delightful', but in Italian it belongs to a different register. In the language of Dante and Petrarch, '*dolce*' is the ever-present epithet for music: '*dolci suoni*', 'sweet', that is to say, harmonious sounds. The Russian '*sladkiy*' is already something not wholly decent, almost kitschy. What do we picture when we hear the words 'a sweet new style'? Certainly not the cool, clear writing of *La Vita Nuova*. The Italian '*dolce*' is free of cloying, of

the crude hedonism lurking in the Russian '*sladkiy*'. This '*dolce*' – it is gentle, harmonious, supple, delicate, courteous, and pleasing. A lady who lacks *dolcezza* ('sweetness' in the sense of an inward suppleness, delicacy) cannot be said to be beautiful.

It is Natalia's genuine, whole-person beauty, that is apprehended by Mandelstam with chaste tenderness, by drawing a connection between her sweet-temperedness (she was known, truly, as a sweet person) and Dante's 'sweet new style', between her uneven gait and the modulations of Italian verse ('typically traduced on our soil into regular iambic pentameter', notes Olga Sedakova), between her profound femininity and the delicacy of feminine rhyme. Everything about Natalia is likened to elements of the Italian poetic form, in such a way that she herself becomes an incarnation of poetry, of its sweet harmony as realized in the '*dolce novo stile*'. One wants to acknowledge this, and the chaste disposition of the poem, yet at the same time differ with Sedakova's outright denial of eroticism:

> This kind of love has a cultural history. Beatrice and Laura join the ranks for beautiful ladies who require but chaste adoration of their admirer, without the slightest thought of possession. This is the 'art of subtle love' of the troubadours, this is *fin amor*.

It seems right to draw a distinction between the absence of eroticism and its suspension, and it is the latter that accounts for the 'chaste' effect of the poem, 'purity' and 'chastity' being ideas energized by a fugitive relation with eros, harnessing eros to perform the unnatural trick of 'sublimation' – an attitude rather distinct from a flat absence of erotic imagination. The sense of restraint, courtesy, even self-effacement of *fin amor* is a product of this tension, of suspended and mastered vital eroticism.

Among memoirists of Mandelstam, Emma Gerstein has left a testimony that can be characterized as 'chaste' in the sense of the suspension of eroticism in the kind of grasping attention that bespeaks genuine love. 'How he would peel a pear with his fine long-fingered hands!' she sighs, as no other memoirist does. 'How beautifully he slept!' she often found herself tempted to exclaim, decades later, whenever Mandelstam's name was mentioned. 'But I would restrain myself, afraid to appear ridiculous.' When mentioning this detail, she substantiates her response with a precise and vivid flashback of Mandelstam when, exhausted by writing protest letters and remonstrating with *FOSP*, he threw himself onto the sofa in mid-conversation and was suddenly asleep:

> He lay on his side, with one hand under his head, knees bent, and his every limb took on a new lightness. It seemed that his nervous but energetic hand, his attenuated features, even the strange build of his body had all surrendered to a mysterious harmony. He did not at all look like a man lying down, but seemed to be afloat in blissful repose, as if listening to something.

Oddly, then – and despite Gerstein's cool resistance to the Mandelstams' various attempts to draw her into an erotic triangle – what she supplies as a friend of the couple is some of the most delicately loving writing about Mandelstam in private, writing that sometimes takes risks reporting details like 'the incorrect placement of his feet':

> heels together, toes apart. This accounted for his gait: in part, dragging his feet, in part, doing something that could not at all be defined. It is possible that Mandelstam's famously raised head, which gave the impression of exaggerated pride, had something to do with this flaw. This habit restored the equilibrium of his whole body when in motion.

There are glimpses, too, of the way he laughed, or the way his eyelashes shadowed his cheek when he slept: vignettes of the very same animating individuality that one finds breathing in Mandelstam's poems, and in Gerstein's writing there is a fair-minded, even wise, sense that these manifestations of the man are no less precious than the poetry, for both sprung from the same fragile, temporal source. At the same time, only Gerstein was capable of discerning, in Mandelstam's love lyrics dedicated to various women, a similar capacity for penetrating insight: 'He knew how to create both the outer and the inner likeness of a woman, very much as an artist, not as an infatuated lover who had "lost his head".' This last phrase, quoted so disparagingly, belongs to Nadezhda Mandelstam and her characterization of Mandelstam's fascination with Maria Petrovykh ('Marusya' to close acquaintances), a married young poet-translator who

> was planning to divorce her husband. This was difficult, because he was profoundly devoted to her. His adoration manifested in writing down things that she said (this I learnt not from Marusya herself but from shared acquaintances).

In the course of her relationship with the Mandelstams, Gerstein would also meet Lev Gumilyov, Akhmatova's son whose father, the poet Nikolay Gumilyov, had been executed by the Bolsheviks in 1921. It was arranged that Lev, whose paternity made his professional life exceedingly difficult, would come to see Emma at her office: it was hoped that she might be able to help him find a job.

> A young man came to the bureau, abstracted and independent, with a rucksack on his shoulders. Having addressed me by name and patronymic, he introduced himself: 'Lev Gumilyov'. Outwardly, he did not stand out from the mass of provincial specialists that crowded the Bureau. Having communicated some basic facts about himself, he asked me lightly, just as he was about to leave: 'Would you like a pop?' – and threw a piece of hard candy on the desk. When he had left town, a couple of days later, and I called on the Mandelstams, Nadya hastened to convey to me his casual impression of my person: 'A regular incompetent'. Such was the son of the executed Gumilyov in the role of a supplicant.

'Nevertheless', Gerstein concluded, 'I took on his case with great alacrity'.

The Mandelstams, who had made the introduction, were well aware of Gumilyov's precarious position. Still, Osip's drive to embroil in his vicissitudes the very people whom he found most sympathetic, prevailed: he recruited Lev to help ambush his adversary, Aleksey Tolstoy, who had presided over the shameful 'community trial' at the Herzen House and had failed to condemn Sargijan's assault on Nadezhda. Now the two friends spent entire days plotting gleefully to give 'Count Tolstoy' a slap on the face. Together, too, they would visit Maria Petrovykh and flirt competitively with 'the artisan of guilty looks', a woman whose significance to Mandelstam would be minimized by other memoirists, but whom Gerstein restores to a much more mysterious and lasting presence in the poet's imagination. (This, too, is a testament to Gerstein's scrupulousness: having found Petrovykh at first quite trivial, Gerstein remains attentive to facts that suggest how much 'Marusya' meant to other people in their circle.) Nevertheless, one day, on her way home from the Mandelstams', she was accompanied by Lev who had been sent by Nadezhda to buy kerosene. Their conversation led Emma to believe 'in Lyova's intellect and spirit, independently of comparisons with his famous parents. I felt him to be the heir to the outstanding Russian minds, not to the talents of mama and papa'. 'Beginning with that day, Lyova began to visit me. This astonished the Mandelstams and alarmed Anna Andreyevna.'

Gerstein would remember the morning when Nadezhda Mandelstam 'flew' into her flat in great agitation, declaring that Osip had composed a dangerous poem that could not be written down and had to be memorized by only one person in addition to 'Nadya' herself: 'That will be you. We are going to die, but you will pass it on to the people. Osya shall read it to you and then you'll memorize it with me. No one should know about this for now. Especially not Lyova.' It was understood that Gumilyov needed special care in being sheltered from political aspersions, and Gerstein complied with Nadezhda's admonition without suspecting being toyed with. The two women went to the Mandelstams' flat, where Osip himself read to Emma the epigram on Stalin, and then, accompanied by Nadezhda, Gerstein retreated to another room to memorize the poem, and there Nadezhda introduced a variant of the fifth line: *Even dogs in his yard are fat*. 'I thought that it was all buried very deep', Gerstein reflected on the experience. 'Until Mandelstam's conviction, I did not mention this poem to a single person, and of course, I never read it to anyone. But once, in front of me, the Mandelstams began talking about the poem, and Nadya declared blithely that Nina Nikolayevna Green prefers another version. It turned out, I was not the only one initiated into the secret.' Nadezhda Mandelstam's warning to Gerstein would have been straightforwardly sagacious – if not for the fact that the Mandelstams themselves had introduced Gumilyov to the Stalin verses.

The recklessness of Mandelstam's induction of Gumilyov into the circle of witnesses to the epigram on 'the Kremlin mountain-man' had to do with the impossibility, for any such witness, of maintaining anything like a neutral position. From the point of view of the state and the secret police, any knowledge of such 'counter-revolutionary' speech or writing compelled the citizen to report it immediately, denouncing the source. Non-reporting, if discovered, could be (and would be, if convenient) interpreted as a form of criminal conspiracy. Any politically flamboyant behaviour in front of one's peers would therefore automatically place them in an extremely uncomfortable, if not outright untenable, moral position wherein one's personal loyalties were pitched against one's very survival. One could remain courageous, principled and loyal in such circumstances, and many people did, like Boris Kuzin who refused to become an informant and was threatened with arrest and his own mother's certain death in the wake of such an event. The peculiar perversion of friendship enacted in the USSR during the purges had to do with pitching the trust and sincerity necessary to friendship against loyalty's requirement that one does not subject one's friends to such moral dilemmas as to what to do with one's exuberant political statements. This did not silence sardonic dissidents like Kuzin and Gerstein (both were known for letting slip fairly reckless statements), but it did complicate the dance of social proprieties exponentially, and life was permeated with risk, with fear – the emotions under whose pressure 'The Stalin Epigram' was propelled into existence:

> Not Hippocrene but a jet
> Of old familiar fear
> Will break through the ramshackle walls
> Of mean Moscow housing.

Gumilyov's case, then, is especially salient for understanding Mandelstam's motives in disseminating the poem, or, to put it more precisely, for understanding the complexity of those motives and their actual imperviousness to rationalization and complete analysis. What is special about this particular witness is his initial political vulnerability, due to the history of the execution of his father. And he was so very young: twenty-one, to be precise, the autumn of the epigram's composition, and it was as true for him as it was for Gerstein (who was thirty) that the consequences of the event had ample time to proliferate, over decades of these two people's lives, to the effect of irrevocable and profound distortion of their entire life-paths.

It is a particularly grave indictment of the regime we are considering that a person could be, and was, routinely forced to entangle or betray the people who mattered to her or him the most. Memoir literature of the period teems with testimonies of this kind, demanding that we notice how deep the effects of the political system reached into the life of private sentiment, hollowing out not just the public life, but life innermost, life most intimate. To substantiate this indictment, we need only consider the depth of Mandelstam's attachment to Gumilyov: the attachment that one might gauge in reference to a number of known episodes but none of them more telling than the evening when Osip brought Lev to his reading of the *Conversation About Dante*. This is also an aberrant and curious kind of biographical incident in which most of the weight of biographical interpretation rests on points of literary criticism. The episode is mentioned in passing by Gerstein, who recalled simply that Osip

> brought Lyova along to Gosizdat, where at the end of a work day he read to several present, editors and authors, his *Conversation About Dante*. 'Was it interesting?' I asked Lyova. 'Very.' 'Did it go well?' 'Wonderfully.' 'Did they discuss it?' 'No.' 'Why not?' 'No one understood a thing. I, too, did not understand it.' 'So what was so wonderful?' 'It was interesting all the same.'

These are the facts. Mandelstam and Gumilyov shared an exuberant evening, walking to Gosizdat and conversing about Dante and about the *Conversation About Dante* – a conversation notable for its absence of an interlocutor. And in the biographical episode of this walk to Gosizdat, to speak about Dante and about dialogue, formal ideas offer cues to the understanding of life, of how Mandelstam thought of it.

The human gait signifies oscillation (hesitation, vacillation, weighing of opposites, dialogue, feedback, correction and self-correction), dialectic and forward propulsion, and, as a function of weight, connection to the earth (life in the real world, and therefore death, in relation to the earth seen as a bed, the love bed and the final place of rest, rest itself being the cessation of movement, of walking). From oscillation, rhythm and prosody are born (Bely's thoughts in *Rhythm as Dialectic* reinforce the connection between dialectical inquiry and prosody), linking bipedal locomotion to the highest forms of poetry (that Dante appears to Mandelstam always on elevation, always with reference to altitude, is not an accident). As dialogue, the *incessus* is related to knowing and not knowing, to the limits that concern epistemology. As a mark of individuality, the walk is a sign of the particular, in contrast with the universal; in this quality, the walk becomes a metaphysical category. With all this teeming richness in mind, to turn to a poem of 1931 meditating on Mandelstam's habitual walks around Moscow is to see in it a meditation of cosmic proportions, or a miniaturization of

Dante's *Inferno*, Mandelstam's Moscow centred upon the Kremlin the way Dante's Hell converges towards its seething pit. On May 17, 1934, in the wake of Mandelstam's arrest, the playwright Aleksandr Gladkov wrote in his diary: 'This morning I had a visit from Leonid Lavrov, who told me of the rumor about O. Mandelstam's arrest the other day. Mandelstam lived somewhere not very far from me, and occasionally I would see him on Prechistensky or Nikitsky Boulevards: a wise old Jew with a stick.' The 1931 poem opened with lines describing these walks:

> I have still a ways to go before becoming
> A patriarch; my age is half-revered.
> I am still cursed behind my back
> In the dialect of tram-car squabbles
> Lacking reason or rhyme:
> You, such and such! And I apologize,
> Without changing inwardly a bit.

'A wise old Jew with a stick'? No, rather, someone of a 'half-revered' age – a humorous allusion to Dante's opening line, 'Nel mezzo del cammin di nostra vita', whose modulated iambic is echoed by the Russian opening line, '*E-schyo | da-**lyo**- | -ko mne | do pa- | -tri–**ar**- | -kha*', which deviates from the regular iamb by leaving several feet unstressed. This contemplative rhythm, replete with feminine endings, was felt by Mandelstam to accommodate his own walking meditations as they unfolded in Moscow's streets:

> And now and then, I'll go and run errands
> In those unventilated, steamy basements
> Where the tidy, honest Chinamen
> Snap up with chopsticks little balls of pastry
> And play at slender cards, and swallow vodka
> Like swallows skimming over Yangtze river.

The poem's emotional crescendo resolves unexpectedly in reaching for an imagined ally, someone to whom it might be possible to say: 'We're going the same way':

> And I would want so much to shake my doldrums,
> To talk, and tell, and empty out the truth,
> Send all this spleen to smoke, to hell, to Pan,
> And take somebody's hand and say to him:
> Be gentle – for we're going the same way.

Gumilyov was one such 'somebody' to whom these words (uttered, as the Russian indicates, to a *male* interlocutor) might be plausibly addressed. The two friends, the old one and the young, would 'go the same way' in many ways, of which the way to the secret police offices was but one. We are not in a position to know how Gumilyov's life would have turned out had he not come into contact with the Stalin epigram. Nevertheless, in 1935 he was expelled from university and arrested. Akhmatova's efforts resulted in his release, but in 1938 he was arrested again and sentenced to five years' hard labour – a sentence he served near the Siberian city of Norilsk located north of the polar circle. In 1944 he joined the Red Army and later was able to use his veteran status to return to Leningrad, but in 1949 he was arrested, once again, and sentenced to ten years' hard labour. After Stalin's death, Gumilyov was officially 'rehabilitated': the charges made against him had been annulled, without acknowledging, however, life's irretrievability – a truth to which poetry has done more justice than any of the epoch's official documents.

CHAPTER 3

'Be Simple Answer'd, for We Know the Truth'

Of Protocol and Interrogations

> once a thing is put in writing, the composition, whatever it may be, drifts all over the place, getting into the hands not only of those who understand it, but equally of those who have no business with it; it doesn't know how to address the right people, and not address the wrong. And when it is ill-treated and unfairly abused it always needs its parent to come to its help, being unable to defend or help itself.
>
> Plato, *Phaedrus*

The textual history of the Stalin epigram brings home an irony: what proved to be the poem's best and most accurate textual witness was not, as it has been claimed, the memory of Mandelstam's friends but the protocol of the poet's interrogation at the secret police headquarters on Moscow's Lubyanka Street – the place that Boris Kuzin termed the poem's 'destination', sensing the undercurrent of fatalistic self-destructiveness implicit in Mandelstam's gesture of exasperated protest. It is true that the Mandelstams' many warnings to the witnesses of the 'Epigram' to keep it in the strictest secret had the quality of courting trouble, waiting to see how soon the precautions would fail and consequences would follow. Because of its unsanctioned ('counter-revolutionary' in the terms of the time) nature, the poem implicated each new witness in the criminality of being in possession of information about 'counter-revolutionary activity'. The official imperative to report the poem immediately to the authorities would not have been, one thinks, entertained as a practical possibility by any of Mandelstam's chosen interlocutors. Yet it is unimaginable that airtight secrecy could have been maintained regarding a poem charged with such explosive potential. As the circle of witnesses widened, the Mandelstams' control over its limits vanished, and by the time the poem reached the ears of the state it had become something of an open secret. The attitude of the state to private secrets is, of course, a litmus test for the condition of democracy, as pointed out by Jacques Derrida:

> I have a taste for the secret, it clearly has to do with not-belonging; I have an impulse of fear or terror in the face of a political space, for example, a public space that makes no room for the secret. For me, the demand that everything be paraded in the public square and that there be no internal forum is a glaring sign of the totalitarianization of democracy. I can rephrase this in terms of political ethics: if a right to the secret is not maintained, we are in a totalitarian space.

It was the task of the secret police to collect and act on the information gathered countrywide with the help of a vast network of informers – many of them coerced into 'volunteering'. Under these conditions, privacy suffered not solely because one's private secrets could be reported by a trusted acquaintance but also because the prerequisite for privacy, private life itself, as constituted and enriched by friendships and casual acquaintances, came to be eroded and corrupted by fear and suspicion. 'It is obvious', wrote Hannah Arendt acerbically, that

> the most elementary caution demands that one avoid all intimate contacts, if possible – not in order to prevent discovery of one's secret thoughts, but rather to eliminate, in the almost certain case of future trouble, all persons who might have not only an ordinary cheap interest in your denunciation but an irresistible need to bring about your ruin simply because they are in danger of their own lives.

Paradoxically, the secret police's task of prying open the secrets of individuals is itself veiled in secrecy. A good secret, in effect, maintains itself even as it crosses the boundary dividing the realm of individual privacy and state secrecy, as what has been kept from public knowledge in the open world once again comes to be insulated from it by the secrecy of state archives. Yet even in a *bona fide* totalitarian society, the machineries of surveillance and of the state itself are but *parts* of the complex social system they supposedly 'control'. Writing on systems of control, Gregory Bateson observed that

> the would-be controller must always have his spies out to tell him what the people are saying about his propaganda. He is therefore in the position of being *responsive* to what they are saying. Therefore he cannot have a simple lineal control.

This lays bare the internal contradiction of control: to the degree that the mechanisms of control depend on feedback – information supplied by those who are 'controlled' – these mechanisms are controlled by the very subjects they are supposed to be controlling. Among the corporeal metaphors of state agency – 'arms' of government, 'heads' of state, etc. – the figure of 'state security *organs*' opens an uneasy view onto the relations of the secret police and the rest of society. In Russian, the euphemistic shorthand for 'organs of internal security' is simply 'internal organs', a figure indicative of the secret police's removal from the society's consciousness (and conscience), as well as a certain sense of ongoing, even involuntary, process. It would not be simple to disambiguate the nature of this apparatus or the nebulous notion of 'secret police'. After all, even the reference edition covering the history of the various organizations encompassed by this term, published in Russian in 2003, bears the title of *Lubyanka*, after the principal location of a chain of entities that, between 1917 and 1960, succeeded one another under the constantly changing designations of VChK, OGPU, NKVD, NKGB, MGB, MVD – all of which proved to be the KGB's successive 'maiden names'. (Apprehension's ubiquitous recourse was to humour. One could not peer into the windows of the big building on Lubyanka Street from the sidewalk, yet the running joke was that the building itself had the longest views: one could 'see Siberia from the basement'. Standing opposite 'Child's World', the country's largest toy store, the secret police headquarters were known as 'Adult's World'.) The shiftiness of the structures within the notorious building is in itself a form of historic evidence: 'The structure of the penal organs VChK–KGB is the best illustration and explanation of certain twists and turns of repressive policy.' Yet here, too, the evidence is insufficient for a coherent historic narrative, as acknowledged by the editors: 'The present volume does not investigate the causes of the constant and significant changes within the administrative apparatus of state security and internal affairs. The relevant decisions of the Central Committee's Politbureau or the Council of Ministers of the USSR simply do not venture their rationales.'

The complicated metamorphoses of the 'apparatus' housed on Moscow's Lubyanka Street have been noted by Peter B. Maggs in his documentary edition of *The Mandelstam and 'Der Nister' Files*. Writing of Mandelstam's final arrest in 1938, Maggs explains:

> During the 1930s and 1940s there were a number of reorganizations and renamings of the agencies handling state security. At the time of Mandelstam's arrest, both ordinary and political arrestees were subject to the jurisdiction of the People's Comissariat of Internal Affairs, called NKVD – the acronym for *Narodnyi komissariat vnutrennikh del*. A division of the NKVD, the Main Administration for State Security, GUGB – *Glavnoe upravlenie gosudarsttvennoi bezopasnosti* – handled political prisoners. During World War II the state security organization achieved separate status as the People's Comissariat of State Security, NKGB – *Narodnyi komissariat gosudarstvennoi bezopasnosti*. Then in 1946, in an attempt to sound less revolutionary and so gain international respectability, Stalin had the 'people's comissariats' renamed 'ministries', with the result that the 'NK' in each Russian acronym became an 'M'. So the People's Comissariat of Internal Affairs (NKVD) became the Ministry of Internal Affairs (MVD) and the People's Comissariat of State Security (NKGB) became the Ministry of State Security (MGB).

1938 was the year when the newly formed NKVD was conducting a mass 'recall' of people who had appeared previously in the penal system's records. In Mandelstam's case, this precedent was constituted by his first arrest of the decade in 1934, occasioned by the composition of 'The Stalin Epigram' and made by NKVD's predecessor, OGPU ('Unified State Political Administration'), an entity founded in 1923. As a descendant of VChK, the OGPU was heir to its broad powers, including licence to carry out executions without trial. Beginning in 1924, a special structure was instituted within the OGPU under the title of OSO ('The Special Commission'). The latter had the power to exile and (according to the editors of *Lubyanka*) 'to detain in a concentration camp for a term of up to three years'. It was the OSO of the OGPU that, on May 26, 1934, sentenced Mandelstam to three years' exile in Cherdyn – a sentence that was hailed as nothing short of miraculous in the terror-ridden Moscow circles. Nevertheless, we know that the arrest and exile of 1934 had set the stage for the fatal events of 1938.

The order for Mandelstam's arrest was signed by Genrikh Yagoda, the acting head of the OGPU, on 16 May 1934. Early in the morning the following day, Mandelstam was delivered to Lubyanka. His dossier contains two interrogation protocols, one compiled on the 18 May 1934, and the other a week later, on 25 May. In the first protocol, 'The Stalin Epigram' was written out by the interrogator, Nikolay Khristoforovich Shivarov (or, as a remote possibility, by a scribe present at the questioning); in the second, Mandelstam is on record requesting permission to write down the poem himself; the autograph is appended to the protocol. The first copy of the poem contains an error, substituting the verb *'pripomnyat'* – 'remember' or 'mention' in the future tense – for *'pripominayut'*, the same verb in the present tense, with two additional syllables breaking up the line's regular anapaest. The change of tense might have been trivial were it not consonant with Nadezhda Mandelstam's recollections of Shivarov: 'In my presence', she writes, he

> said to M. that it was useful for a poet to experience fear ('you yourself told me so') because it can inspire verse, and that he would 'experience fear in full measure'. Both M. and I noted the use of the future tense.

The protocols of Mandelstam's interrogations make the sequence of the questioning appear straightforward. The first protocol is structured by a series of basic identifying questions, followed by further interrogatories establishing Mandelstam's authorship of the Stalin epigram and a list of eight people to whom the poet had recited it. On May 19, the protocol was supplemented by two additional names – Maria Petrovykh and Vladimir Narbut – and a correction excluding the previously mentioned David Brodsky from the list. Mandelstam's testimony reads:

> In supplement to my prior testimony, I must add that among the persons to whom I read the above-mentioned counterrevolutionary poem was the young poet Maria Sergeyevna Petrovykh. Petrovykh wrote down this work as I read it, promising, however, to destroy the copy later.

> On the fifth and sixth lines, the words 'David Grigoryevich Brodsky, a man of letters' are crossed out in accordance with my request as testimony that does not correspond to reality and was made by mistake during my interrogation yesterday. I must add to my previous testimony that I also read the above-referenced counter-revolutionary work to V. I. Narbut. After hearing the poem, Narbut said to me: 'This never happened' – meaning that I was not to tell anyone that I had read that work to him.

The testimony about Narbut is alarmingly at odds with the men's relationship, as described by Boris Kuzin:

> For O. E. friendship was a necessity. He was in warm, even close relations with many people, beginning with the relatives, his own and his wife's. His most faithful friend and companion was, of course, N. Y. But she was his wife. A friend is a different thing. Among the people I had encountered at the Mandelstams' flat, I cannot name a single close friend of O. E. V. I. Narbut was probably closer to him than anybody else.

The revised list of nine people is reiterated in the protocol of 25 May, a week after the first deposition. Points established on 18 May are rehearsed and developed in detail on 25 May. The record of that day shows Shivarov eliciting from Mandelstam a series of admissions: first, a detailed history of his political views and unorthodox musings; next, a new admission of authorship of the Stalin verses and of their political malignancy; a full text of the poem is written down by Mandelstam; a numbered list of people who had listened to the poem is produced, followed by the details of each person's reaction upon hearing the verses. Mandelstam omits from this report his wife's and Akhmatova's responses, and Shivarov pursues this line of questioning only on Akhmatova's account (possibly because Nadezhda Mandelstam was already sufficiently incriminated by association and her case needed no further development). After establishing some evidence of what could be worked up as heretical sympathies among this immediate circle, Shivarov leads Mandelstam to characterize the poem as a 'widely applicable means of counter-revolutionary insurgency' that could be used 'by any social group whatsoever'.

Black's Law Dictionary defines 'interrogation' as 'the formal and systematic questioning of a person; esp., intensive questioning by the police, usu. of a person arrested for or suspected of committing a crime'. Part of this 'formal and systematic' character is the practice of recording the interrogation – or of maintaining a 'protocol': a document structured as a series of question–answer pairings attested by the respondent's signature at the end. The last detail marks, and bridges, the distance separating this modern 'protocol' from the original Greek term, *'protokollon'*, which referred to the 'first page' inscribed with the date and the name of the scribe and appended to a scroll. We know the dates of Mandelstam's interrogations, but if we were to assume that, apart from Mandelstam's autographs, the interrogator himself was the scribe, it would be good to remember that nothing in the dossier confirms this assumption. However that may be, Mandelstam's signature beneath the words attributed to him does still more to divert attention from the interrogator's active role in producing the document. The question-and-answer pattern of the text, and especially the form of direct speech given to the answers, contribute to the impression of a direct record of a conversation taking place between the questioner and the answerer – a conversation in the course of which Mandelstam divulges – unresistingly, it would seem – incriminating information about himself and his social circle. But a closer examination of these records suggests that the reality of what it is that they document is more complicated. To set this difficulty in its basic, lexicographic context, here is the *Oxford English Dictionary*, which gives a range of meanings for 'protocol' spanning from notions of exactitude and authority ('a formal or official statement of a proceeding') to fraudulent pretences of exactitude and authority ('*Protocols of the Elders of Zion* and variants: a fraudulent, anti-Semitic document first printed in Russia in 1901, purporting to be a report of a series of meetings held in 1897 to plan the overthrow of Christian civilization by Jews'). Interceding between contradictions, we find that 'chiefly in Russian contexts' a protocol may constitute 'a record made by the police of an incident or case'. Among Russian dictionaries, the *Popular Dictionary of Foreign Words* defines '*protokol*' as 'a document containing a complete record of all that occurs in the course of a meeting, proceeding, judicial process, etc., e.g. ~ of an interrogation'. What is ambiguous in this definition is the meaning of 'all': does this 'all' include the form and sequence of the locutions, or only the information they contain? Can, for instance, a detailed summary qualify as 'all' whilst omitting items deemed irrelevant? And could the same items become highly germane if considered from a different perspective? The *Greater Law* Dictionary, acclimated to Russia and its legal praxis, does permit that a protocol might be something like a digest of the facts previously elicited by the interrogator: 'PROTOCOLS – procedural documents, fixing in written form the proceedings and results of procedures conducted by an investigator or an interrogator while investigating a criminal case or by a court in considering a criminal or a civil case. P. are also compiled as part of the constitutional and administrative due process and arbitration.' It appears that the 'and' in 'proceedings and results of procedures conducted by an investigator' need not insist on the presence of *both* elements in the protocol; it can contain either, and can be limited to the latter – that is, to the results of the questioning.

If their question-and-answer form invites us to read the Mandelstam protocols as records of the interrogation as it unfolded in real time, as if it were a live dialogue, much of our understanding of Mandelstam's situation at Lubyanka, as well as our subsequent moral appraisals, depends on the truth of this assumption. If it were true, it would appear that, a week into his investigation at Lubyanka, Mandelstam was on record accepting compliantly every self-incriminating formula suggested by Shivarov. In his commentary on the documents of the Lubyanka dossier Pavel Nerler was moved to remark contemptuously that Mandelstam 'trilled like a nightingale', incriminating himself with 'basketfuls of nonsense' – yet nowhere in his study does Nerler question the protocols' accuracy or the appearance of uninterrupted speech they give. Only some curious line breaks early in the protocols, and the equally curious choice of a journalistic present tense, reflect the off-the-record dynamics, as Mandelstam furnishes his political autobiography, beginning with 1917:

> My reception of the October revolution is starkly negative. I view the Soviet government as a government of usurpers and this finds an expression in my poem 'Kerensky' published in *The Will of the People*. This poem represents a relapse into the social-revolutionary cast of mind: I idealize Kerensky, calling him the scion of Peter, and by contrast, I call Lenin an accidental favourite.
>
> Approximately a month later I make a sharp turn towards the Soviet activities and people, and this finds an expression in my involvement in the work of Narkompros on establishing a new school.

> At the end of 1918, a political depression sets in, motivated by the harsh methods of establishing the dictatorship of the proletariat. By this time I had moved to Kiev, and after it was taken by the Whites I moved to Feodosia. There, in 1920, after being arrested by the Whites, I confront the problem of choice: emigration or Soviet Russia – and I choose the Soviet Russia. The impetus for my escape from Feodosia was, incidentally, my acute revulsion against the White Guard.

One striking thing about these confessions is their remarkable succinctness. Key identifications with political groups, allegiances and doubts, are organized with precision for the purposes of the investigation. In 1927, Mandelstam's 'increasing trust in the politics of the Communist party and the Soviet government' wavered under the influence of 'not very deep, but fairly ardent Trotskyist sympathies'. Faith in the communists was again restored in 1928. The record continues in the present tense, lending a brisk dynamism to the narrative of the prisoner's changing political convictions, which he appears to report without a shadow of hesitation or evasiveness. These statements are precisely, as the definition of a protocol indicates, 'results of procedures conducted by an investigator' – 'procedures' conducted off the record, prior to the composition of the protocol and in the white spaces indicated by line breaks between the statements, line breaks being a record of elapsed time whose content is being silenced. The dates of the protocols – the first being dated two days after the arrest, and the second following a week later, on 25 May – support the conjecture that preliminary work had been done in advance of the two interrogations. (Nadezhda Mandelstam's memoirs, too, confirm this reading, but, for the moment, let the protocols speak for themselves.)

> In 1930 a deep depression sets in within my political consciousness and social self-awareness. The social underpinnings of this depression had to do with the liquidation of *kulak*s as a class. My attitude towards this process is reflected in my poem 'Cold Spring' – attached to the present interrogation protocol and written in the summer of 1932 after my return from the Crimea. By that time, I am already experiencing the feeling of social persecution, exacerbated by a number of confrontations of the personal and socio-literary sort.
>
> Transcribed after my spoken testimony correctly and read by me.
>
> O. Mandelstam

The reference to the attachment of a copy of the Crimean poem is a clear indication both of preliminary conversation and the preparation of the attachment, before the statement is set on record. So, too, is the repetition of 'depression' – 'this depression', the first in a series of repetitions, highly unusual in Mandelstam's inexhaustibly rich conversational manner (not to speak of his poems teeming with profligate variants). Whether one might blame Shivarov's ghostwriting or Mandelstam's own striving to establish a rapport with the interrogator, the unnatural, reduced, stifled and jargon-laden quality of this language evidences a yielding to some form of external force, under which Mandelstam is not recognizably himself. The merest hint at a new element of the narrative in Shivarov's questions is met with acquiescent disclosures, detailed, unambiguous and organized as only the 'results' of unrecorded 'procedures' can be.

> QUESTION: Do you acknowledge yourself guilty of composing works of counter-revolutionary content?
>
> ANSWER: Yes, I acknowledge myself guilty of the fact that I am the author of a counter-revolutionary lampoon against the leader of the communist party and Soviet state. I request permission to write down this lampoon separately, as an appendix to the present interrogation protocol.
>
> QUESTION: How did the individuals previously named by you respond to your reading of the lampoon in their presence?
>
> ANSWER: Kuzin B. S. noted that this work is the most full-blooded of all the works that I had read to him in the last year, 1933. Khazin Y. Ya. noted the vulgarization of the subject matter and the incorrect interpretation of personality as a dominant of the historic process. Aleksandr Mandelstam shook his head disapprovingly without comment. Gerstein E. G. praised the poem for its artistic qualities. If memory serves, there was no extended discussion of the topic. Narbut V. I. said to me: 'This never happened', which was meant to signify that I should not tell anyone that I had read this lampoon to him. Petrovykh – as I said – wrote down this lampoon and praised the work for its high poetic qualities. Lev Gumilyov endorsed the work by saying it was 'swell' or some other indeterminate, emotive expression, but his response was not fully independent from that of his mother, Anna Akhmatova, in whose presence he had first heard the poem.

The placement of initials after the persons' last names is a convention of official writing in Russian, but it is inconceivable as a spoken form: another clue that the phrasing belongs to Shivarov, not Mandelstam himself. The steady progression of the interrogation, from one incriminating finding to other, graver findings towards the end, suggests that Shivarov had a chance to structure in his mind the information he had previously obtained. It is unsurprising that Mandelstam signed the protocols without having read them – something for which even his interrogator rebuked him, during Nadezhda Mandelstam's prison visit. 'He must have trusted you', Nadezhda snapped. Certainly, he had been drawn into some form of collaboration with the questioner, a collaboration involving fear, resignation – and, sinisterly, trust.

None of the women mentioned by Mandelstam as witnesses to 'The Stalin Epigram' were arrested. Nadezhda Mandelstam, Emma Gerstein, Anna Akhmatova and Maria Petrovykh continued their existence as women of letters, albeit in exceptionally difficult circumstances. When Nadezhda announced to Emma Gerstein that Mandelstam had named her during the interrogation, Akhmatova, who was present, remarked with characteristic coldness: 'Congratulations! Now you, too, have a dossier.' Gerstein recalled her shock at 'those sensible words', concluding: 'If only I could survey the twenty years that followed, when in every organization, every human-resource department, every publishing house and qualifying commission, and in the Writers' Union I would hear the same formula, *your application has been denied*. But that day I had other things on my mind.' On the other hand, three of the men named by Mandelstam were subsequently distinguished by tragedy. One was Lev Gumilyov. The other two were Mandelstam's close friends, Vladimir Narbut and Boris Kuzin. Narbut was arrested in 1936, on the accusation of membership in a Ukrainian nationalist conspiracy. He was sentenced to five years' hard labour and by the fall of 1937 found himself on the banks of Kolyma. The following spring, he was shot by special order of an NKVD *troika* – a 'committee of three'. As for Kuzin, his arrest in 1935 was his second in three years, and it was understood to have been precipitated by Mandelstam's testimony. Kuzin reflected on these events with calm disinterestedness: 'In 1934 O. E. was sent into exile, and in the spring of 1935 it was my turn to be arrested. After more than two years in a camp, I was released and wrote to the Mandelstams, who had then moved to Moscow.' 'I always thought it unjust to demand heroism of people. We admire those capable of heroism. But not to be a hero is not the same thing as to be a scoundrel.'

Shivarov, who had the reputation of a literary specialist at Lubyanka, was interested in what Akhmatova had to say about the Stalin 'epigram'. The care with which he states his question is matched by Mandelstam's reply on the record:

> QUESTION: How did Anna Akhmatova respond when hearing this counter-revolutionary lampoon and what was her appraisal of it?
>
> ANSWER: Anna Akhmatova, in her characteristically concise and poetically astute manner, pointed out the work's resemblance to a monumental *lubok* and its crude character. This assessment is correct because this virulent, counterrevolutionary, slanderous lampoon – which contains tremendously potent social poison, political hatred, and even disdain for its subject, alongside the concession to his enormous power – has the qualities of a greatly potent propaganda poster.

Apparently satisfied by this characterization (the Russian '*lubok*' referring to a certain kind of cheap woodcut or poster), Shivarov moved into the final phrase of the interrogation, opening first an avenue for persecuting potentially any member of the old intelligentsia, and then broadening the reach of the accusations to members of 'any social group whatsoever':

> QUESTION: Does your counter-revolutionary lampoon 'We live …' express only your own, Mandelstam's, perception and disposition, or does it express the perceptions and dispositions of some particular social group?
>
> ANSWER: The counter-revolutionary lampoon 'We live …' which I have written is not a document of my personal perception and disposition but a document of the perceptions and dispositions of a particular social group, namely, that part of the old intelligentsia that considers itself the bearer and transmitter of the values that belonged to past cultures, in our own time. From the political standpoint, this group has extracted from the experience of various revolutionary movements a habit of using historical analogies that distort contemporary reality.
>
> QUESTION: Does this mean that your lampoon happens to be a weapon of counter-revolutionary insurgency only in the hands of the group you have characterized, or can it be deployed in the interests of counter-revolutionary insurgency by other social groups?
>
> ANSWER: In my lampoon I followed the path that has become traditional in old Russian literature, using the devices of simplified exposition of the historic situation

that reduce it to a contrast of the country against the ruler. Beyond doubt, this lowers the quality of the historic interpretation on the part of the previously characterized group, to which I belong, but precisely this permitted me to achieve the poster-like expressiveness of the lampoon that makes it a widely applicable means of counter-revolutionary insurgency that can be used by any social group whatsoever.

If there was at Lubyanka such a thing as *protocol* – in the sense of proprieties attendant upon a particular setting – it was certainly violated by Shivarov's entertaining one of his literary friends, Pyotr Pavlenko, by letting him sit, hidden in a closet, at one of Mandelstam's night-time interrogations – apparently during preliminary questioning that has not been set on record. Nadezhda Mandelstam remembered, corroborating Gerstein's memories:

> As far back as 1934, Anna Andreyevna and I heard of the writer Pavlenko's stories about how he had accepted out of curiosity an invitation from his friend who was leading the investigation of O. M. and how he was present at a nighttime interrogation, hiding in a closet or between some double doors. I myself had seen several identical doors in the investigator's office – there were too many doors for just one room. Later someone explained that some of the doors opened up into closets for trapping, and others served as escape doors.
>
> Pavlenko talked about Mandelstam looking pathetic and lost during the interrogation; his trousers kept falling down, and he kept pulling at them while answering the questions, always off the mark – not a single clear and distinct answer, he talked nonsense, was nervous and writhed like a fish in a frying pan, and so forth...

'Not a single clear and distinct answer' – in contrast to the succinctness of the record which Nadezhda Mandelstam had not seen. It is therefore Pavlenko who, while boasting of his nocturnal adventure in the belly of the beast, supplies crucial testimony regarding Mandelstam's testimony to Shivarov. Pavlenko's testimony makes the protocols of Mandelstam's interrogation travel from one end of the range defined by the *OED* to its polar opposite: from their appearance of exactitude and authority, the protocols shift all the way to a fraudulent *pretence* of exactitude and authority. Yet they tell us nothing about how Mandelstam was conditioned to produce his on-the-record testimony.

On 25 May, the OGPU issued a decision declaring the investigation complete and finding Mandelstam guilty of 'the composition and dissemination of counter-revolutionary literary works'. This conclusion was signed by Mandelstam and directed to the Special Committee (OSO) for consideration, which on 26 May issued in a sentence: exile in Cherdyn for three years. The dossier was to be archived. Yet, in spite of this official 'end of story', life's events continued their unfolding. Mandelstam's encounter with Shivarov may have implicated yet another person in the play of contested loyalties set in motion by the Stalin verses. In 1936, Nikolai Shivarov was transferred to Sverdlovsk. This may have been a sign of a distancing from power: in December 1937 Shivarov was arrested on the charges of espionage. He was sentenced to five years' hard labour. In 1940, he committed suicide at a labour camp near Vandysh – a village slightly south of the Polar Circle.

CHAPTER 4

Double Bind, 1934

> The after-math seldom or neuer equals the first herbage.
> Andrew Marvell, *The Rehearsal Transpros'd*

When Virginia Rounding wrote, in *The Guardian*, of Mandelstam's 'less than saintly behaviour', the phrase, with its casual opprobrium, implied that some form of 'saintly behaviour' could have been expected of the prisoner under the circumstances. A 'saintly' or heroic Mandelstam would not have given Shivarov a list of witnesses to the Stalin poem. The disappointment seems to rest on fictions about human nature and the nature of the penal system. One such fiction is that excellence under duress must manifest in silence. This assumes that the person under interrogation has something like 'the liberty of silence' – an assumption put in doubt by Geoffrey Hill in his essay 'Language, Suffering, and Silence'. 'Taciturnity', he writes,

> does not have an absolute value, any more than suffering itself has or any more than the words 'absolute value' have. R. W. Chambers, in his biography of More, writes of the martyr's 'great plea for the liberty of silence'. Chambers modulates that air of expansiveness inseparable from the hallowed commonplace 'freedom of speech', words which, for citizens of democracies, lie somewhat lightly upon the tongue.

Hill adduces the example of Robert Southwell, the sixteenth-century Jesuit who 'remained as dumb as a tree-stump' under interrogation by torture. 'Dumb as a tree-stump' does say something about human nature and how much against its grain muteness in pain appears to run. Similarly, he tells us of the seminary-priest John Ingram, who was 'called a "monster" of "strange taciturny" by his baffled inquisitor'. Baffled indeed, because silence is not something one would expect under the circumstances.

The question of what 'liberty of silence' and what other liberties were available to Mandelstam rests on the matter of duress. Prevailing opinion seems to be that he was not tortured, since torture in the conventional sense was not sanctioned by Lubyanka until 1937, and techniques employed there prior to that year are not generally considered to constitute physical coercion. This, however, conflicts with the facts that Mandelstam was not allowed to sleep for long stretches of time, that he was fed salty food but was not given anything to drink, and that when he demanded water, he was restrained in a straightjacket. Emma Gerstein notes that after his stay at Lubyanka, Mandelstam's eyelashes fell out and never grew back; what had been done to his eyes remains unexplained. What is clear, then, is that other kinds of pressure, manipulations of circumstances enacted chiefly in the language, can and did inflict unbearable anguish, and are witnessed by the later records of characteristic post-traumatic behaviour observed in Mandelstam by his friends and family.

To Mandelstam, who had in 1933 declared himself to be first and foremost 'a friend of his friends', surrender to Shivarov meant loss of self in a situation where the alternative was loss of life. This untenable situation was a species of the dilemma that stood, in actuality or potentiality, before each citizen of the totalitarian state: the choice between 'going free' within a prison state, on the one hand, and being imprisoned within its penal system, on the other hand, left no possibility of genuine freedom – such as, in this instance, 'the liberty of silence'. Even friends whose futures had been threatened by Mandelstam's testimony, hesitated to reproach the man who had emerged from prison in a state of profound shock repeatedly characterized as psychosis and who attempted suicide by leaping out of a hospital window shortly after arriving in Cherdyn, the designated place of his exile. Even after his recovery from this initial, acutely paranoid phase, Mandelstam remained a changed person – anxiously irritable, demanding and profoundly dependent on constant care, from Nadezhda or, when she herself was in need of reprieve, from someone who could take her place – her own mother or Emma Gerstein. The latter choice is particularly chastening in view of the damage to Gerstein's professional life caused by Mandelstam's indications to Shivarov. Her memoirs are matter-of-fact on this point:

Shortly after the already described events of the summer of 1934 I was removed from my job with a 24-hour notice and an abominable character evaluation. I searched for work until 1936, when I was hired by the Literary Museum, but only as a freelancer, not a staff member. As soon as I received the first money, I set out for Voronezh.

On this very first visit, Gerstein was asked to take some time off, in order to keep Mandelstam company. 'Nadya was determined to go to Moscow, someone had to take her place, but it could not be just anyone, they needed someone who was close'. This plan involving Gerstein took shape as the alternative to the Mandelstams' first idea, which had been that Emma should visit the Central Committee of the Party in Moscow to advocate for Mandelstam, explaining to the officials that he was starving in Voronezh without work. No one had taken into account that Gerstein herself was only marginally and precariously employed. Gerstein could not imagine herself making demands at the Central Committee, but the prospect of overstaying her leave in Voronezh also appeared dangerous. The Mandelstams insisted. Nadezhda used guilt and Osip pleaded, finally forcing Gerstein to raise the delicate matter of his role in complicating her own situation, 'which I had not previously permitted myself to mention during my encounters with Nadya in Moscow'.

> But in the face of Mandelstam's increasing demands I finally decided to place the dot over the 'i'. Our trust in our friends must, after all, be reciprocal. Osip Emilyevich began to explain: 'But you must understand that I could not have named someone else. Could I have named Akhmatova or Pasternak? Kuzin was out of the question, you know perfectly well...' (He meant the recent arrest of Boris Sergeyevich and his under-surveillance status.) 'And Lyova...' he said significantly, playing on my particular feelings for L. Gumilyov.

Of course, just as before, when she was made to believe she was the only witness of the Stalin verses, Gerstein was being misled, yet new truths emerged amongst the unpleasant admissions.

> It is fairly sad to realize that you had been chosen to be sacrificed in order to save others. I did not say that, of course, but Mandelstam sensed the awkwardness. In order to smooth it out, he brought up the interrogator, who had called me a 'perfectly Soviet individual'. None of this mattered anymore. I already knew that Mandelstam's initial intentions, no doubt agreed upon with Nadya, had come to naught. Pasternak and Akhmatova had both ended up on the list of people who heard his epigram on Stalin.

> ... He began to tell me how frightening his time at Lubyanka had been. I remember only one episode, which Osip described to me with amazing frankness: 'They were taking me somewhere in an internal elevator. Several people were in it. I fell to the floor and thrashed about... And suddenly there was a voice above me, "Mandelstam, Mandelstam, shame on you!" I raised my head. It was Pavlenko.'

Was this 'internal elevator' one of the spaces concealed behind the various doors of the investigator's office? Was this the 'less than saintly behaviour' imputed to Mandelstam by a writer in *The Guardian*? Nadezhda Mandelstam's indignation was justly directed at the standards of morality and honour set by sheltered 'impartial observers' like Pavlenko:

> Why are we supposed to be brave enough to stand up to all the horrors of twentieth-century prisons and camps? Are we supposed to sing as we fall into the mass graves? Face death in the gas chambers with courage? Travel cheerfully to prison in a cattle car? Engage our interrogators in polite conversation about the role of fear in poetry, or discuss the impulses that lead to the writing of verse in a state of fury and indignation?

Beyond these powerful rhetorical questions, Nadezhda Mandelstam poses a highly specific question indicative of the clinical gift that animates her writing, at its best, with such keen insight.

> Why is it that members of the intelligentsia and nervous, sensitive people in general react so strongly to arrest, often developing a mysterious traumatic psychosis that passes quickly without leaving a mark –

'this remains an open question', she concluded. Yet, this is a question to which certain psychiatric evidence can now be adduced.

As 'The Stalin Epigram' made its way through the secret police headquarters on Lubyanka Street, rumour had it that Genrikh Yagoda, the acting head of the OGPU, 'liked the verses so much that he deigned to memorize them. It was he, after all, who read them to Bukharin.' Ensconced at the upper rungs of the political hierarchy, these men felt themselves immune from being implicated in the poem's criminality, and relished the blasphemous verses, albeit *sotto voce*. But, in 1938, Bukharin, once known as 'the love of the Party', was executed as one of the key defendants in the Third Moscow Process – the last in a series of major public trials of

Double Bind, 1934

high-ranking party officials, where Yagoda, who had become the head of the newly formed NKVD in July 1934, also figured as a defendant and would be shot in prison, after a trial whose transcript preserves the spectacular animus of his questioning by Andrey Yanuaryevich Vyshinsky, a prosecutor nicknamed 'Jaguaryevich' on account of his predatory penchant for the death penalty.

> VYSHINSKY: Tell us, traitor Yagoda, is it possible that in all your abominable, treacherous activities you never felt the slightest remorse, the slightest regret? And now, as you answer at last for your despicable crimes before the court of the proletariat, can it be that you do not feel any regret for what you have done?

Vyshinsky – awarded the Stalin Prize for his theory of evidence that changed Soviet jurisprudence – was the man who dispensed with the idea of the presumption of innocence, placing the burden of proof on the defendant. In the absence of sufficient incriminating evidence, Vyshinsky's doctrine held that the defendant's fate should be determined by 'the revolutionary conscience of the prosecutor'. Vyshinsky's gambit in interrogating Yagoda could not be more reminiscent of Gloucester's interrogation in *King Lear*: ushered into the room 'by two or three', Gloucester is heralded, 'Traitor!' – *before* Regan commences the interrogation with the injunction: 'Be simple answer'd, for we know the truth.' This is not a contradiction that could simply be objected to ('Well, if you already know the truth, I shouldn't have to answer, should I?') – we, too, know the truth of what happens next. Gloucester's untenable situation is comprised of the contradictory injunctions to speak the truth as if to inform, *and* to say just what the interrogator claims to already know, although the answerer himself does not know what that might be. A third injunction, implicit in the situation, is that the answerer not even attempt to protest these contradictions.

> CORNWALL: And what confederacy have you with the traitors
> Late footed in the kingdom?
> REGAN: To whose hands have you sent the lunatic king? Speak.
> GLOUCESTER: I have a letter guessingly set down,

>   Which came from one that's of a neutral heart,
>   And not from one opposed.
> CORNWALL: Cunning.
> REGAN: And false.

That the victim is in a bind is underscored by the enjoinder: 'Bind fast his corky arms' – the doubled 'Hard, hard', followed by 'To this chair bind him', alerting us to the deadlock of binding injunctions upon which Gloucester is crucified. This deadlock is *not* achievable solely by a single pair of contradictions. The *double bind*, as conceptualized by Gregory Bateson, depends on the central contradiction being secured by the tertiary injunction not to question it, which is in turn upheld by the power differential between the victim and the other person. All three key features of the double bind are present in this scene: apart from the contradictory orders (the explicit one running against the implicit) and the tertiary prohibition, the answerer's relationship to his tormentors is one of intense dependence. This, once again, resurrects the coercive pattern of double bind evident in the Mandelstam-*Ulenspiegel* affair. In revisiting its formal features, we shall be quicker to notice it reasserting itself in other contexts – notably, its pervasive presence in the experience of imprisonment as such.

It is a requirement of a double bind that the contradictory messages involved in it must be interpreted by the victim as *commands*, but these can be either explicit or implied: the contradiction may take the form of a simultaneous injunction to 'move to the left' and 'move to the right', or 'move' and 'stand still', or 'forget and forgive'. It may also take the form of the cobra's hypnotic enjoinder in Kipling's 'Riki-tikki-tavi': 'Keep very still, all you three. If you move, I strike, and if you do not move, I strike.' But the commands can also be tacit: a simple change of facial expression is an implicit command, as it calls for something like a reciprocal change of expression or acknowledgement from the other person in the relationship. It is the mark of an 'intense relationship' that even its minute communicative aspects represent urgent commands to act reciprocally and appropriately in relation to what is being expressed. The contradiction can be expressed

Double Bind, 1934

in a verbal statement incompatible with the tone of voice in which it is made. One's mother saying, in an aggrieved way, 'I am perfectly happy', will be interpreted, correctly, as a pair of contradictory injunctions: to seek to comfort her, and not to.

R. D. Laing, who underplayed the importance of the tertiary rule in a double bind, nevertheless acknowledged that

> it would not exhaust the rhetorical situation to point out that the victim is caught in a tangle of paradoxical injunctions, or of attributions having the force of injunctions, in which he cannot do the right thing.

The 'rhetorical situation' as conceived by Bateson is richer than that: the tertiary injunction, prohibiting the victim from commenting on the situation or questioning the questioner, is key to the disposition of forces. At the end of his discussion of the case of the young schizophrenic patient who, after being visited and repeatedly invalidated by his mother, 'assaulted a orderly and was put in the tubs', Bateson proposes:

> this result could have been avoided if the young man had been able to say, 'Mother, it is obvious that you become uncomfortable when I put my arm around you, and that you have difficulty accepting a gesture of affection from me.' However, the schizophrenic patient doesn't have this possibility open to him. His intense dependency and training prevents him from commenting upon his mother's communicative behaviour, though she comments on his and forces him to accept and to attempt to deal with the complicated sequence.

Yagoda, with his thorough insider's understanding of 'the rhetorical situation', had something admittedly much better and more effective to say to Vyshinsky than this unrealistic 'Mother, it is obvious, etc.'; this was made possible for him through sheer contempt for the prosecutor.

> VYSHINSKY: Tell us, traitor Yagoda, is it possible that in all your abominable, treacherous activities you never felt the slightest remorse, the slightest regret? And now, as you answer at last for your despicable crimes before the court of the proletariat, can it be that you do not feel any regret for what you have done?
>
> YAGODA: Yes, I do regret – I regret very much –

VYSHINSKY: Attention, comrade justices! The traitor Yagoda feels regret. What is it that you regret, spy and criminal Yagoda?

YAGODA: I greatly regret – I greatly regret that, when I had the power to do so, I did not have all of you shot.

Unlike the 'intense dependency and training' of the schizophrenic patient, Yagoda's 'training' was blessedly rich in memories of standing at the apex of the system that now prosecuted him, and this enabled him to comment freely on the process and maintain a certain internal equilibrium, until the very end. This situation was, nevertheless, entirely atypical for a prisoner locked into a state of dependence upon the mercies of his interrogators, without so much as an imaginative recourse to the kind of immediate experience of power that had been so familiar to Yagoda: a criminal indeed, though not against the regime.

The tertiary injunction is ubiquitously present in our encounters with authority: it is silently expressed by the policeman's uniform, by the 'official' setting in which a private person is inevitably made to feel self-consciously unofficial, by the distribution of roles, so that it is clear who the doctor is and who the patient – the latter thereby implicitly instructed to behave accordingly, etc. The moment we are told that the situation we are in is called an 'interrogation', the performance begins, in accordance with the performative rules implicit in 'the name of the game', and we can be sure who will be asking the questions and who will be answering, under the force of the tacit prohibition against challenging the rules. It is one thing to say that where there is power there can be the abuse of it; it is something different to see just how easily an encounter with an official can turn into a coercive situation. With the tertiary prohibition already in place, with some form of dependence, too, entering easily into the mix (*I* need the official to issue me a new passport, while *he* does not need anything from me), it is sufficient for the person in power to begin behaving somewhat inconsistently for the other person to start feeling distress at the sensation of being at once paralyzed and torn apart. The concept of the double bind can be formulated as an equation: the greater the quotients of dependence and inconsistency, the greater the distress. What emerges from this analysis is the unsettling conclusion that Lubyanka's practices, whilst not, at the time of Mandelstam's arrest in 1934, physically coercive, nonetheless involved a deliberate heightening of dependence anxiety in the detainees. This dependence was carefully cultivated through their maximal isolation from contacts with the outside world and by fostering separation anxiety so as to condition subsequent engagement with the investigators. Nadezhda Mandelstam recorded her insight into the investigation's pressure tactics:

> Methods like these are possible only if a prisoner's links with the outside world are broken from the moment of his arrest. Apart from the signatures of the receipt book for packages, he is left completely in the dark about the people he has been torn from – and by no means everybody is allowed to receive packages.

What ensues under these conditions is typically the involuntary transfer of all prisoner's hopes for human emotional support to the cell-mates furnished by the prison (and often charged with the task of covertly 'incubating' their confessions, as in the case of the 'broody hen' assigned to be Mandelstam's cell-mate) and to the interrogator. The dynamics of this process have been analysed by W. R. D. Fairbairn in a 1952 essay (treating principally of anxiety endured by soldiers deployed abroad and its influence on their relations with authority) whose core assertion is already familiar to the reader:

> it is better to be a sinner in a world ruled by God than to live in a world ruled by the Devil. A sinner in a world ruled by God may be bad; but there is always a certain sense of security to be derived from the fact that the world around is good – 'God's in his heaven – All's right with the world!'; and in any case there is always a hope of redemption. In a world ruled by the Devil the individual may escape the badness of being a sinner; but he is bad because the world around him is bad. Further, he can have no sense of security and no hope of redemption. The only prospect is one of death and destruction.

Subjected to this dilemma, the victim becomes unable to think ill of the authority figure and sacrifices his own judgement 'to maintain the sacred illusion' that the actions of the figure in power 'make sense'.

Yet it is also true that the would-be controller of the situation, the investigator, cannot control it without depending, in turn, on feedback from the detainee. In other words, the person who is supposed to be strictly dependent under the circumstances proves nonetheless to have a certain degree of influence over his captor. The memoirs of Nadezhda Mandelstam make it clear the extent to which Shivarov himself was captivated by his prisoner, who appeared to inspire in him a not wholly calculated curiosity:

> The interrogator's approach was to seek an explanation for every single word in the poem on Stalin. He was particularly concerned to find out what had prompted the writing of it. He was flabbergasted when M. suddenly told him in reply to this question that more than anything else he hated fascism. M. had not intended to speak so frankly to the interrogator, and he blurted this out despite himself – he was by then in such a state that he just didn't care. As he was in duty bound to, the interrogator stormed and shouted, demanding to know what M. thought was fascist about our system. This question he repeated in my presence during the interview, but, astonishingly enough, he didn't pursue the matter when M. replied evasively. M. later assured me that there was something ambiguous about the interrogator's whole behaviour, and that behind his blustering manner one could constantly sense his hatred for Stalin.

Under the aspect of the double bind, this ambivalence can easily be seen as an asset for Shivarov's investigative role. A penchant for making statements in a tone of voice suggestive of a wholly different meaning would have made him a natural at instigating distress in his charges. But there is more in Nadezhda Mandelstam's account of her prison visit: it supplies a remarkable record of Shivarov's efforts to control the narrative, in a way prescribed by Bateson's requirement for a tertiary injunction. For the duration of Nadezhda's visit, Mandelstam had a close, beloved person to support his own sense of reality, and later she would again come to his aid in reconstructing his prison experience and separating the hallucinations from the inconceivable things that nevertheless did happen. She would write of Shivarov's insistence on monopolizing the metacommunicative dimension of the conversation, on imposing his own interpretations on Mandelstam's experience. Shivarov's 'obvious purpose'

> was to impress on me his view of the case as a whole and various aspects of his inquiry into it. I was, as it were, being given authoritative guidance on how the whole thing should be seen. . . . M.'s cellmate tried to frighten him with the thought of his trial, assuring him that all his family and friends had been arrested and would appear in the dock together with him. He went through all the articles of the criminal code under which M. might be accused, as though giving him 'legal advice', but in fact

trying to alarm him at the prospect of being charged with terrorism, conspiracy and the like. M. would return from his nighttime interrogation to the clutches of his 'fellow prisoner', who gave him no respite.

Mandelstam noticed that his cell-mate had clean, neatly pared fingernails – improbable for someone who claimed to have spent several months in prison. Another time Mandelstam was brought to the cell and found it empty; some time later, his cell-mate returned, supposedly from being interrogated – and smelling of onions. After being openly confronted by Mandelstam, this 'broody hen' was removed from Mandelstam's cell. Shivarov insisted that he had been placed in Mandelstam's cell in accordance with the mandate against solitary confinement. He 'declared that solitary confinement was forbidden on humane grounds', adding that Mandelstam's cell-mate had had to be transferred to rescue him from Mandelstam's harassment. 'This kind of deception', Bateson wrote in 'Toward a Theory of Schizophrenia',

> will provoke the patient to respond to it as a double bind situation, and his response will be 'schizophrenic' in the sense that it will be indirect and the patient will be unable to comment on the fact that he feels that he is being deceived.

Mandelstam's indirect, incomplete response, too, was recorded by his wife. '"What touching concern!" O. M. only managed to insert.' Shivarov spoke in a way that did not permit interruptions, implicitly discounting and discouraging the interlocutor's contribution. Joined to the deceptive narrative about Mandelstam's cell-mate and the overarching imperative of the investigation, even this vignette exhibits all the features of the double-bind situation; further, these features arise not from singular details of a given day but from Shivarov's own conversational habits, which appear to have played out continuously in his involvement with Mandelstam. Distorted valuations, for example, are witnessed by Nadezhda Mandelstam at a different point in the conversation:

> At the interview I saw that M. had bandages on both wrists. When I asked him what was wrong with them, he just waved his hand, but the interrogator delivered himself of an angry speech about how M. had brought forbidden objects into his cell – an offense punishable under such-and-such an article. It turned out that M. had

slashed his veins with a razor blade. He had been told by Kuzin, who in 1933, after two months in jail had been released on the intervention of a Chekist friend with a passion for entomology, that the thing you want most in prison is a knife or at least a razor blade. He had even thought of a way of providing for an emergency by hiding one in the sole of his shoe. Hearing this, M. persuaded a cobbler he knew to secrete a few blades in this way for him.

Nothing could witness the life-or-death intensity of the prisoner's plight like this account, which strengthens the connection of imprisonment under investigation with the first requisite of the double bind: the intensity of the subject's relationship with a person in power, the investigator in this instance. (Other kinds of power reside, for example, in intimate relationships, but what matters in this discussion is the vital importance, for the subject of the double bind, of interpreting correctly the communications of his *vis-à-vis*.) What is evident in Mandelstam's case is a life-and-death dependence on Shivarov and the urgent need to satisfy the demands of the investigation. The testimony further implicates other people important to the respondent, contributing to the urgency of the situation and the importance of placating the interrogator. Yet here we uncover the basic contradiction of the situation. To put it crudely, (1) in order to be released, the prisoner must satisfy the investigation; but if the investigation is bent on extracting incriminating information (be it about the prisoner or people close to him, then (2) in order to satisfy it, he must incriminate himself or others, in a manner which would result in (3) his own continued imprisonment or the arrest of persons implicated. But any venture to address this contradiction directly would issue in 'an experience of being punished precisely for being right in one's own view of the context', which is Bateson's most concise definition of a double-bind situation, whose disastrous reach we witness at the end of Gloucester's interrogation in *King Lear*.

The double-bind model enables us to see that the process of eliciting information from the prisoner actually *depends* on the contradictory nature of the situation in which self-incriminating divulgence is *both* the condition of release and the grounds for continued imprisonment (and, possibly, increased severity of treatment). This implies that the more confusing and self-negating the interrogator's messages are, the more effective she or he will be in getting the needed information. It is the confusion that arises as the person is clasped in the forceps of the double-bind situation that can result, when crushing force is applied, in chaotic and unexpected behaviour – unexpected even to the prisoner himself – and in statements whose implications cannot be fully pre-calculated by the respondent. Being at the mercy of his captors, the prisoner is in no position to comment on the contradictory demands made on him, a situation which conforms to Bateson's third requirement, securing the structure of a deadlock, shown clinically to have devastating effects on the subject's psyche.

What ensues from a 'traumatic situation which involves a metacommunicative tangle' is that the victim will eventually experience 'trouble in identifying and interpreting those signals which should tell the individual what sort of a message a message is'. In general, 'severe pain and maladjustment can be induced by putting a mammal in the wrong regarding its rules for making sense of an important relationship with another mammal', resulting in debilitating disorganization of the subject's perceptions and responses.

> His metacommunicative system – the communications about communications – would have broken down, and he would not know what kind of message a message was. If a person said to him, 'What would you like to do today?' he would be unable to judge accurately by the context or by the tone of voice or gesture whether he was being condemned for what he did yesterday, or being offered a sexual invitation, or just what was meant. Given this inability to judge accurately what a person really means and an excessive concern with what is really meant, an individual might defend himself by choosing one or more of several alternatives. He might, for example, assume that behind every statement there is a concealed meaning which is detrimental to his welfare. He would then be excessively concerned with hidden meanings and determined to demonstrate that he could not be deceived.

In short, what we would witness when a healthy person is caught in a double-bind situation is that he or she 'will respond defensively in a manner similar to the schizophrenic' – in other words, will be rendered incapable of commenting on the communications of others 'without considerable help'. 'Without being able to do that', Bateson goes on, 'the human being is like any self-correcting system which has lost its governor' – or, to borrow the words of Robert Lowell, like 'something simple that has lost its law'. Nadezhda Mandelstam confirms that, after his release, her husband needed her help in sorting out the nature of his psychotic experience, particularly in separating delusional ideas from memories that appeared incredible but must have been genuine and correct. This is why Mandelstam's consultation with a Moscow psychiatrist who visited Voronezh, where he was transferred after his suicide attempt in Cherdyn, had such a memorably therapeutic effect.

> O. M. asked why it is that now people get sick after a few days of detention, whereas before the revolution one could spend years in a fortress and come out healthy. The physician only gestured his dismay.

Nevertheless, in the absence of a theory, this clinician was able to address the root of Mandelstam's distress:

> he invited O. M. to accompany him on his rounds. Afterwards, he asked O. M. whether he could find anything in common between himself and the various patients of the clinic. Which category would he assign himself to? Dementia, senility? Schizophrenia? Circular psychosis? Hysteria? The doctor and the patient parted as friends.

By lifting the prohibition on the patient's right to comment on his own painful situation, the visiting psychiatrist achieved – in a single therapy session – a lasting improvement in the state of the traumatized man he had just met. The self-alienation of victims of trauma implies that 'people can never get better without knowing what they know and feeling what they feel' – in the words of Bessel van der Kolk, a leading clinical researcher, in his popular book, *The Body Keeps the Score*. Contemporary studies of trauma have recovered the sense that inhibited communication must be a manifestation of something central to the aetiology of trauma. Yet 'the way medicine approaches human suffering has always been determined by the technology available at any given time', and since the early 1990s, brain-imaging tools have become the means of explaining the symptoms that restructure the lives of traumatized people. In a study of brain scans organized by van der Kolk and performed on people experiencing induced traumatic flashbacks, the most surprising finding 'was a white spot in the left frontal lobe of the cortex, in a region called Broca's area'. The neuroscientist explains:

Broca's area is one of the speech centers of the brain, which is often affected in stroke patients when the blood supply to that region is cut off. Without a functioning Broca's area, you cannot put your thoughts and feelings into words. Our scans showed that Broca's area went offline whenever a flashback was triggered.

This was 'visual proof that the effects of trauma are not necessarily different from – and can overlap with – the effects of physical lesions like strokes'. (This discovery should be important to arguments involving the word 'physical' – particularly, arguments about the nature of 'physical coercion' and torture.) Even years after the traumatic events, van der Kolk observes from a clinical point of view, 'traumatized people often have enormous difficulty telling other people what has happened to them'. 'This doesn't mean', he qualifies, 'that people can't talk about a tragedy that has befallen them'. Sooner or later, most survivors

> come up with what many of them call their 'cover story' that offers some explanation for their symptoms and behavior for public consumption. These stories, however, rarely capture the inner truth of the experience. It is enormously difficult to organize one's traumatic experiences into a coherent account – a narrative with a beginning, a middle, and an end.

A 'cover story', with its promise of uncovering and its unspoken covering up, is an unintentionally apt term for this resistance of traumatic memory to fluent, eloquent witnessing. (Philomela, the ancient survivor-witness, attains the eloquence of a nightingale – but how intelligible is nightingale-speech to us?) This very concrete struggle with words and memory is what we see in Mandelstam's lines recalling his journey into exile:

> One cannot recall what has been:
> The lips are hot and the words hardened –
> The white curtain flapped in the wind,
> The rustle of iron leaves rushed by.

All trauma is preverbal, van der Kolk observes, invoking the lines of Shakespeare's *Macbeth*: 'Oh horror, horror, horror, / Tongue nor Heart cannot conceive, nor name thee. / . . . / Confusion now hath made his masterpiece'. What the neurological account does not explain is why trauma should be linked specifically to an area of the brain responsible for communication, or how Broca's area comes to be reconditioned in the way reported in the study. Closer to an explanatory account is the historic excursus that takes us to Pavlov's famous early conditioning experiments, and specifically to the discovery of traumatic 'learnt helplessness' in 1924.

> The thaw in St. Petersburg during the spring that year caused the River Neva to flood Pavlov's basement laboratory, inundating the cages of his experimental dogs who were trapped in the icy water with no means of escape. The dogs survived, but after the water receded the dogs continued to be terrified, even though they were physically uninjured. A significant proportion, though physically unscathed, 'broke down' emotionally, behaviorally, and physiologically. Many of them laid around motionless, barely paying attention to what was going on around them.

'Pavlov interpreted this as a sign of ongoing terror, which had obliterated any curiosity in their surroundings. We now know that physical immobility and loss of curiosity are also typical of frightened, traumatized children and adults.' Such immobility has been conceptualized as maladaptive since Darwin's publication of *The Expression of Emotions in Man and Animals* in 1872:

> Behaviors to avoid or escape from danger have clearly evolved to render each organism competitive in terms of survival. But inappropriately prolonged escape or avoidance behavior would put the animal at a disadvantage in that successful species preservation demands reproduction which, in turn, depends upon feeding, shelter and mating activities all of which are reciprocals of avoidance and escape.

The consequences of being trapped in a dangerous situation were disastrous to Pavlov's animals, and persistent:

> Pavlov showed that after exposure to extreme stress, animals find a new internal equilibrium different from the previous organization of their internal housekeeping. The traumatized dogs kept acting as if they were in grave danger long after the waters of the Neva had receded. When he measured their physiology he found both markedly increased and depressed heart rates in response to minor stresses, signs of instability of the autonomous nervous system, as well as full-blown startle reactions in response to slight changes in their environment, like approaching laboratory assistants.

In Pavlov's interpretation, the key feature of the situation that resulted in this dramatic reconditioning was *conflict* between the dogs' impulses to escape and the impossibility of acting on that impulse for animals entrapped in their cages. 'To this chair bind him.' Again, Pavlov's conceptualization relies not simply on the experience of fear and danger but on the sense of *deadlock*: 'the collision between the two contrary processes: one of excitation and the other of inhibition', which could not be accommodated together, leading to 'a breakdown of equilibrium'. In the contemporary encapsulation of trauma as 'inescapable shock', the first word carries at least the same weight as the second. The remaining step required to connect this account with Bateson's double-bind theory is to note that this inescapability need not be the product of physical conditions. Bateson's work makes it evident that, in an animal with highly developed cognition (such as a porpoise), the sense of inescapability can be effectively engendered by purely communicative means. This makes intuitive sense: it is as true for humans as for other members of the animal kingdom that the environment to which our impulses respond includes other beings. Conversely, van der Kolk's findings suggest that imprisonment in itself supplies one of two prerequisites of 'inescapable shock'. The addition of threat to the situation of a person already imprisoned will automatically issue in a pathogenic situation. Yet again, in the light of Bateson's analysis, we can see how this sense of threat can be generated purely through spoken and nonverbal means, opening the avenue for traumatic stress. The integration of these findings amounts to a new perspective on the notions of *duress* and coercion, whose scope reaches beyond the judicial and penal systems.

Mandelstam's acute 'psychosis' would resolve in changes that persisted for the remainder of his life. Van der Kolk observes that, in contrast to the healthy pattern, the stress hormones of traumatized people

> take much longer to return to baseline and spike quickly and disproportionately in response to mildly stressful stimuli. The insidious effects of constantly elevated stress hormones include memory and attention problems, irritability, and sleep disorders. They also contribute to many long-term health issues, depending on which body system is most vulnerable in a particular individual.
>
> After trauma the world is experienced with a different nervous system. The survivor's energy now becomes focused on suppressing inner chaos, at the expense of spontaneous involvement in their life. These attempts to maintain control over unbearable physiological reactions can result in a whole range of physical symptoms.

Mandelstam's Lubyanka files contain their own evidence of these changes. Photographs taken in prison after each of Mandelstam's arrests – in 1934 and in 1937 – show two different people: a confident, lean Mandelstam with his arms crossed and a sharp stare directed back at the photographer in 1934, and, in 1937, a much older man, whose lustreless gaze appears resigned and weary. The much heavier body has lost its tone and strength; his facial muscles are no longer supple and mobile. One wonders, looking at the two sets of photographs – facing front and profile – whether Stalin's famous directive to 'isolate but preserve' was not in itself a self-contradictory injunction, for isolation, first in prison, and then in exile, spelled out the destruction of the person subjected to these profound cruelties. By the time of his second arrest, Mandelstam's health and sanity had been shaken, in a way that, much later, upon his return from exile in 1937, he saw reflected in the faces of Muscovites. Emma Gerstein recalled:

> On one of those first days Osip Emilyevich stood facing the window, next to the daybed, about to go to sleep. Instead of this, he began to speak about Moscow. It disturbed him. Something about it was no longer recognizable to him. He would not speak of the friends who had disappeared and died. No one did that. Such losses fell to the very bottom of every person's soul, and from there they emitted a secret radiation that permeated all of one's actions, words, even laughter. Anything but tears – such was the character of that time.

Mandelstam, a changed man, was looking for words to describe his impression of a Moscow that appeared to him changed. He was having trouble finding words, and the word he finally did find was recorded by Gerstein in dilated capitals:

> 'And the people have changed. They're all ...' He moved his lips in search of an epithet. 'They're all ... they all seem to have been ... DEFILED.'

INTERLUDE

Under the Stars

Poetry as Courage and Resistance

> Two things fill the mind with ever new and increasing admiration and reverence, the more often and more steadily one reflects on them: the starry heavens above me and the moral law within me.
>
> Immanuel Kant, *Critique of Practical Reason*

There are poems that convey a deep peace, which appears to be achieved against a backdrop of an equally deep unrest. These poems give voice to an overcoming of internal division through straddling the opposed terms of conflict, and it is this that lends them their majestic calm. What is achieved by these creations is not merely a linguistic trick, but a mobilization of deep internal resources by means of art. It is the presence of this moral effort that lends them their emotional authority; yet the source of these energies remains mysterious, resting deep within the *hiatus irrationalis*. What does, though, remain open to our examination, apart from the poem itself, is the form of the biographical situation, suggestive perhaps of the kinds of stimuli that had to be transformed in the poet's imagination before becoming concomitant in a poem of particular power and beauty.

In 'Double Bind, 1969', Gregory Bateson speculated that, if the situation's pathogenic potential be successfully warded off, 'the total experience may promote *creativity*'. Creativity, in turn, has long been appreciated as one of the possible avenues of therapy, yet the reasons why creativity should assist healing remain obscure. What will follow, then, is an exploration of how literary imagination may help us rise above imminent danger so as to preserve psychic integrity. To frame this in Bateson's terms, what turns a mere dilemma into a double bind is the 'tertiary prohibition', forbidding the person caught in the bind to remonstrate or comment on the untenable situation in which she or he is caught. Creativity is therefore therapeutic when it specifically addresses this prohibition, enabling the object of the double bind to resist the silencing that, in Bateson's statement of the problem, is an integral part of the 'pathogenic situation'.

Nikolay Zabolotsky's memoir, 'The History of My Imprisonment', contains an affecting description of his state while under interrogation at the Leningrad division of the NKVD. Faced with hostile pressure, and in the absence of outside emotional support, Zabolotsky found himself hallucinating visions of role reversal with his tormentors, tapping spontaneously and effectually his inner resources and drawing from these hallucinations the power to resist traumatic collapse:

> I remember that I myself began to shout at the interrogators and to threaten them. Symptoms of hallucination became evident: on the wall and on the parquet floor of the office I was seeing figures in constant motion. I recall once sitting before a whole conclave of investigators. I was no longer afraid of them in the least and felt instead only contempt. The pages of some huge book I myself was imagining were turning before my eyes, and on each of its successive pages I would see new images. Paying no attention to anything else, I expounded the contents of these pictures to my investigators. It is hard for me now to define the state that I was in, but I recall the feeling of inner relief and exaltation before those people, who were then failing in their attempts to dishonour me.

In the closed freight train-car that took him and others to Siberia, Zabolotsky composed 'The Forest Lake' – according to the poet's son, the only poem of substance written in Zabolotsky's eight years in labour camps. 'The History of My Imprisonment' gives a brief account of the harrowing circumstances that preceded the poem's emergence:

> Once, we were not given water for about three days, and on New Year's Eve 1939, somewhere near Baikal, we were forced to lick the black, smoke-covered icicles that had grown on the walls of the car out of the vapors we ourselves had produced. Never, not even at the end of my life, will I be able to forget that New Year's feast.

Under the Stars

Suffering from thirst in the vicinity of Baikal, the world's largest freshwater lake, the prisoner was visited by a consolatory vision:

> Once more it gleamed at me, fettered by slumber,
> The chalice of crystal in the forest dark.

Nature in this poem is seen under an aspect of violence. Even the trees are engaged in their own slow-motion massacre:

> Through the battles of trees and the carnage of wolves,
> Where insects drink life out of flora prostrated,
> Where flowers groan in the debauchery of stems,
> And nature lords over its creatures, insatiate:
> I made my way through this – and froze at your gates,
> Just parting the rustling brush with my hands.
> In a crown of lilies, a necklace of reeds,
> And wearing a vegetal vestment of sedges,
> A piece of chaste moisture lay there before me,
> The haven of fish and the game birds' refuge.
> Yet strange is the quiet: how solemn it is;
> Can grandeur surprise one amidst such a shambles?
> Why isn't the bird army yowling and screeching
> But is instead sleeping, lulled into sweet slumber?
> The snipe is alone in resenting his lot
> And blows indignantly into a reed.

At the heart of the poem is the chilling recognition of being immersed in the inescapable violence that is the order of the animal world. The pervasiveness of this violence leaves no sensible venue for lament. The snipe's indignation at this state of affairs is not mocked or derided but understood – and yet, found to be senseless, as there is no one to turn to for sympathy in such a world. When, farther along in the poem, an inanimate and silent consciousness is found in the lake, whose calm countenance reflects the flaming evening sky, it is not obvious in what way this entity could be an ally. The magnificent colour, that is not proper to the lake but a reflection of the sunset's display, then becomes a manifestation of deep feeling. This transfer of colour makes possible the transfer of emotional experience to this mysterious other consciousness, capable of embracing and containing profound emotion the way it contains the flaming sky while remaining itself immobile, undisturbed.

One way of looking at this is to notice that the poem poses and contemplates a problem of conflicting attitudes that it is attempting to balance, as against ending in a deadlock, to borrow a schemata from Empson, whose comparison of *balance* and *deadlock* runs parallel to Bateson's contrasting of the 'beneficial' and 'pathogenic' forms of the double bind. In March 1933, Empson compared these logical shapes in a letter to I. A. Richards: 'the very crucial "balance – deadlock" opposition where *balance* suggests a man walking on a tightrope – able to do what he *wants* on it – and *deadlock* two men fighting and neither getting what he wills'. The comparison can be extended to the realm of play, including the kind of play that is mental process. Once arrived at, the disconcerting recognition of the violence pervading animal life (human life not excepted), must be dealt with like any other truth. The difficulty is that if submitted to, such knowledge can amount to despair, while resisting it would threaten self-deception. The sentimental solution of resignation and acquiescence was what Empson deemed an undue and objectionable 'pacification' in his commentary on Gray's 'Elegy Written in a Country Churchyard'.

> Full many a gem of purest ray serene
> The dark unfathomed caves of ocean bear;
> Full many a flower is born to blush unseen
> And waste its sweetness on the desert air.

'What this means, as the context makes clear', Empson writes of these lines,

> is that eighteenth-century England had no scholarship system or carrière ouverte aux talents. This is stated as pathetic, but the reader is put into a mood in which one would not try to alter it. (It is true that Gray's society, unlike a possible machine society, was necessarily based on manual labour, but it might have used a man of special ability wherever he was born.) By comparing the social arrangement to Nature he makes it seem inevitable, which it was not, and gives it a dignity which was undeserved. Furthermore, a gem does not mind being in a cave and a flower prefers not to be picked; we feel that the man is like the flower, as short-lived, natural, and valuable, and this tricks us into feeling that he is better off without opportunities. The sexual suggestion of blush brings in the Christian idea that virginity is good in itself, and so that any renunciation is good; this may trick us into feeling it is lucky for the poor

man that society keeps him unspotted from the World. The tone of melancholy claims that the poet understands the considerations opposed to aristocracy, though he judges against them; the truism of the reflections in the churchyard, the universality and impersonality it gives to the style, claim as if by comparison that we ought to accept the injustice of society as we do the inevitability of death.

This was written at a time when Empson already admired Buddhism, as he would thereafter, defending in it a religion most conducive to real-world virtue. This admiration was chiefly attributable to Buddhism's courageous acceptance of suffering as one of the 'noble truths' about the world – though 'noble' perhaps only in the sense that a certain disinterestedness is required to embrace a proposition so galling. It is the acceptance of pain, without denying the essential fact that pain is undesirable, that requires courage. This is congenial to Zabolotsky, who notices the snipe's lament in a way that equates its loneliness with futility.

> The snipe is alone in resenting his lot
> And blows indignantly into a reed.

A complaint unheard is all the more a sadness, but in witnessing it with compassion, the poem recognizes that the plight is not without its own absurd, wistful comedy. This momentary and not at all malicious irony dissipates in the surrounding silence. The forest, representing not only the natural order but also the psyche with its clamouring, conflicting and conflicted aspects, is silenced in order for the powers of the lake to come into focus:

> Embraced by the quiet flames of the night's eve,
> The lake lies within its own depth, still and shining,
> And fir-trees, like candles, stand up high above,
> Closing their ranks from one end to another.

This is a moment outside time yet encompassing all of time and all of memory. The so-called 'pathetic fallacy' (which is, in actuality, not a fallacy but an epiphany) is employed here to generate a profound sense of absolution as the lake itself becomes an eye of suffering. The eye, an organ of perception that cannot perceive itself (except in a mirror), is easily interpretable as a symbol of consciousness, which reflects the world without being able to reflect itself, unless reflecting upon another's reflection. The implications of this might be dizzying, but it is sufficiently clear that the lake's reflexive (and not merely *reflective*) property is beautifully commensurate with the symbolism of an eye (present in the English pun, *eye/I*), which is the mind, and subjectivity. The effect of the comparison reinforces the trance that we are led into as the poem itself becomes a liturgy.

> The bottomless chalice of water so pure –
> It shone, as if thinking distinctly and clearly,
> The way that the eye of a despairing man,
> When sighting the light of the first evening star,
> No longer in sympathy with the sick body,
> Burns, fixed singly upon the night sky.

Coleridge's poem 'To William Wordsworth, Composed on the Night after his Recitation of a Poem on the Growth of an Individual Mind' (1807) is invoked by Geoffrey Hill in 'Poetry as "Menace" and "Atonement"' in a way that is germane to Zabolotsky. Hill quotes from the poem:

> In silence listening, like a devout child,
> My soul lay passive, by thy various strain
> Driven as in surges now beneath the stars,
> With momentary Stars of my own birth,
> Fair constellated Foam, still darting off
> Into the darkness; now a tranquil sea,
> Outspread and bright, yet swelling to the Moon.

'The beauty of the image of "fair constellated foam"', Hill writes,

> does not conceal the nature of the experience which Coleridge is evoking. The brightness is ephemeral, it moves outward from the centre into the darkness where it is quenched or lost. But we note also that there are other stars; and, bearing in mind the broodingly complex nature of Coleridge's inspiration, it may be legitimate to relate the first reference to the 'stars' to those of the prose gloss (virtually a marginal prose poem) added to the 1817 edition of 'The Ancient Mariner': in particular to a passage which Humphry House rightly calls 'that one long sentence of astounding beauty' and which I would call an outstanding image of the attainability of atonement:

> In his loneliness and fixedness he yearneth towards the journeying Moon, and the stars that still sojourn, yet still move onward; and every where the blue sky belongs to them, and is their appointed rest, and their native country and their own natural homes, which they enter unannounced, as lords that are certainly expected and yet there is a silent joy at their arrival.

The consciousness overpowered by its confinement (though it may be that the stars and the planets are even more constrained, in their determined orbits) surrenders to a recognition of the dignity of the inanimate and finds consolation in a realm free of emotion, and liberation in the calm progress of the universe. Similarly, in 'The Forest Lake', we find the mind of the poem at one with both the lake and the forest fauna in a moment of sacrament when the animals come to drink from the lake, partaking of a supreme cosmic sentience reflected in the calm water:

> And crowds of animals and feral beasts
> Poking their antlered faces between the firs,
> Bowed towards their baptismal font,
> To drink the life-giving water of truth.

The magnificent resolution of these lines, the gentle comedy of the 'antlered faces' and the completeness of the consolation derived from a vision so entirely impersonal (but, nevertheless, communal), all point to a buoyancy of spirit from which the poem appears to have issued. The beauty of the communion realized in the poem, as well as its therapeutic power, proceed from its abstention from dismissing its opening claims: before being at one with any emergent realization, the poem is deeply at one with itself and succeeds in maintaining within itself the recognition of pain, and the concurrent recognition that there are things above pain, and witnesses other than those whose absences pain us. The poem arches over these recognitions, liberating itself into supreme independence from conditions. Its subject, then, becomes *atonement*, rendered by Geoffrey Hill as 'at-one-ment' and seen by Hill not only as a subject for poetry but also as its function – a view that needs to be considered so as to differentiate from it the claims made here. 'Ideally', Hill writes in 'Poetry as "Menace" and "Atonement"', my theme would be simple; simply this: that the technical perfecting of a poem is an act of atonement, in the radical etymological sense – an act of at-one-ment, a setting at one, a bringing into concord, a reconciling, a uniting in harmony; and that this act of atonement is described with beautiful finality by two modern poets: by W. B. Yeats when he writes in a letter of September 1935, to Dorothy Wellesley, that 'a poem comes right with a click like a closing box' and by T. S. Eliot in his essay of 1953, 'The Three Voices of Poetry':

> when the words are finally arranged in the right way – or in what he comes to accept as the best arrangement he can find – [the poet] may experience a moment of exhaustion, of appeasement, of absolution, and of something very near annihilation, which is in itself indescribable.

Anyone who has experienced that moment in which a poem 'comes right' must, I believe, give instinctive assent to such statements.

'Ideally' itself appears to be an admission of difficulty – or difficulties, one of them being that the equivalence of 'at-one-ment' and 'atonement' will not be achieved simply by refusing to notice the work done by the hyphens that set the morphological parts of 'at-one-ment' apart while holding them together – as one word that will not be at one with 'atonement'. Yet 'the words of Eliot', points out Christopher Ricks, 'are not at one with those of Yeats', with the consequence that

> Hill's search for at-one-ment has led him to two descriptions of 'this act of atonement', each of which has indeed a 'beautiful finality' in its evocation of atonement as a finality, but the two of which are finally irreconcilable, tonally and totally.

The imaginative absolution achieved in a poem depends on a recognition of irrecoverable loss with no hope of atonement, for which the 'at-one-ment' of a finished poem is not a substitute or an equivalent. Similarly, the liberating and therapeutic potential of literature cannot be equated with setting things right in the world at large. This, again, is a recognition on which great poetry depends. In this light, the courage marshalled in Mandelstam's poem written in 1921 in Tiflis becomes distinct. The poem is alive with foreboding, a presentiment of large-scale terror.

> I washed myself at night in the yard.
> The firmament shone with hard stars.
> A star's ray, like salt on the blade of an axe.
> The barrel, full to the brim, was cooling.

The gates under a lock,
The Earth severe in earnest.
No purer foundation will be found
Than the truth of a fresh canvas cloth.

A star melts in the barrel, like salt,
And the cold water is turning blacker.
Death gets purer, sorrow saltier,
And the Earth more truthful and terrible.

The feeling is of anticipating irredeemable errors and irrecoverable losses – all that is meant by the term 'injustice'. In its sense of scale and of the conflicted relation of a part to the whole (of the individual to the nation's monumental collective), this is both a metaphysical poem and a political one. Yet it would be decidedly wrong to interpret it as a poem of 'resistance'. It is actually about something much more modest, yet also more concrete and practicable than 'resistance': *not running*, a resolve borne out of an impulse precisely to *run*. 'Fight-or-flight' is a phrase that both obscures and reveals the unity of the impulse *to go on being* (Winnicott's phrase for the continuity of healthy psychic functioning) that can be channelled through either end of the dilemma. What matters is that one not be paralyzed in the act of decision, where indecision spells deadlock and the frustration of the impulse to go on being. Nevertheless, the tension of the dilemma is proportionate to the strength of the impulse, as recognized by Empson, in 'Courage Means Running', an immaculately analytical poem tracing the transformations of the self-preserving impulse:

> No purpose, view,

> Or song but's weak if without the ballast of fear.
> We fail to hang on those firm times that met
> And knew a fear because when simply here

> It does not suggest its transformation. Yet
> To escape emotion (a common hope) and attain
> Cold truth is essentially to get

> Out by a rival emotion fear.

And 'attain cold truth' may not suggest its transformation by Mandelstam (in 1932), into siding with the 'fiery Lamarck', in a duel to defend 'Nature's honour':

> There was an old man, timid as a boy,
> A lumbering and bashful patriarch.
> Who will draw a rapier for Nature's honour?
> But of course, our fiery Lamarck.
>
> Everything that lives is but an error,
> Blotted in the course of one brief, orphaned day.
> Let me occupy the lowest rung
> On Lamarckian mobile stairway.
>
> I'll descend down to the Annelidae,
> Rustling past the lizards and the snakes,
> Down elastic gangways and grooves
> I shall slide and shrink, Protean.
>
> I shall don a mantle of horn substance
> And forsake the warming rush of blood,
> Overgrow with tentacles and suctions,
> Like a tendril, sink into the foam.

At this place in the poem, Lamarck is quite unexpectedly transfigured into a Virgilian figure as he leads the narrator down the rungs of the evolutionary *Inferno*:

> We have filed past the insect classes,
> With their liquid goblet-eyes.
> He said: Nature everywhere fractures,
> Sight no more, you see for the last time.
>
> He said, No more symphony; in vain,
> Here, your love of Mozart; this great chasm
> Opens here only to remain;
> An Arachnid deafness has advanced.

As if awakening from this reverie, Mandelstam observes something about the human species' condition: that no such retreat is possible, for the reason that we are not 'God-forsaken' but forsaken by Nature, orphaned by *Her*. The drawbridge is raised, and what we are left with is our *humanity* – nothing more, and nothing less, than a set of distinguishing features in the style of Darwin's cameos in *On the Origin of Species*:

> Those whose graves are a verdant green,
> Whose breath is red, who have a pliant laugh.

In relation to the inescapable situation it contemplates, the poem becomes the single available avenue of escape, that escape being of the imaginative kind. To this imagined possibility the poem then attends – responsibly, for in countenancing the impossibility of the longed-for retreat, it arrives unflinchingly at its conclusion, which happens to be a *dead end*. This is in line with the way courage is displayed by other poems evoked on the preceding pages: regardless of which side of the fight-or-flight dilemma they entertain, be it the metaphoric 'running' or declining to, they do so without losing *integrity* – that is, without surrendering under the pressure to split away aspects of consciousness, with the result that a certain wholeness of vision is maintained and that, in dynamic terms, deadlock is avoided and a commitment made with the full backing of the poem's energies, including the necessary risks and sacrifices. It is this fullness of apprehension that determines the therapeutic potential of the poem, first experienced by the poet (as feelings of release we have seen described by Yeats and qualified differently by Geoffrey Hill and by Christopher Ricks), and secondarily by the reader (in the singular, because the experience is always inward, private, individual). In the poet's mind, the poem can, rather apparently, become the means of breaking Bateson's 'tertiary injunction' to make no comment on the unresolvable contradictions of a situation, with the result that the double bind is ameliorated. This was just the kind of magical creativity enacted by Zabolotsky in 'The Forest Lake'. The therapeutic effect of the composition on the consciousness of the poet is mirrored in the poem's vision of the 'crowds of animals and feral beasts' who,

> Poking their antlered faces between the firs,
> Bowed towards their baptismal font,
> To drink the life-giving water of truth.

It is one of the central therapeutic potentials of literary art to become such a 'baptismal font' for all those who inhabit the language and to proffer, in a specific and necessary way, 'the life-water of truth'. Mandelstam, washing himself at night in Tiflis in 1921, the year he had turned thirty, came upon the same convergence of senses when the barrel brimming with cold water reflected the stars above. The scale of the looming realization is signalled by the omission of the first-person pronoun in the opening ('Washed at night in the yard'), and it is in keeping with the poem's prophetic reach and meditative pacing that the poet-translator George Kalogeris made the bold decision to let the three quatrains of Russian unfold in a cascade of rippling triplets twice the length of the Russian original. The extra space, upon which the poem is allowed to unfold its every image, is purchased at the risk of dilution, or loss of unity, where integration is more than usually important as a realization of the poem's subject, *integrity under duress*. What prevents an unmooring of the poem over this double line-count is the translator's decision to tether it thrice over by its opening line, 'As I was washing myself in the dark':

> As I was washing myself in the dark,
> Washing outside where the ice-cold water
> Kept spilling over the rim of the barrel,
>
> The evening stars against the horizon
> Glistened like salt on the blade of an axe.
> As I was washing myself in the dark,
>
> I saw the locked gate that couldn't keep out
> The menacing look of my surroundings,
> Once it had entered my state of mind.
>
> . . .
>
> As I was washing myself in the dark,
> Washing outside where the ice-cold water
> Kept spilling over the rim of the barrel,
>
> The earth edged closer to truth and terror.

Dialogos, Kalogeris's collection of 'paired poems in translation', pursues its own kind of straddling act, bringing together poems from across the tradition and inviting us, implicitly, to observe their interplay and the kinds of reciprocity, illumination and balance (i.e. freedom, in Empson's sense of 'balance') that may arise from it. Mandelstam's Tiflis poem appears opposite Baudelaire's 'Le Cygne', trumpeting of loss.

> And just as old memories trumpet
> Their tired refrains, I thought of loss that memory
> Cannot restore, and the blank look of a castaway's
> Empty horizon;

The capacious reflective melancholy of 'The Swan' leads us towards Mandelstam's poem that isn't, by contrast, melancholy, even as it begins with an outline of empty horizons – empty, yet teeming with unintelligible life, graspable only as a looming, ineluctable danger. The heart of this poem lies in marshalling carefully chosen words to achieve the effect of concentrated silence. There is unstated resolve in this abstention even from a mention of flight, far from crying out one's despair, as does Baudelaire's hampered swan,

> its webbed feet imprinting
> The dirty pavement as it dragged its plumage
> Across the cobbles, whose ruts looked even ruttier
> Swept by the swan's feathers. But then it demurred,
> Pointing its open beak at the empty gutter,
> And let out a shriek –

to be answered, in the translator's imagination, by the silence of Mandelstam's meditation under the stars, grounded in hopelessness, so deeply felt as to approach shrewdness: there's no point in crying out, no one is listening, nor can anyone change anything. What we see, instead, is a star dissolving, like salt, in the overflowing contents of a water barrel, transubstantiating water into saline solution. If this invention strikes us as wholly unconscious and spontaneous, the impression has to be related to the nature of helplessness and other feelings of being overwhelmed, all of which have powerful ties to earliest and most basic experiences – the kind that animate a completely different work, Carroll's *Alice*:

> 'And things are worse than ever', thought the poor child, 'for I never was so small as this before, never! And I declare it's too bad, that it is!'
>
> As she said these words her foot slipped, and in another moment, splash! she was up to her chin in salt-water. Her first idea was that she had somehow fallen into the sea, 'and in that case I can go back by railway', she said to herself.

'However', we learn a few sentences later, 'she soon made out that she was in the pool of tears which she had wept when she was nine feet high'. A child's psyche can easily be drowned in the sorrows of the full-grown giants that are adults, similarly to an adult's psyche when confronted with overwhelming political realities that may threaten one's readiness to carry on being. It is this parallel that brings *Alice* into the scope of Empson's consideration of the pastoral and its political implications, when he writes, in 'The Child as Swain':

> The only passage that I feel sure involves evolution comes at the beginning of *Wonderland* (the most spontaneous and 'subconscious' part of the books) when Alice gets out of the bath of tears that has magically released her from the underground chamber; it is made clear (for instance about watering-places) that the salt-water is the sea from which life arose; as a bodily product it is also the amniotic fluid (there are other forces at work here); ontogeny then repeats phylogeny, and a whole Noah's Ark gets out of the sea with her.

This intertwining of ontogeny and phylogeny is responsible for the therapeutic effect of the scene, aimed at curing the very impulse to recoil that inspired Mandelstam's 'Lamarck'. The solution to the problem of entrapment is escape and absolution through dissolution in the oceanic saline solution, which is magically equivalent to a birth, with its felt integration into a new state of solidity and resolution: the Protean liquidity of related nouns – *solution, dissolution, absolution, resolution* – is itself suggestive of the capacity for escape and renewal they indicate. Mandelstam's poem does not specify the exact nature of the fluid in which a star has just dissolved, for this is to be understood unconsciously, at once multiply and singly. It might be water sampled from the primordial ocean, amniotic fluid, or even tears flowing over the brim in the night (another instance of the 'pathetic fallacy', a misnomer). Through this hypnotic work of words, the poem succeeds in conveying the wordless ruminations of a consciousness imprisoned in history, ruminations about what *liberty* might still be there, as judged by the cold and detached light of the stars, whose inexorable procession in their orbits is a powerful intimation of the implacable. Even the relatively slighter forces that rage outside the locked gates turn any attainable security into imprisonment: the solitary half-naked man washing himself under a starry sky is no less locked inside the gates than kept safe from the outside chaos. This is, then, a poem of containment and its discontents, a poem of self-containment in the face of what obtains, at one in its dignified sobriety and calm with a far-ranging constellation of poems contemplating inaction as one honourable form of courage. Such is Andrew Marvell's 'An Horatian Ode upon Cromwell's Return from Ireland' and its portrayal of Charles I and the dethroned monarch's conduct before execution:

> He nothing common did or mean
> Upon that memorable Scene:
> But with his keener Eye
> The Axes edge did try:
> Nor call'd the Gods with vulgar spight
> To vindicate his helpless Right,
> But bow'd his comely Head
> Down as upon a Bed.

The family resemblances enfold Mandelstam's 'salt on the blade of an axe', along with an element of the nocturnal calm, here enacted by the gentle, downward gliding of the vowels in 'bowed' and 'down', evocative of rest ('Down as upon a Bed'), and the ensuing clear detachment that develops into a certain vulnerable indomitability, a supreme and majestic independence from violent events, of what might be 'looming there, in the near future'. In the same constellation, or family, we find William Empson's 'Aubade' of the fateful year 1937, in which lovers are awakened by an earthquake ('It seemed the best thing to be up and go').

> I slept, and blank as that I would yet lie.
> Till you have seen what a threat holds below,
> The heart of standing is you cannot fly.

The last line once again reminds us of the swan's situation, as seen by Baudelaire,

> its webbed feet imprinting
> The dirty pavement as it dragged its plumage
> Across the cobbles, whose ruts looked even ruttier
> Swept by the swan's feathers.

'The heart of standing is you cannot fly.' Indeed. And the heart of this line is in the contrast, with 'a gem' that 'does not mind being in a cave', or 'a flower' that 'prefers not to be picked': it reminds us that a natural, unhampered being would prefer to 'fly' or to flee, to be 'up and go'. There's modesty in this line and its pragmatism, as it takes our attention off the considerable self-possession that the admission requires. So, too, in the instance of Mandelstam's countenancing of what's 'looming there', 'like salt on the blade of an axe':

> Salt of the earth and stars of the sky
> Dissolving now in the water's reflection,
> This briny water that keeps turning blacker,
>
> Like some purer shade of appalling death –
> As if our lips had already tasted
> What's steeped in the salt of worsening luck.
>
> As I was washing myself in the dark,
> Washing outside where the ice-cold water
> Kept spilling over the rim of the barrel,
>
> The earth edged closer to truth and terror.

In 1922, the year following the composition of that prescient poem, Jurgis Baltrušaitis, the Lithuanian diplomat (and poet), would offer Mandelstam an opportunity to leave Russia. Mandelstam would decline.

CHAPTER 5

In the Cross-Vault

The Stalin 'Ode' as Metaphysical Poetry

> and at last for the highest event in ethics, the moral discovery,
> which gets a man called a traitor by his own society.
> William Empson, '*The Ancient Mariner*'

The term of Mandelstam's Voronezh exile was to end in May 1937. The looming prospect of return to Moscow and reintegration into its literary life (the couple did not yet know that they would be prohibited from residing in the capital) required with utmost urgency that Mandelstam prove himself a *bona fide* proletarian poet. In view of his recent past, the prospect of emergence from exile put Mandelstam, a professional man of letters, in a perilous situation. Unable to make a living if not by public utterance, he was certain to be scrutinized by the regime's ideological vigilantes – yet, given the internal contradictions of the reigning ideology, it was not at all clear *how* he might have prepared for the scrutiny.

Having emerged as a minority ideology, Bolshevism had, as it rose to power, turned its puritanical insistence on absolute conformity into a criterion for dividing the society into 'those who are with us' and 'those who are against us' – a division that did not permit of degrees, be it of doubt or belief. Revising or retracting one's prior, ideologically 'misguided' views was a matter of humiliating penitence which put one at the mercy of the Party. Regardless of the immediate outcome, such a tainted past would remain one's biographical Achilles' heel, a ready vulnerability, should prosecution ever need an opening. By 1937, the Communist Party's ambition of establishing an ideological monoculture had taken the form of a fully-fledged programme of eradicating nonconformity, down to purging former members of non-Bolshevik revolutionary factions. As Bolshevism increasingly insisted on undiluted ideological purity, the category of 'counter-revolution' became proportionately broader. (Stalin's purges of the upper echelons of power in 1938 would reveal the extent of the systemic autoimmune malaise represented by a trend of aggressive orthodoxy that would inevitably core itself by its own insistence on absolute loyalty.) The metaphors necessary for the regime's propaganda of this standardization of human thought came from the language of industrialization concurrently sweeping the country. Stalin, who addressed writers as 'engineers of human souls', set Soviet society on its own course of mass production – the product, in this case, being the mass human: hardy, innocent of private property, devoid of personal life, minimally attached to family, happiest when submerged in a collective and, above all, studiously trained to attune her or his consciousness – and conscience – to the dictates of the regime. The resistance of human material to such radical reshaping was thought to be rooted in the atavistic pre-revolutionary mores, and the language in which the Party furthered its vision of the reformed society was rife with metaphors of eradication 'at the root', amputation, liquidation – all in the interest of establishing an even ideological monoculture, as if to spite the idealist Kant, who had observed that 'out of such crooked wood as the human being is made, nothing entirely straight can be fabricated'. Stalin, though, appears to have thought that there was plenty of human timber to go around on the construction site of Socialist future: 'when you chop wood, chips go flying'. To change the metaphor, Soviet society would enter a new phase of historic development as a camel through the needle's eye, and the necessary sacrifice would be the total eradication of heterodoxy.

This sketch is intentionally general, so as to bring into focus the internal contradiction of Bolshevism, which is its self-destructive insistence on ideological purity. Supposing, in very simple terms, that the social system was designed to progressively rid itself of nonconformity through repeated cycles of self-examination and expulsion of heterodox elements, the result would depend on whether we were to believe that absolute conformity to a given standard could be achieved in a critical mass of the population. Kant's admonition, if taken seriously, would mean that the answer to this question is simply No, and that, in the basic algorithm of its operation, the system has no effective governor to stop it from hollowing itself out through progressive purging. Yet, where Kant saw human difference as inherent in human nature (and thought uniformity unachievable in principle), Bolsheviks understood difference as a mere accident of historical conditions and thought it both desirable and possible to isolate and remove all that went against the grain of their vision. (Against this backdrop, Stalin's directive concerning Mandelstam, 'isolate but *preserve*', reveals its peculiar, calculated inventiveness.) Yet the matter of *isolating* whatever might be deemed 'extraneous', 'alien', 'foreign', 'other', nonconformist and heterodox, is itself vexed with metaphysics and the question of what it would mean to accomplish such a carving-up of reality with artificial hermetic boundaries.

The continuum of the language itself (language being the medium of politics, among other things) appears to resist such endeavours. *Roget's Thesaurus of English Words and Phrases* – a monument of lexicographical thought on likeness and difference, concord and contradiction – is organized on the principle of opposition among antonyms, 'synonym' itself being an antonym of 'antonym', standing in paradoxical opposition to *opposition* in a way reminiscent of Andrew Marvell: 'Ballance thy Sword against the Fight'. Where *Roget* attends to *Relation* (Section II, immediately following the disposal of *Existence*, Section I), the first pair of opposed relations is that of 'relation' and 'irrelation'. The latter, variously manifest in 'dissociation', 'inapplicability', 'inconnection', 'disconnection', 'independence', 'incommensurability', 'heterogeneity' and 'nonconformity', is established largely by negating relation by means of negative prefixes. Negation itself is, of course, a function of the positive statement – in other words, the very idea of unrelatedness is logically dependent upon the prior idea of relatedness. The paradox of irrelation is, then, that irrelation is but one of the possible kinds of relation, relatedness itself thus becoming intractable and pervasive. Severance of relations – for instance, through exclusion of the outer world by monastics – opens vertiginous vistas such that only Marvell was fit to contemplate consummately:

> These Walls restrain the World without,
> But hedge our Liberty about.
> These Bars inclose that wider Den
> Of those wild Creatures, called men.
> The Cloyster outward shuts its Gates,
> And, from us, locks on them the Grates.

The boundary erected so as to isolate and keep apart is also that which joins the two sides, becoming the ground of their redefined relation; 'within' and 'without' are hinged upon the preposition 'with', swinging both ways, like doors that keep apart but also connect. The gates, with their grates, are shut and locked 'from us' within, 'on them' without – though someone might think the nuns imprisoned in the convent, rather than 'the World without' being locked up to preserve their 'Liberty'. What we're presented with, unexpectedly and rather thrillingly, is the reversible nature of exclusion, the sense that something is being conserved on both sides of the divide, amounting to a reciprocity. What of irrelation, then? It is subsumed under the species of relation, which demonstrates that some complex ideas encompass their own opposites.

In this manner, *Roget* lists 'bolshevism' and 'revolution' under the category of *Disobedience*, reminding us that Bolshevik orthodoxy, now so insistent on *Obedience* ('allegiance, loyalty, fealty, homage, deference, devotion, fidelity, constancy', along with 'submissiveness', 'ductility', 'servility' and more yet), had itself sprung up as revolt against its predecessor (autocratic monarchy), and was therefore plagued from the inception by philosophical inconsistency. Lenin's note concerning Trotsky ('tell Comrade Trotsky that he is a radish – red on the outside, white underneath') should have met the objection that the 'redness' of a true Bolshevik depends on the 'whiteness' of the opposition, and that red, in virtue of its dialectical relation to white, subsumes and contains it, just as the outwardly red radish contains the white flesh within. The language of colour itself is, of course, another venue in which opposition and complementarity are essential to meaning – as encapsulated by Kuzma Petrov-Vodkin in his theoretical notes on colour:

> There is much that is paradoxical in the nature of colour. For example this: we see a red object, but what does that mean? It means that this object does not accept and

In the Cross-Vault

instead deflects all the red rays whilst absorbing the blue and the yellow; and so it turns out that the object, while being in itself green, envelops itself, so to speak, in red.

The object, in other words, 'wears' the colour complimentary to the colour that it absorbs and, in a certain sense, contains. 'It is curious, too', remarks Petrov-Vodkin, 'that daltonists perceive exactly this inward colour contained by the object'. This observation concerns specifically a person's sensitivity to red and green parts of the spectrum – and these are the colours subjected to just such an inversion by Mandelstam, in his poem 'Bolshevik', written in the spring of 1935:

> The world's inception, great and fearsome:
> In the green night, a black fern.
> The aching strata roused the Bolshevik –
> Single, continuous, indisputable.

'Single, continuous, indisputable': uniform, monolithic and tolerating no dissent. The poem is evidently preoccupied with the metaphysical matter just raised, but what commentary upon the problem can we glean from the puzzling transposition of green (night) and black (fern)? The impression is akin to a photographic negative: the light values exchanging places with the dark, inverting the tonal scale of the whole composition in chiaroscuro. Yet, considered as a colour negative, the line should invert into the following positive image in colours complementary to green and black:

> In the *red* night, a *white* fern.

The political significance of these colours is now unambiguous: in the predominantly red (Bolshevik) environment, some kind of otherness blossoms, however small: the white fern of 'counter-revolution' – a term then applied, as we know, to anything that wasn't pro-revolution, and therefore permitting or acknowledging nothing outside of the schema in which everything somehow stood in relation to revolution and Bolshevism. If the slight white figure against a red ground is to be indicative of the nascence of 'white', counter-revolutionary reaction amidst the dormancy of the 'red' state, then the next inversion (repeating the transposition of black and green in the poem itself) would yield the line:

> In the *white* night, a *red* fern.

The 'white night' in this permutation readily invokes Petersburg, the revolutionary Petrograd, the place where the 'red fern' of Bolshevism unfolds and blossoms, like the magic fern in the nocturnal rites of Ivan-Kupala, the midsummer festival of ancient Rus, the animistic night from which the Russian world flourished like an unfolding fern: the inception invoked in the first line of the quatrain. The mutability of the line, suggested by the first colour inversion, invites the thought of painful inherence of the red moment in the white, and vice versa, resulting in the grandiose collision of elemental forces and the rise of the supreme Bolshevik,

> Persisting and respiring in the wall.
> Hail to you, who volunteered to bind
> The labourers; let this coal-cornerstone,
> Your mighty brain, light the country, light!

What this poem makes absolutely clear is that this universal and single Bolshevik – Stalin – is not just another private and accidental human being. Stalin's existence is a matter of historic necessity; unlike anything accidental and partial, he is encompassing, and therefore paradoxical ('volunteered to bind'), a universal phenomenon whose volcanic glow lights the land in the colours of Dante's *Inferno*. The Kremlin's significance is notably a function of Moscow's plan without a plan, as the city's peculiar shape was a product of growth starting from the Kremlin and moving outward in concentric circles, so that the city's map resembles the rounded sack of the human heart, with radial roads reaching out like blood vessels. Mandelstam associated Moscow's archaic shape, its crooked streets and circular boulevards centred around the Kremlin, with decay and dormant threat of contagion, writing in 1931:

> Midnight in Moscow. Splendid is the Buddhist summer.
> With fine clatter, the streets part, in their tight iron clogs.
> Boulevard rings lie resplendent in the repose of smallpox.

If the clatter of these 'clogs' sounds to us distinctly Spanish, this may be owing to Mandelstam's intuition of his own time's consonance with the history of Muscovite religion. The Eastern Church's moment of fascination with the Inquisition in the fifteenth century had since been carefully redacted from cultural memory (so very successfully that Orthodox Christians today are seldom aware of Fyodor Kuritsyn's limited success in burning heretics in Russia, prior to the decisive intervention of St Nilus of Sora). While the linear streets of St. Petersburg give opportunity to long unbroken strides, taking a stroll in Moscow means meandering down curving lanes, turning corners and sometimes noticing that one walks in circles: one firm reason for associating Moscow with Dante's circular pilgrimage, and the Kremlin and its chief inhabitant – 'Persisting, respiring in the wall' – with the centre of *Inferno*'s vortex.

It is against these sentiments that Mandelstam labours in 'Bolshevik', whose preoccupation with the metaphysical matter of relation is continuous with the problem of patronage and the question of what possible relation to Stalin the poet might hope to secure. 'Would you feel pleased if someone called your brain a "coal-cornerstone"?' Mandelstam is known to have asked an acquaintance upon composing these lines, apparently well aware of how urgent the question would become in the space of two years. The answer to that question rests largely on how believable the flattery, which has been, for centuries, the challenge of artists under the conditions of patronage, where the mark of a true artist has been his or her capacity to bridge the gap between truth and flattery. The capacity to 'interpret' the subject of the portrait (portraiture being the foremost expression of patronage) into an ennobling vision, whose persuasiveness is essential to the enterprise, relies, in turn, upon the artist's supreme command of both reality and imagination. The two quatrains of 'Bolshevik' make evident the presence of these questions in Mandelstam's mind, together with an idea of how one might proceed with the justification of Stalin's immense power: the leader, whose biography's particulars have been cast aside as mere accidents, is here felt to contain all of the country's human potential. The potentiality of Stalin's energies, expressed in the immobility of the energetically charged 'coal-cornerstone', converts directly into the kinetic energy of individual industrial workers, who take their rhythmic cues from the even breath within the Kremlin wall. Dark, impenetrable, animistic, indifferent to good and evil because absorbing of all difference – Mandelstam's Stalin is invested with an ambivalence suggestive of a power to reconcile all contradictions within the industrial cauldron of his inert yet fearsomely energetic being, itself forged of an alloy, as indicated by Stalin's self-chosen name. Mandelstam's early intuition concerning the portrayal of Stalin was, thus, immediately metaphysical – that is, concerned with the relation of the One to the Many, and with justifying Stalin through depicting him in a relation to the proletariat that is like the relation of a universal to particulars. All this constitutes the case for speaking here of metaphysical poetry, as defined by James Smith:

> verse properly called metaphysical is that to which the impulse is given by an overwhelming concern with metaphysical problems; with problems either deriving from, or closely resembling in the nature of their difficulty, the problem of the Many and the One.

This will be the operative definition of metaphysical poetry, as it is subtler and more penetrating than, say, W. H. Auden's in introducing the *Elizabethan and Jacobean Poets*:

> 'Metaphysical' is a somewhat misleading term, for it suggests that the poets to whom it is applied had a unique interest in the science of Being, in contrast, say, to 'Nature' poets. This is not the case: the subject matter of Donne and his followers is not essentially different from that of most poets. What characterizes them is, first, certain habits of metaphor: instead of drawing their images from mythology, imaginative literature of the past, or direct observation of nature, they take their analogies from technical and scientific fields of knowledge, from, for example, cartography.
>
> > My face in thine eye, thine in mine appeares,
> > And true plaine hearts doe in the faces rest,
> > Where can we finde two better hemisphaeres
> > Without sharp North, without declining West?

Auden's sense of the primacy of metaphor over subject in defining the convention is also 'somewhat misleading', for Donne's metaphor in the above example is felt to be so precisely fitted to the subject in virtue of its conveying Donne's actual discovery of patterns inherent at once in the love relation described and in the phenomena of the wider world, so that the love secluded in the private world of two people is made to breathe the turbulent open air of oceanic travel. This sense of breadth, of escape from the stifling accidents of the purely personal into a broader, more elemental and more encompassing sense of belonging and embracing, came as an unheralded reward of the early enthusiasm for a conceptual vision of the world, proclaimed by Donne's contemporary, Galileo (e.g. by insisting on the primacy of quantity over quality). Yet what is concept in science and philosophy is metaphor in literature, a metaphor being a relational schema superimposed upon the object of comparison; for this reason, it is not at all surprising that the advent of modernity, marked by a sudden emphasis on quantitative categories and certain other kinds of universals proper to science, would have been accompanied by a corresponding shift in literary convention expressed in an altered repertoire of metaphors. Again, metaphor functions not as a spurious embellishment but as a model of the world which encompasses both that which is being compared and that *to* which comparison is being made (the 'tenour' and the 'vehicle' in Donald Davie's conception of metaphor). What makes a metaphor metaphysical is its exposition of relations between the One and the Many, the universal and its proper particulars, where we might not have suspected the presence of such a relation. 'Metaphysical problems', Smith writes, 'rise out of pairs of opposites that behave almost exactly as do the elements of a metaphysical conceit'; 'If any conceit is taken, of the kind I have called metaphysical, I think it will be found that its elements are either a pair of opposites long known to metaphysics, or reducible to such a pair.' Having seen examples of this in Bolshevism, in Marvell and in the structure of *Roget's Thesaurus*, we shall see it, in due course, in Mandelstam's 'Ode' to Stalin: 'He leaned out of the tribune as from a cliff / Over the hills of heads'; 'The debtor by far stronger than the credit'; 'The sculptural, complex and convex eyelid: it must work / Out of a million frames'; 'All – candid honesty, all – confession's brass, / His hearing sight tolerates no falsehood'; 'Towards all who stand, ready to live and die, / Run, rippling, his severe wrinkles'. To foreshadow the pervading presence of these conceits is to suggest also that we notice, in

Mandelstam, the turbulence, elusiveness, unrest and searching perplexity that James Smith observes in Donne and Thomas Aquinas (in contrast with Dante or Lucretius), generalizing these as the characteristic mood of metaphysical poetry. To quote at length,

> it is Donne's verse that is disturbed, and his lines that are the battleground between the difficulty of belief and the reluctance to doubt. Lucretius is bellicose, Dante submissive; but both have an assured peace.... I think it can be said, of both Dante and Lucretius, that they were not so much themselves metaphysicians, as the disciples of metaphysicians; and disciples have a way of being more certain than their masters. There is, for example, an obvious contrast between Thomism as one meets it in Dante, and as one finds it in Thomas himself. To the lips of those who know Thomas only through Dante, or through compendiums devised for the study of the *Commedia,* there rises inevitably one adjective for the description of his work: the adjective 'neat'. There is, of course, a neatness about Thomas: one of language, which has scarcely, if ever, been rivalled. But his thought, or any fragment of that thought, is rich, suggestive and haunting. It has a thousand ramifications, of all of which the mind is to some degree aware, few of which it can clearly grasp and follow, and these perhaps not to their very end; further, they are fine and interpenetrating, so that they seem to be alive.

So much of this is true also of the Voronezh notebooks, teeming with metaphysical oppositions and conceits, that the reader can only be invited to consider the figures that crop up, one after another, to testify to this. 'The Birth of a Smile' alone contains figures of a child (potentiality and actuality), a smile (expressing bitterness and sweetness), a snail (evolution and retreat), a rainbow (multiplicity ordered in a spectrum and Heraclitean 'reciprocal harmony' inherent in the bow shape), an ocean (multiplicity without form or order) and the Russian word *'privivka'* which can mean (by homonymy) either of a pair of metaphysical opposites: a graft (nature enhanced by artifice) or an inoculation (contagion and immunity). This choice of figures is not simply a mannerism, as Auden thought, but evidence of being haunted by the pervasive contradictions of existence that resist unambiguous resolution. Yet, as Smith observed about metaphysical thought, its value

> depends on what is held in suspension ... rather than on what is precipitated. Once precipitation takes place, it loses in value; nor has the precipitate a value which makes

up for the loss. Yet it is this precipitate that the disciples collect, and of it they make their 'neat' display.

It is by metaphysical means that Mandelstam would address the problem of patronage in constructing his portrayal of Stalin in relation to the proletariat – and to himself as the artist. That apologia, foreshadowed by the two brief yet capacious quatrains of 'Bolshevik', would become plainly necessary by 1937, if Mandelstam were to defend his poetic legitimacy – nay, his *utility* to Soviet literature. Conceivably, it was perhaps to see him navigate this treacherous moment of re-emergence that Stalin granted him exile instead of death back in 1934. Now a *persona ingrata* on the verge of reentering public life, Mandelstam had to establish a relationship with Stalin – the target of his 'Epigram' – as his patron, the subject of a portrait. In the winter preceding his return from exile, he wrote: 'I stare into the frost's face, all alone.'

The artist's problem in flattering a person in power is not a trivial one, if Kant's vexation be any measure of its difficulty.

> This problem is at the same time the most difficult and the latest to be solved by the human species. The difficulty which the mere idea of this problem lays before our eyes is this: the human being is an animal which, when it lives among others of its species, has need of a master. For he certainly misuses his freedom in regard to others of his kind; and although as a rational creature he wishes a law that sets limits to the freedom of all, his selfish animal inclination still misleads him into excepting himself from it where he may. Thus he needs a master, who breaks his stubborn will and necessitates him to obey a universally valid will with which everyone can be free. But where will he get this master? Nowhere else but from the human species. But then this master is exactly as much an animal who has need of a master. Try as he may, therefore, there is no seeing how he can procure a supreme power for public right that is itself just, whether he seeks it in a single person or in a society of many who are selected for it. For every one of them will always misuse his freedom when he has no one over him to exercise authority over him in accordance with the laws. The highest supreme authority, however, ought to be just in itself and yet a human being. This problem is therefore the most difficult of all; indeed, its perfect solution is even impossible; out of such crooked wood as the human being is made, nothing entirely straight can be fabricated. Only the approximation to this idea is laid upon us by nature. That it is also the latest to be worked out, follows besides from this: that it requires correct concepts of the nature of a possible constitution, great experience practised through many courses of life and beyond this a good will that is prepared

to accept it; three such items are very difficult ever to find all together, and if it happens, it will be only very late, after many fruitless attempts.

Given the grim equality of all the variously 'crooked' representatives of humanity, what individuates one in their midst – sending him, in Robert Lowell's phrase, 'clawing up the tree of power'? Lowell's answer was, of course, a dark and undemocratic one: something had to be deeply *wrong* with a person endeavouring upon a life in politics. Kant, though, wrestled with the internal inconsistency of representation: what's *representative* of the human race cannot possibly be fit to serve as a *political representative* by virtue of excellence – the perennial justification of leadership (this paradox echoed by Marvell's lines, 'The double Wood of ancient Stocks / Link'd in so thick, an Union locks'). Consequently, those who are elected or strive to represent the interests of a group are typically far from typical for that group, and must be instead, in some way, deeply aberrant. The puzzling thing about personality cults is that in order for the person in a crowd to see oneself reflected and realized in the figure of the leader (the phenomenon loosely referred to as 'identification'), a deep chasm of otherness must be felt to separate one from the other, a difference as cardinal as that between a particular and a universal in philosophy. This difference resembles the distance between a 'regular person' and a person of genius, which, to Mandelstam, appears to be a special form of proximity:

> Schubert on the water, Mozart in the din of birds,
> Goethe, whistling on the winding path,
> Hamlet, who thought by anxious steps,
> All counted the crowd's pulse, and believed the crowd.

This, together with the mentions of Schubert's deceptive calm, bespeaking the deep anxiety of *Auf dem Wasser zu singen*, of Mozart losing himself, on the brink of his own death, in *Die Zauberflöte*, of Goethe's own nervous whistling, can only be read as a confession arising from a deep uncertainty, and an attempt to calm oneself. Yet, once again, persuasion can only work if it relies on some truth, and to Mandelstam the truth was that a genius cannot be insane. Sanity, in turn, meant to him a sympathetic awareness of other people – as attested by the entirety of his meditation 'On the Interlocutor', but also by his letter to his father,

Emil Mandelstam, whose orthodox communist convictions prompted the latter to scold his son in 1931. Mandelstam wrote back:

> Could I have thought that from you I would hear the Bolshevik sermon? But on your lips, it is far more powerful for me than if heard from anybody else. You have spoken of what is the most important: one who doesn't get along with his epoch, one who hides from it, will give nothing to other people and will find no peace with himself. The old is gone, and you have understood it so late, yet so well. Yesterday is gone, and what remains is only the very ancient and the future.

If our lives are in some sense portrayals of the parents who raised us, those early relationships can easily be cast in terms of patronage, with their insistences that one must be truthful, yet must also please. Depending on the tension between the two imperatives (and the presence of the 'tertiary prohibition' on comment), sanity can be threatened and suffer. It is felt to be similarly imperilled in Voronezh poems, which confront us with a consciousness oppressed by contradictions and wishing sometimes to cut through their Gordian knot, to be rid of one or another half of a contradiction, where the two halves operate like crushing forceps.

> I must live, although I have twice died.
> Of swollen water, the town is in half-mind.

It was April 1935, and the poem opening with these lines contemplated not only the two suicide attempts of the preceding year, or perhaps two kinds of death, private and public, inherent in one's removal from society, but also the treacherous political implications of the past for the future. The springtime swell of the river ('*polovod'ye*') is inventively enfolded in '*opoloumel*' – gone mad, a verb derived from the adjective '*poloumnyi*' ('mad', etymologically 'of hollow mind'). Although their shared root, '*pol*', stands for hollowness (as in the noun '*polost*'', 'a hollow', or the adjective '*polyi*', 'hollow'), its homonymy with '*pol*' as in '*polovina*' ('half') suggests that the city has lost half of its mind – gone mad through a diminishing of its former full and ambivalent consciousness to some kind of stunted single-mindedness. The root '*pol*' again shows up in January 1937:

> Unhappy is the one, who, shadow-like,
> Shudders at the barking, mowed by the wind.
> Poor is the one who, *half*-alive,
> Pleads for alms with his own shadow.

If the half-aliveness of which the poem speaks proceeds from the impossibility of living fully, this can mean many different things, one of which is that the fullness of life amounts to an untenable contradiction. A poem written early in 1937, opening with the question 'Where can one escape to this January?', is far from the travel agent's meaning of 'escape'; it is a poem of inescapability, of dead ends.

> The stockings of these barking lanes,
> The broom-closets of these crooked streets –
> And scamper hurriedly into corners
> And run out of corners – the dark bewhiskered cornerers…

The murky town's public spaces are felt to be faintly threatening in unfamiliar, unpredictable ways. Though menacing, they appear populated by alien life: the only living creatures in the poem are those named by the ingenious neologism '*uglan*' (similar to '*ulan*', a type of cavalry-man in the imperial army, and rhyming with '*tarakan*', 'cockroach', the word is derived from '*ugol*', 'corner') with its impression of furtive and shadowy creatures darting in and out of corners, not so much street-corners – intersections where friends meet – as the unkempt recesses of claustrophobic *cul-de-sacs*. The poem develops into a tumbling nightmare, prescient of Mandelstam's burial within two years:

> Into a pit, into a warty dark
> I slide towards the frozen water-pump
> And, stumbling, eat the morbid air

This is significantly darker than the dark forebodings of 1935, which start with the already familiar ideas of crookedness and linearity but end in the form of a memorial plaque, a kind of epitaph:

> What street is this?
> Mandelstam street.

> What sort of a devil's name is that?
> However you turn it,
> It sounds crooked, not straight.
>
> Little about him was linear,
> His temper unlike a lily,
> And that is why this street,
> Or, more precisely, this pit
> Bears the name
> Of that Mandelstam...

In her memoirs, Nadezhda Mandelstam adduced none of this ferment to her account of the composition of the 'Ode'. When *The Slavic Review* published the poem for the first time in English translation, the poem, anonymously translated and prefaced, was framed as a straightforward case of the poet's utter denigration and enslavement:

> Near the window in the room at the seamstress's stood a square dining table which served us for absolutely everything. O. M. took possession of the table and spread out his pencils and paper on it. He had never before done anything of the sort: paper and pencils, after all, were necessary only at the end of his work. But for the sake of the 'Ode', he decided to change his habits, and from then on we were forced to eat on one little corner of the table or even on the window sill. Every morning O. M. seated himself at the table and took pencil in hand: a real writer. A regular Fedin. I even waited for him to say 'at least one line a day', but that, thank God, never happened. After sitting for a half-an-hour or so in the writer's pose, O. M. would suddenly jump up and begin to berate himself for his lack of craftsmanship. 'Now Aseyev, there's a craftsman. He wouldn't even stop to think, but would get it down right off.' Then, suddenly calming down, O. M. would lie down on the bed, ask for tea, get up, feed sugar to the neighbour's dog through the *fortochka* ... once again pace the room and, brightening up, would begin to mutter. This meant that he had not been able to smother his own poems, and they had broken loose and conquered the evil spirit.

The work of this alien 'evil spirit', supposedly at war with Mandelstam's 'own poems', would emerge as the culmination of the entire Voronezh period – only to become Mandelstam's most misunderstood poem, condemned on all sides, from Stalin's functionaries to the poet's own wife and his foremost champions. Yet the surrounding poems can no more be isolated or insulated from the 'Ode' than dissent can be sealed off from orthodoxy. Oddly, though, literary studies betray a persistent wish to cordon off the 'Ode' as something unrelated to the rest of Mandelstam's *oeuvre*, which itself has come to resemble an orthodoxy, jealously guarded against heresy – for fear, to change the metaphor, that one bad apple might spoil the cartload. To be more exact, the fear has to do with the poem's supposed servility, bowing down to political necessity, and failure of personal principles – all such arguments being involved with the poem's intention, not its contents, and drastically oversimplifying its *raisons d'être* and the nature of its engagement with those conditions. Considered generally to be an embarrassment (similarly to the way John Ruskin's Communism is often felt to be an embarrassment and passed over by Ruskin scholars), the 'Ode' is avoided or evaded where its mention would be germane – supposedly out of tact, as a service to the poet – or else hedged by excuses and apologies for its existence that, in all their benign intent, belittle the intensive philosophical work Mandelstam had poured into the 'Ode' and the other poems written in the winter and spring of 1937 – poems continuous with it in their subject matter and in their spirit. To read these poems with an eye to the genuinely difficult philosophical problems with which it wrestles is to realize that this thought unfolded in utter dignity, as a free and genuine philosophical investigation and could not possibly be any farther from the servility that is so often, so readily and so wrongly attributed to it. Regardless of what we might think and feel about it, the 'Ode' came into existence, and at eighty-four lines it is not an easy thing from which to avert one's eyes, so we might as well read its opening lines.

> If I were to pick up the charcoal in high praise,
> For the indisputable ecstasy of drawing, –
> I would section the air into cunning angles,
> Both carefully and anxiously, so that
> The present would resound in every feature,
> Verging on impudence in art,
> I would speak of him who found a fulcrum,
> Honouring the custom of a hundred and forty tribes.
> I would raise that eyebrow's little corner, and
> Would do so again, resolving differently:
> Prometheus has blown alive this ember –
> Behold, Aeschylus, how I draw – and weep!

J. M. Coetzee, who took his cues in this regard from Nadezhda Mandelstam, came up with perhaps the cleverest device for cordoning off the 'Ode' and its odd contents in his essay 'Osip Mandelstam and the Stalin Ode'. Seizing upon the subjunctive mode of its inaugural line, he concluded that the entire poem was a kind of performative trick predicated on the opening qualifier, *If*, which supposedly 'brackets', or suspends, the truth of the eighty-odd lines that follow. The sense, then, comes out to be something like this: '*If* I were to endeavour to praise Stalin, I would say what I'm about to say, but in fact (*if* you pay attention to my *ifs*), this is all purely speculative.' In other words, the poem, as viewed by Coetzee, and not only by him, is little more than a specimen of a 'fig in the pocket', a survival tactic adopted by much of the Soviet intelligentsia and amounting to doing what the regime asks, but with a covert attitude of great defiance. Now, if the poem were in need of a moral justification, this account would hardly suffice, since it attempts to extricate a person from charges of cowardice by attributing to him a cowardice of a different and rather more distasteful sort. Coetzee is right to draw our attention to the inaugural qualification; where he is mistaken is his interpretation of the hesitancy in 'If I were to pick up the charcoal in high praise', for Mandelstam himself expands upon it: 'I would section the air into cunning angles.' Now, in spite of the work being putatively a portrait, the 'angles' (partly because envisioned in the 'air', i.e. three-dimensional space) belong to architecture, suggesting that the opening 'If' of the poem has to do with the poet's taking up an unusual task: accustomed to seeing himself as a craftsman working in stone (to which he had so often likened language), he now ventures for the first time to conceive of himself as a master architect, framing the poem as an architectonic monument – as if to say that this is the only form appropriate to his subject. To portray Stalin, we understand, is to portray the grandiose phenomenon of his multiplicity as reflected in the minds of the Many and in the 'million frames' that bring the Leader's likeness before every person, making him the cynosure of all eyes. The fleetingness of the moment in the poem which indicates architectonics as a mode of portraiture, the delicacy with which only the 'air' and the geometry of the 'angles' intimate, but briefly, that we are in an architectural space, have led critics to miss the moment when the charcoal of portraiture emerges out of its prior stage as the charcoal of architectural draftsmanship. Yet the entirety of the grandiose poem affirms this intention to portray Stalin in a mode of equivalence and reciprocity with the great edifice of state – an edifice composed of the Many, each of which looks upon and praises the One: Stalin. This conjecture flashes in a freestanding quatrain, written in the same period:

> There are such things as living mosques –
> And I have just divined:
> We, too, might be an Hagia-Sophia
> With a countless multitude of eyes.

This idea was, of course, nothing new in the history of poetry and political patronage. Andrew Marvell had to solve the problem of justifying Cromwell's power, and harnessed the disparate and clamouring wills of the many into a rigid unity of the political edifice in 'The First Anniversary of the Government under O. C.':

> The Commonwealth then first together came,
> And each one enter'd in the willing Frame;
> All other Matter yields, and may be rul'd;
> But who the Minds of stubborn Men can build?
> No Quarry bears a Stone so hardly wrought,
> Nor with such labour from its Center brought;
> None to be sunk in the Foundation bends,
> Each in the House the highest place contends,
> And each the Hand that lays him will direct,
> And some fall back upon the Architect;
> Yet all compos'd by his attractive Song,
> Into the Animated City throng.

Among the elements that contribute to the effect of these lines is the use they make of the capacity of English words to accommodate opposite meanings. Words and phrases like 'willing' (signifying both malleability and assertiveness), 'who the Minds of stubborn men can build' (one 'builds' a political edifice out of the minds of the many by first 'building' *them*, that is, shaping them through education or propaganda), 'each the hand that lays him will direct' (the pliancy of the word order allows to read this in two opposite ways). The poem's argument is tested and enriched by the presence of these alternate readings, indicative of reciprocal tensions throughout, in the spirit of Heraclitus: 'Whilst being at variance, it is in agreement with itself.' It is Heraclitus' idea of 'reciprocal harmony, like that of a bow or a lyre' that surfaces again in Marvell, as he elaborates his vision:

> The Common-wealth does through their Centers all
> Draw the Circumf'rence of the publique Wall;
> The crossest Spirits here do take their part,
> Fast'ning the Contignation which they thwart;
> And they, whose Nature leads them to divide,
> Uphold, this one, and that the other Side;
> But the most Equal still sustain the Height,
> And they as Pillars keep the Work upright;
> While the resistance of opposed Minds,
> The Fabrick as with Arches stronger binds,
> Which on the Basis of a Senate free,
> Knit by the Roofs Protecting weight agree.

This is a justification of political union, as imposed by Cromwell, in terms of architectonics – one possible metaphor (i.e. relational schema, or concept) of a system. The interlocking oppositions are subsumed within the edifice that derives its strength from the tensions resolved in the shape of an 'Arch', showing the productive and benign potential of opposition, as compared to the negative unproductive sense of deadlock. Among the great figures of speech for *e pluribus unum*, the arch is a centuries-old metaphor. It is, of course, Gothic architecture – defined by John Ruskin as '*Foliated* Architecture, which uses the pointed arch for the roof proper, and the gable for the roof-mask' – that made possible this rhetoric of unity achieved through an elastic tension amongst all of its parts:

> Egyptian and Greek buildings stand, for the most part, by their own weight and mass, one stone passively incumbent on another; but in the Gothic vaults and traceries there is a stiffness analogous to that of the bones of a limb, or fibres of a tree; an elastic tension and communication of force from part to part, and also a studious expression of this throughout every visible line of the building.

'When Gothic is perfect', Ruskin observed, specifically with respect to the arch, 'it will follow that the pointed arches must be built in the strongest possible manner'. This necessitated foliation, and

> the forms of arch thus obtained, with a pointed projection called a cusp on each side, must for ever be delightful to the human mind, as being expressive of the utmost strength and permanency obtainable with a given mass of material.

Significantly for the rhetorical implications of the Gothic style, the apex of the building, too, had the form of an arch. Only the roof-mask – the external structure protecting the roof proper from the elements – had the shape of a gable. The gable, in turn, 'built on a polygonal or circular plan, is the origin of the turret and spire; and all the so-called aspiration of Gothic architecture is nothing more than its development'. What the vertical of the gable celebrates, then, is the 'reciprocal harmony' of opposite forces engendering the strength of the arch at the basis of the edifice. It is in virtue of this development that the Gothic becomes a visual rhetoric compatible with the tradition of thought leading back to Heraclitus' earliest known statement of *harmonia* as a reciprocal elastic tension of opposition, 'reciprocal harmony, like that of a bow or a lyre' – the elastic tension we witness in both the opening and the closing lines of a Heidelberg poem, written in the autumn of 1909 but not included by Mandelstam in the collection of the period, *Stone*. The poem – a meditation in four stanzas – opens by invoking the cold and iridescent sound of the lyre, and concludes with the already familiar image:

> And slender fingers tremble,
> Pressed against their own counterparts.

We have already attributed this gesture to the Heidelberg art historian Henry Thode, and the Gothic figure formed by his fingers, paired into Gothic arches, could not have been lost on Mandelstam, who attended his course on sixteenth-century Venetian painters and another course on the foundations of art history at the time of the poem's composition. Shortly after the composition of this poem, in 1913, the whole Ruskinian complex of feelings and ideas about the Gothic as systematic, encompassing, emblematic of rational thought and responsible and noble craftsmanship, would ripen into Mandelstam's own manifesto, 'The Dawn of Acmeism', claiming to 'introduce the principles of the Gothic into the relations among words':

> Acmeism is for those who, possessed by the spirit of workmanship, do not recoil from their heavy load but accept it joyfully, so as to awaken and to harness its dormant architectural powers. The master-builder says: 'I build, therefore I am right'. ... What madman would agree to start building if he did not believe in the reality of the material whose resistance he must conquer? Stone becomes pure substance in the hands of a master-builder, and he was not born for building who does not discern a metaphysical proof in the sound of a chisel breaking the stone.

Referring to Tyutchev's reticent miniature poem, 'Probleme' (written in 1857), Mandelstam continues:

> Tyutchev's stone – which, 'having rolled down the mountain, rested in the valley, started on its own or pushed down by a thinking hand' – is word. The voice of matter in this sudden fall sounds like intelligible speech. This challenge can only be met with architecture. Acmeists lift reverently this mysterious stone of Tyutchev's and lay it at the foundation of their edifice. ... The stone has, as it were, thirsted for another existence. It discovered within itself the capacity, potentially dormant within it, for the dynamic – and asked to be taken into the cross-vault, to partake in the joyous interaction with others of its own kind.

These sentences breathe the same recognition of elevation as potential energy that Ruskin expresses as the 'mountain brotherhood between the cathedral and the Alp', their shared 'magnificence of sturdy power' that moved young Mandelstam to write the same year:

> The more attentively, O rock of Notre Dame,
> I contemplated your tremendous ribs,
> The more often I thought that I, too, some day
> Would create beauty from a sinister mass.

If we sense a presentiment of great power, here and in the bidding made in 'The Dawn of Acmeism', it is partly due to the encompassing sense of the architectonic and the sheer reach of the metaphor. The *Oxford English Dictionary* registers a tension between the predominant material senses of 'architectonic' ('pertaining to architecture' and to 'construction') and the philosophical, systemic sense: the relationship that unites these two predominant senses is metaphoric, as the material sense of the word is used for representing the relations of ideas within a system. Being historically the latest to arrive, the latter sense ('*esp.* in *Metaph*. Pertaining to the systematization of knowledge') relies on notions of mass and gravity to intimate similar configurations of forces in the realm of ideas. William Whewell's *History of Inductive Sciences* supplies an illustration: 'Classification is the architectonic science, to which Crystallography and the Doctrine of External Characters are subordinate.' Between the material and the metaphysical senses, the political is found: 'having a function of superintendence and control, i.e. having the relation that an architect bears to the artificers employed on the building'. Yet we have seen the political sense itself figure within Kant's metaphor of 'reason's government' over cognitions, which reinforces the impression that centuries of elaboration have enriched the idea of an *edifice* as a representation of both comprehension and control. In 'The Architectonic of Pure Reason' (part of the architectonic of the 'Transcendental Doctrine of Method'), Kant explains:

> By an *architectonic* I mean the art of systems. Since systematic unity is what first turns common cognition into science, i.e. turns the mere aggregate of cognition into a system, architectonic is the doctrine of what is scientific in our cognition as such; and hence it necessarily belongs to the doctrine of method.
>
> Under reason's government our cognitions as such must not amount to a rhapsody; rather, they must amount to a system, in which alone they can support and further reason's essential purposes. By a system, however, I mean the unity of the manifold cognitions under an idea. This idea is reason's concept of the form of a whole insofar as this concept determines a priori both the range of the manifold and the relative position that the parts have among one another. Hence reason's scientific concept contains the whole's purpose and the form of the whole congruent with this purpose.

These ideas were as intimately familiar to Mandelstam as Gothic architecture, but the rhetoric of the Gothic, which Mandelstam would ingeniously deploy in the composition of the 'Ode' supplies a distinctly humanistic, unexpectedly warm aspect to what would otherwise remain a sterile abstraction. Mandelstam's understanding of the Gothic, which shines scattered through his personal writings, is distinctly Ruskinian, revealing affinities with the latter's paradoxical 'red Toryism'. When leaving the Federation of Soviet Writers in the wake of the *Ulenspiegel* affair, Mandelstam addressed the institution in a letter of protest: 'I, dear comrades, am not an angel in starched vestments', he wrote, recommending himself instead as 'a worker, a heavy labourer of words' who 'turned the boulders of books with my own hands'. 'My work has never been slave labour', Mandelstam continued in his letter, 'and I am ready to defend, foaming at the mouth, my right to failure, my right to have a breakdown'. Once again, the sentiment is informed by a comprehension of the craft that early on became Mandelstam's model of literary art – the Gothic. The craftsman's right to imperfection is part of the political polemic mounted by Ruskin in connection with the Gothic, understood by him as a deeply Christian architecture: 'to banish imperfection' he writes, 'is to destroy expression', and this is because perfection – absolute adherence to an ideal – is at odds with richness, a profligate love of variation characteristic of the art of the Middle Ages and reliant on the forgiveness of imperfect skill among the workmen called to adorn the common edifice:

> It seems a fantastic paradox, but it is nevertheless a most important truth, that no architecture can be truly noble which is *not* imperfect. And this is easily demonstrable. For since the architect, whom we will suppose capable of doing all in perfection, cannot execute the whole with his own hands, he must either make slaves of his workmen in the old Greek, and present English fashion, and level his work to a slave's capacities, which is to degrade it; or else he must take his workmen as he finds them, and let them show their weaknesses together with their strength, which will involve the Gothic imperfection, but render the whole work as noble as the intellect of the age can make it.

> in the mediaeval, or especially Christian, system of ornament, this slavery is done away with altogether; Christianity having recognized, in small things as well as great, the individual value of every soul. But it not only recognizes its value; it confesses its imperfection, in only bestowing dignity upon the acknowledgment of unworthiness. ... Therefore, to every spirit which Christianity summons to her service, her exhortation is: Do what you can, and confess frankly what you are unable to do; neither let your effort be shortened for fear of failure, nor your confession silenced for fear of shame. And it is, perhaps, the principal admirableness of the Gothic schools of architecture, that they thus receive the results of the labour of inferior minds; and

out of fragments full of imperfection, and betraying that imperfection in every touch, indulgently raise up a stately and unaccusable whole.

On the other hand,

> Wherever the workman is utterly enslaved, the parts of the building must of course be absolutely like each other; for the perfection of his execution can only be reached by exercising him in doing one thing, and giving him nothing else to do. The degree in which the workman is degraded may be thus known at a glance, by observing whether the several parts of the building are similar or not.

The salience of these lines might not be immediately obvious, since it has been proposed that Mandelstam's relation to the 'Ode' is that of a master architect's to an edifice. Who are, then, the workers about whose liberty we are concerned? In this regard, Oleg Lekmanov supplies the crucial evidence, having examined practically all the Soviet poetry portraying Stalin in the year 1937 and finding practically all of its recurrent tropes and metaphors carefully incorporated into Mandelstam's 'Ode'. Lekmanov's study, positioning the 'Ode' against 'the backdrop of poetic Staliniana of 1937', enumerates such motifs as the leader's 'childhood in the Caucasus'; his life of 'arrests, imprisonments and exile'; his 'oath over Lenin's body'; his authorship of the USSR Constitution (gleaned by Lekmanov from the lines 'I would speak of him who found a fulcrum, / Honouring the custom of a hundred and forty tribes'); the image of Stalin in a soldier's overcoat and mentions of his wise gaze, his encouraging smile, his voice, his mighty hand, his closeness to the Soviet people, his steely name and the Soviet people's readiness to give their lives for his sake. His handshake and the familiar features of Stalin's omnipresent portraits are drawn into the poem, which likens him also to a mower ('a mower of handshakes' implicitly likening each man reciprocating the handshake to a blade of grass, one among multitudes). Yet the leader is also seen as ruling nature 'and, it is cautiously suggested, even the sun' – which would ordinarily rule both the mower and the grass. All said, out of the entire array of this genre's accumulated devices, only one (the image of a leader who 'never sleeps') is found by Lekmanov missing from an otherwise complete set of similes, metaphors and biographical allusions. What all this suggests is that, in the 'Ode', Mandelstam elects to be at one with his fellow poets, to whom he will not deny their

In the Cross-Vault 189

expression but will rather act as the master builder, assembling into a single edifice the work of a plurality of craftsmen. This appears to have been a judicious solution to a whole sheaf of problems. Mandelstam's principled reluctance to contradict the voice of his own epoch is satisfied in this act of solidarity with the men and women of letters, his contemporaries. The superlative and monumental nature of the 'Ode', which threatened to single out its author among other poets, is diffused by the openly 'collaborative' approach to the form, in which Mandelstam gives his assent to other voices, not necessarily proclaiming that they are *right*, but unequivocally affirming their *right to be*. In light of such a reading, the muttered 'Now Aseyev, there's a *craftsman*', remembered by Nadezhda Mandelstam, acquires an entirely different tone from the sarcasm with which she had injected it, and the conditional opening line of the 'Ode' appears to say: *If* I were charged with such a portrayal, it could only be a polyphony, and my own voice in it could only be a part of a chorus of praise, sung by

> Not me, and not the other, but his kin,
> His Homer-people triples praise upon him.

This was, once again, in the spirit of the conjecture made back in November 1933 – almost concurrently with the composition of 'The Stalin Epigram':

> We, too, might be an Hagia Sophia
> With a countless multitude of eyes.

These lines, considering the idea of a union under a single architectonic principle – and doing so in the immediate vicinity of the 'Epigram' – bring into relief the vertiginous complementarity and mutual dependence of the 'Epigram' and the 'Ode' (with but one of them, instead of both, we feel, Mandelstam himself is 'in half-mind'). The lines of 'Hagia-Sophia' singing out with Apocalyptic echoes:

> And the first beast was like a lion, and the second beast like a calf, and the third beast had a face as a man, and the fourth beast was like a flying eagle. And the four beasts had each of them six wings about him; and they were full of eyes within: and they rest not day and night, saying, Holy, holy, holy, Lord God Almighty, which was, and is, and is to come.

With all eyes turned to a single cynosure, with all perspectives converging to a point, that intersection, the cross-vault of the complex edifice, can become a centre of tremendous strain – the tension of actuality, with its bristling 'crooked timber', against the ideality of an imaginative construct in which all variance is resolved.

> Perhaps it is the point of madness,
> Perhaps it is your conscience –
> The knot of life within which we are known
> And untied into being.
>
> So the cathedrals of crystals overarching life
> Are taken apart into ribs
> By the diligent spider, light,
> And gathered again into a single bundle.

These lines were Mandelstam's own commentary upon the 'Ode' and its genuine preoccupations, corroborated by Empson's cognate poem, 'Arachne':

> Twixt devil and deep sea, man hacks his caves:
> Birth, death; one, many; what is true, and seems;
> Earth's vast hot iron, cold space's empty waves:
>
> King spider, walks the velvet roof of streams:
> Must bird and fish, must god and beast avoid:
> Dance, like nine angels, on pin-point extremes.

Read with a correct sense of what it probes – the relation of the One and the Many, the dependence of the Many upon the One, and the chasm that separates the one and the other – the 'Ode' proves to be highly serious, filled with an honourable yearning for the common good, audacious, searching and *tragic*, as does, in James Smith's view, metaphysical poetry in general, when properly understood. This tragic aspect of the 'Ode' would be developed by Mandelstam in a poem so overtly representative of the metaphysical type that the reader should not need any further assistance in discerning its salient features. This poem is 'Verses For the Unknown Soldier', which stands, at ninety-eight lines, as a formidable

In the Cross-Vault

complement to the 'Ode'. In relation to the new universal contemplated therein, Mandelstam avows his own particularity within history with a conviction that could not have been mustered in the 'Ode', in relation to Stalin:

> As aortas swell up with blood
> And a whisper is heard in the ranks:
> I was born in the year ninety-four,
> I was born in the year ninety-two;
> And I squeeze in my fist the worn-out
> Year of birth, with the rest of the mob,
> Whispering with my bloodless mouth –
> I was born on the night, from the second
> To the third of the month of January,
> In the year ninety-one, and the centuries
> Encircle me with their flames.

The Parisian Arc de Triomphe stands over the Tomb of the Unknown Soldier, interred on Armistice Day in 1920 to memorialize those, who, in Wilfred Owen's words, 'die as cattle', the Arc and the Tomb acting as opposites in a metaphysical conceit involving the state and the individual, victory and sacrifice, commemoration and oblivion. It appears that the relation of the 'Ode' to the 'Verses for The Unknown Soldier' parallels this relation of the Arc to the Tomb, in which the one monument necessitates the existence of the other. The elusiveness of the 'Ode', attributable either to humility or indecision ('If I were to pick up a charcoal', 'Not me, and not the other, but his kin'), is continuous with its turbulence:

> Crushing the charcoal intersecting all,
> Voracious hand imploring a resemblance,
> The likeness-axis preyed upon by the hand-carnivore,
> I shall crumble the coal in hunting for his features.

It shares, too, the spirit of Marvell's 'Last Instructions to a Painter':

> His desperate Pencil at the work did dart,
> His Anger reacht that rage which past his Art;
> Chance finish that which Art could but begin,
> And he sat smiling how his Dog did grinn.

> So may'st thou perfect, by a lucky blow,
> What all thy softest touches cannot do.

This is a turbulence continuous with the mood of 'The Unknown Soldier', as with 'turbulence in Donne, elusiveness in Thomas' –

> both are signs of something very different from the certainty to be found in Dante and Lucretius. I am not suggesting a resemblance between Donne and Thomas in the possession of a negative quality merely. I do not believe that anyone who lacks certainty, who is puzzled and therefore in his account of his studies puzzling – for instance, the cross-word fanatic or the half-wit – is for that reason to be called metaphysical. Metaphysics is 'puzzling', if I may retain the homely word, in a peculiar way. It is not that, to the matters it studies, there is an abundance of clues, so that the mind is lost among them; or that there is a shortage of clues, so that the mind is left hesitant; but rather, that such clues as there are, while equally trustworthy, are contradictory.... The contradictions in metaphysics ... spring from essence. The very nature of things brings them forth. It seems impossible that the nature of things should possess either the one or the other of a pair of qualities; it seems impossible that it should possess both together: it seems impossible that it should not possess both.

The official commentary on the 'Ode', issued in March 1938, reflected these qualities, too, but in its own peculiar assessment. The review belonged to Pyotr Pavlenko (whom Mandelstam would have been right to call 'my dark person', after Pushkin's Mozart when speaking of Salieri), who had now been charged with evaluating Mandelstam's new poems for the NKVD, stating:

> There are good lines in the 'Verses about Stalin', a poem of great feeling, which sets it apart from the rest. But overall the poem is not as good as its select stanzas. There's much in it that is muddled, which has no place in a Stalin theme.

On May 5, Mandelstam was arrested again; on August 2 he received a five-year hard labour sentence. Mandelstam's last known poem, dated July 4, 1938, remains faithful to the contradictions that had inhabited his poetry until then; in his final poem, though, they reach the pitch of madness, and then simply wash away: 'as if over the meadow ... walk mad mowers; the downpour mows the meadow in a bow'.

CHAPTER 6

Quarrels on the Witness Stand

Posthumous Mandelstam

> No human face is exactly the same in its lines on each side, no leaf perfect in its lobes, no branch in its symmetry. All admit irregularity as they imply change; and to banish imperfection is to destroy expression.
>
> John Ruskin, *The Stones of Venice*

'Posthumous Mandelstam' is a phenomenon that is no less a monument to the will and determination of his varied champions than to the poet himself. In the most generous assessment, it is akin to an edifice in the Ruskinian Gothic style, whose coherence is a product of variance among the (sometimes grossly) imperfect contributions of the disparate witnesses. To judge more stringently, the construct is ridden with flaws that, to extend the architectural metaphor, are in themselves a record not solely of Mandelstam himself but also of the struggle for the title of his posthumous reputation's Master Architect. This inkling is corroborated by Emma Gerstein's scrupulous recollections of her acquaintance with the Mandelstams, which furnish an explicit account of the editorial contentions that unfolded between the three principal memoirists of Mandelstam (all of them women) from the moment when it was decided that all three – Nadezhda Mandelstam, Anna Akhmatova and Gerstein herself – should write down their memories.

When the original of *Hope Against Hope* began to circulate in *samizdat* in the early 1960s, Akhmatova learned of it only from her granddaughter, who had read the book and said to her: 'Akuma, there's a lot there about you.' Akhmatova, ever attentive to her own public persona, was bewildered: 'It seems that Nadya should have told me before publishing her book.' 'On her part', Gerstein reports, she treated the poet's widow with great attention. *Leaves from a Diary* do not depart, not by a word, from Nadya's versions of events. This, given that they were conceived as a tendentious work in their own right.

Consistency was thus a principle to which Akhmatova adhered, expecting others to do the same, which required a concord as to what could and couldn't, should and shouldn't be mentioned. Gerstein recalls that, 'following Akhmatova's wishes',

> I began to put my scattered notes about Mandelstam in some order. I showed her the very first drafts of a continuous text. Without reading to the end of the second page Akhmatova cried out: 'No, no! You can't write about that!' This prohibition referred to passing mention of the squabble between Mandelstam and Gornfeld. I was astonished. That literary row was widely known, it had been discussed repeatedly in the press, and a great many documents relating to the affair had survived – Mandelstam's entire *Fourth Prose*, after all, had sprung from the conflict. 'Why can't we at least mention it?' 'Because, because' (she was incoherent with agitation), 'because Osip was in the wrong!'

Having already traced the history of the *Ulenspiegel* affair, with the surviving documents mentioned by Gerstein, we may well be convinced that 'Osip' had not, after all, been in the wrong, and that Gerstein, too, was right in her sense that an attempt to suppress the episode would come at too high a cost. Yet this was not the only area of Mandelstam's biography to be redacted. His testimony to the OGPU in 1934 and his composition of the 'Ode' to Stalin in 1937 were also subject to this unofficial censorship, since those events, too, ran against the grain of the lapidary image that Akhmatova thought proper to a poet. While cultivating a self-consciously stylized image of herself, 'the Cleopatra of Neva' thought it best to preserve Mandelstam in similarly stylized – but immune to criticism – lineaments. That 'sin does not befit a poet' is a guiding sentiment of her 'Poem Without a Hero', but when applied to biography, this apophatic approach can only result in a hollow idea of the man who was once Mandelstam, for to subtract these supposed embarrassments from his biography is to vacate it of every event that tested and thereby revealed his character, of every organizing crux around which other events cluster and find their order. All the same, as Gerstein recalled, this was 'the guiding principle' responsible for the background against which her own memoirs would stand in relief.

> There was prior agreement that the literary portrait of Osip Mandelstam should ignore entire layers of his tangled and stormy life. I could not accept this set of rigidly enforced omissions. Moreover, the one-sided description of Mandelstam's personality led to a series of distortions. In *Leaves from a Diary* one encounters episodes where this supposedly ennobling deception becomes translated into the crudest of untruths.

Gerstein's gifts included the rare combination of scruple and great tact, and it seems that without the latter she could not have remained a lifelong friend both to Akhmatova and to Nadezhda Mandelstam – in contrast, for instance, with Boris Kuzin, a close friend of Mandelstam's who severed all relations with the latter's widow, remarking in his reminiscences: 'Had I continued my relations with N. Y., I would inevitably have formed some ties with those who are now creating – and I cannot find a different word for this – the cult of Mandelstam.' The religious overtones of 'cult' are apt with regard to the notions of 'sin' that informed a policy which led, by 1957, to the situation in which Akhmatova was

> utterly confounded by her permanent commitment to idealizing the image of Mandelstam ... The 'Poem without a Hero' speaks about amnesty for a sinner, but the *Pages* reject the very fact of sin as such. Without doubt, Anna Andreyevna was not free in writing her *Pages*, since she was greatly influenced by the guiding hand of Nadezhda Yakovlevna.

(Gerstein's characteristic, though not consistent, use of her friends' patronymics acknowledges their personal acquaintance, still taking a degree of courteous distance – so as not, one thinks, to slight the reader by flaunting their closeness. Russian names vary so as to reflect the speaker's relationship to the subject; the choice of form, then, is always significant and telling, with respect to the relationship itself, but also to the speaker's judgement.) More to the point, this brief passage shows an immediate concern of all three memoirists with matters of culpability – personal, political and artistic – and with establishing a rhetoric that would best redeem Mandelstam and protect him from judgement. The touching side of this is the wish (the widow's and Akhmatova's) to continue sheltering

Mandelstam posthumously from persecution, not now by Stalin's regime but by those who were against it. Yet among the three parties to this conversation, only Gerstein appears to have felt that more would be lost than gained in trying to render Mandelstam's reputation immune to criticism by over-pruning the facts. (Mandelstam himself would probably have agreed with her, even judging by his rebuke, in the *Conversation About Dante*, of Blok's portrayal of Dante – his 'immaculate hood' and 'aquiline profile' – that was more commemorative medal than man of flesh and blood.) Not coincidentally, it was Gerstein who preserved memories of how Mandelstam conversed ('Of course, you are unhappy', he said to her when still a young woman, early in their acquaintance, 'but, you know, sometimes unhappy people can be very happy'), how he slept on the sofa, walked, or peeled a pear: variegated, rich, teeming reminiscences that are the opposite of 'lapidary'.

It might, of course, be objected that towards the end of her life Nadezhda Mandelstam herself would go on record (in conversation with a foreign correspondent) as if under a banner of '*épater le bourgeois*':

> Here's what I can tell you about Mandelstam, if you don't know anything about him. He was a remarkable person, we often laughed together, I was never bored with him, and we were very happy together even in the hardest of times. And I was not the cause of it – he was. Sometimes we would fight, we both had insufferable personalities, but at night we always made love, and very successfully. It may be ridiculous to talk about sexual accomplishments at 73 years of age, but that was the reason we lived together. We could not live without one another. I tried to be unfaithful to him, but it never worked. Because he was the best.

What do we make of this surprising invitation into the couple's bedroom (recorded in 1972 or 1973), so far removed from the idea of Mandelstam on a pedestal, classicized and stylized, 'in profile'? If this be a rhetorical figure, what sort of ground does it depend on for its effect? It seems evident that this statement and its backdrop of decent, 'bourgeois' poetic respectability are like two hands clapping. The final impression is that the widow's unconventional admission of the extent of the Mandelstams' marital happiness is far less revealing than it might seem at first, since it stymies the conversation ('Questions, anyone?'), diverting it away from the difficult territory that is Mandelstam's public biography and framing the poet instead as a private being: her *husband*, no less and no more.

The idea of 'sin', as one possible conceptualization of moral failing, belongs to a system of metaphors that includes 'witness', 'martyr', 'sacrifice', 'redemption', 'atonement', etc. – all such metaphors informed by Christian theodicy and based on the tacit premise of a hermetic boundary between Good and Evil. A similar idea of a clear boundary, between legality and illegality, resurfaces in judicial matters, attributable not to active metaphysical conviction but to a kind of 'dead metaphysics' that has long since become the basis of court practice – that of issuing decisions in the form of verdicts. For this reason, whether we invoke explicitly religious language or speak, as did Czesław Miłosz, of 'putting culture on trial' (resorting to the legal metaphor), the implication is of accepting the metaphysical premise of the radical discontinuity of Good and Evil (with the concomitant belief in the comprehensiveness of these categories). There is, arguably, a principal difference between perceiving the world in categories of Salvation and Damnation, scapegoats and sacrificial Lambs, saints and sinners, Madonnas and whores – and adopting, for lack of direct evidence, a sceptical attitude to the effect that 'life involves maintaining oneself between contradictions that can't be solved by analysis'. Corollary to this realization is the sense that biography can only succeed where it addresses itself to the genuinely unresolvable contradictions in the life of its subject. Unless the subject be trivial, such contradictions will necessarily arise, and it is from the heart of such contradictions that comprehension and forgiveness have opportunity to emerge.

What verdict, for example, could be issued in the case of Mandelstam's year-long involvement with Sergey Rudakov, an aspiring textual scholar exiled to Voronezh in 1935, who, within a year, had been appointed heir to Mandelstam's archive and his sole literary executor? Had Nadezhda Mandelstam's been the sole known testimony about Rudakov, we would only know him as an inconsequential pedant with a penchant for copying out poems and drawing India-ink silhouettes.

> He had a bunk in a room which he shared with a young worker named Tosha, but he came to us for all his meals. This was a relatively good period for us when we had earnings from translation, the local theater and the radio, and it was no hardship

for us to feed the poor fellow. While I was in Moscow he had carefully collected all the drafts of 'Black Earth', which M. was composing then, and after my return, when M. and I began trying to remember the poems confiscated during the house search, Rudakov copied them all into a notebook for us. Overnight he copied them on drafting paper, in a rather comic copperplate hand with curlicues, and brought them along to us in the morning. He despised my spidery handwriting and complete lack of concern for the appearance of manuscripts. He thought, for instance, that it was scandalous to write with ordinary ink, and insisted on using India ink. (He also drew silhouettes in India ink, and the result was no worse than those done by street artists.) He showed me his beautifully executed copies of M.'s poems and said: 'This is what they'll keep in the archives, not the messy things you and Osip Emilyevich do.' We only smiled, and tried not to hurt his feelings.

This 'annihilating' portrayal (to use Rudakov's own characterization of Nadezhda's way of dealing with him), rendered long after his death in the Second World War, met substantial resistance from Gerstein, despite Rudakov's disastrous role in the fate of the Mandelstam papers. Gerstein took it upon herself to balance this portrait – characteristically, by adducing further evidence. (Though she was not in a position to censor anything expressed by others, she betrays no desire to do so, either.) Yet no memoir could narrate Rudakov's conquest of Mandelstam better than his own letters to his wife, Lina Finkelstein, to whom he wrote daily, sometimes twice, which were published in near-entirety in 1997, by Alexander Mets and E. A. Todes. In April 1935, Rudakov wrote to Finkelstein, showering her with pet names: 'Linusya, is this clear or not? Lika, this is Mandelstam . . . I did not know that he was in Voronezh. They (he, and she, who is now in Moscow) are inviting us and Anna Andreyevna to visit at the dacha (they'll be just outside Voronezh 20–25/IV).' The 'lightless black night' of their first acquaintance culminated in Rudakov's departing, like an old intimate, 'through the rear balcony door of the little house that stands at the edge of the railway village'. The result: 'I feel amazing. The game of silence is over. One can speak, think. And I could never think without speaking.' He was indisputably thrilled by the chance to see Mandelstam 'not on a stage, not in the dressing room'; what he discovered was not a public persona but 'a profoundly unhappy person'. 'His habits and manners', he mused, 'are wholly understandable'. Soon afterwards, he reported on his own positive role: 'I force him to shave and to clean his boots outside.' 'I write seemingly about him', he continued the same month, 'but in reality, about myself and my world'.

He persuades us easily of his own narcissism, which Finkelstein appears to have accommodated quite easily, since her husband's letters poured forth with the enthusiasm of a man being encouraged:

> During the day, walking from room to room, I was telling Lilya some of the easier pieces of my literary conception. And suddenly I found a scheme (however arbitrary), according to which Gumilyov and Khlebnikov are the limits, the poles of poetry. Between them, there's Oska, myself, etc. Everything to the right of Gumilyov is bad poetry (in gradations), what's to the left of Khlebnikov may be very good but it is only life, not literature (i.e. thought, Academician Pavlov, for example, or Marr, as an idea of language). From this – without simplification – may spring the roots of composition. This is not vulgar because it is not an end in itself, only a preliminary construct. It would be intoxicating to fill it out with names (literally make a diagram). This is for personal use only – but the conclusions will be real. Do you think it interesting? Will it be of any use?

The speed with which familiarity bred contempt is astonishing: this 'Oska' (a name that Rudakov could only have used in the third person, out of earshot of Mandelstam), placed right next to 'myself' in the spectrum of Russian poetry, foreshadowed some truly bizarre developments. By May 8, Rudakov was referring to Nadezhda ironically as 'Nadine' (mannered and foreign), and to Mandelstam himself with most casual familiarity: 'Osyuk'. 'Nadine left today', he registers.

> At the station she flew off her handle and drove poor Osyuk into such a state that he was saying, in a trembling voice, 'Nadenka, you cannot get angry, you are leaving'. He lost his walking-stick, which, luckily, was found in the cupboard. He was awfully pitiful. He became quiet and was making cocoa for me and for himself. He smudged his hands on the saucepan, wiped them on his own forehead, and looked quite a zebra for the rest of the evening.

Two days later, an excited letter reported that 'Nadine (the shrew) is in Moscow' and 'a beautiful stretch has begun'. The fruit of this 'beautiful stretch' would be that (by May 26, Nadezhda Mandelstam still in Moscow) all of Mandelstam's papers were bequeathed to Rudakov: 'These are his own words: "You will be my sole executor and the publisher of

Mandelstam".' Consideration of Nadezhda, Mandelstam's longtime amanuensis, entered only as 'now Nadine will perhaps bring the old pieces from home'.

Having insinuated himself successfully into the day-to-day life of the deeply unhappy, ailing and emotionally volatile Mandelstam, Rudakov – whose chief scholarly achievement to date had been the transcription of Wilhelm Küchelbecker's poems for Tynyanov's edition – was evidently exploiting the acquaintance with all boldness, reporting cheerfully on his own editorial interventions with Mandelstam's new compositions: 'I have composed another half-verse with white nights for "Chapayev".' Mandelstam himself appears to have been uncertain as to how to respond. As of May 29, 'M. has entered a new stage – he praises me almost publicly, talks about "collaboration" on his things, and, when reciting, he announces lines written or corrected by me with horrific roaring. Savage arguments over the final version of "Chapayev".' And yet: 'Now, of 1930–1933 we have 406 lines (and there are only 250 in the magazines, and there should be around 150 more lines of dictation).' On June 1, Rudakov took stock of the achievement: 'His poems as they are now are unthinkable without me.'

The day after Nadezhda Mandelstam's return, he was met with a new wave of resistance: 'Nadine is "annihilating" me in her female way, and engages in polemics against my corrections of his things.' Three days later, 'we' (Mandelstam and Rudakov) 'dictated (to me) around 150 lines'. On June 23, he gloried in 'a scene': 'He lies on the sofa, I lie beside him'.

Their manic activity continued into the high summer, when Mandelstam's apparently increasing anxiety about the poems gave way abruptly to depression. Rudakov took careful notes of Mandelstam's monologues:

> Again I'm standing before this dilemma. The Soviet reality will not accept me. I'm lucky yet that they are not persecuting me. But I cannot do what it is that they let me. I cannot go, look and see. One cannot write as if one were a bull staring at a cow. I fought against that my whole life. I cannot describe, only the Lord God or a clerk of the court can describe. I am not a novelist, I cannot do that.... I have *sinned thrice*: I wrote a sycophantic poem (about the pilots) – and it's brisk, muddy, and vacuous. I wrote an ode without sufficient reason for it. Ah, ah! and nothing more. I wrote reviews – under pressure and on ridiculous subjects – and an essay (a variant of one review). I loathe myself. Everything noxious is rising from the depth of my

soul. I've been starved into opportunism. I wrote a tiny quantity of true verse and then, because of conformism, broke my voice on the last one. This is the beginning of a huge void. I thought that with a good attitude life itself would come and pick me up with 'facticity'. But that wasn't literature, and I cannot penetrate through something that thick into tomorrow or any other day, I simply lack the strength. ... My preliminaries are awful, either I give nothing at all or something energetic. I wanted to please them with my essay. And it became an embarrassment. With those verses I put an end to poetry; in the reviews I wrote stupidities and nonsense; with the essay, I've exposed my ineptitude (he showed it at the office of *Pod'yom* and they told him it was bad). This is the end to everything. Both moral and financial. And it casts a shadow of doubt on everything I do and on my verse.

'Kitty', Rudakov reported excitedly,

this is almost a verbatim record, only abbreviated a great deal. In real life, he laments, he is near tears. But there is no madness. It's all sober, and he has assessed this whole period. I hope that it passes. That no new madness, no suicides will follow. But by the way Nadine has suddenly pulled herself together, and from her descriptions of the previous episode, and even from my own observations – I see that this is serious.

'Mandelstam is howling', he went on. 'It is not the same Osip Emilyevich (or Osya) who ate dinner with us but the genius, Ovid's equal, the one who feels that his poetry is in shambles. I cannot even be ironic here and only call him Oska out of habit.' The depression persisted into the new year 1936. On January 20, Rudakov noted: 'M. is in a state of dumb resignation, he seems reconciled and simple-minded. Where did they go, all the storms and polemics of the recent months? O. E. has aged a great deal and sagged somehow.' The morning following this observation, Mandelstam was speaking of suicide. Their friendship had soured, but when Pushkin House approached Mandelstam with an offer to purchase his papers, he refused, insisting that the archive was for Rudakov to work on. They argued – 'about my importance', Rudakov wrote, concluding that the Mandelstams had failed to appreciate him: 'Even his best intentions would change nothing... it is offensive to watch the swinish devouring of my acorns, and disgusting to listen to the ungrateful oinks.' When leaving Voronezh at last the following summer, he referred to the Mandelstams in the plural, as 'Oskas', noting that they were now 'known consummately'. In a letter to 'Nadine's mother' (appended to the letter sent to Finkelstein) he requested that she give him Mandelstam's old photographs. 'This, and yesterday's Dante, are simply marvelous achievements.'

No editorial achievement would issue from this assiduous collecting, for Rudakov would soon be killed on the front. The craftily assembled archive was left in the keeping of Lina Finkelstein. Once established as someone with whom papers might be deposited in advance of an ever-looming search, Finkelstein received additional documents to keep – notably, multiple folders of the executed Nikolay Gumilyov's archive, which was transferred to her by Akhmatova and had to be transported to her flat on a child's sled (the load was too heavy to be simply carried). Both sets of papers, Mandelstam's and Gumilyov's, would disappear, over the long term of Finkelstein's charge of the archives.

It was Gerstein, not either of the two widows, who embarked on a painstaking reconstruction of what had happened to the papers of the two dead men. Having maintained contact with Rudakov's widow, too, Gerstein recalled that, in 1944, Finkelstein returned to Leningrad from her Sverdlovsk evacuation. Shortly afterwards, she met Akhmatova at the Philharmonic. In the intermission, she came up to Akhmatova and whispered to her: 'Everything's intact'. Gerstein, too, had been assured, in a letter, that 'All is well' (the circumspect phrase itself being a model of communicating under surveillance). Based on the date on an autographed copy of Akhmatova's poem 'In Memory of a Friend', dedicated to Rudakov, which she had given to Lina, Gerstein concludes that Finkelstein saw Akhmatova on November 8, 1945, when it would have been agreed that Gumilyov's papers should remain, for the time being, with Finkelstein. Akhmatova kept busy, and it alarmed no one when Finkelstein wrote, in the spring of 1946, that she had not gone to see her in a long while. Zhdanov's campaign against Akhmatova made any transfer of Gumilyov's papers a moot point. On August 2, 1947, Finkelstein once again wrote to Gerstein: 'I have not seen Annushka, but I think that in the nearest future I'll work up the courage to go and see her.' Late that year, Gerstein herself came with a visit to Leningrad.

> I stayed with Lina Samoylovna. In our free time we spoke often and a great deal about Sergey Borisovich and about the manuscripts which, it appeared, she was keeping like a holy relic. She did not show me Gumilyov's letters to Akhmatova

and his other autographs, but I did not think I had the right to look at them. But we did look at Mandelstam's autographs, I held them in my hands and read them. Nevertheless, Lina Samoylovna did not show me everything, explaining that the suitcase with the manuscripts was under her mother's bed and that she did not want to open it in front of her. She complained that her mother was a stranger to her, did not understand her fidelity to the memory of Seryozha, and kept asking that she sell his library and archive. Naturally, her mother wished secretly that Lina would get married again, but she only kept saying: 'There's never been and never will be anybody better than Seryozha.'

On her next visit the following year, Gerstein found the two women in a state of poverty. The late 1940s were a difficult time of tenuous respite from the hardships of war; unemployment was high, especially among the Jews, and frugality was the norm. Given all this, Gerstein was understandably surprised when Finkelstein remarked that she was planning to purchase a coat of curly lamb, for which she would pay in instalments. Gerstein subsequently dated the beginning of Finkelstein's sale of the archive to 1948, the year marked by the arrival of the wonderful curly coat – and by Finkelstein's noticeable new nervousness around Lev Gumilyov. In the spring of 1949, Finkelstein was passing through Moscow and, naturally, met with Gerstein. What she said now astounded the latter: Finkelstein did *not* have Gumilyov's papers, having 'confused' them with a different envelope, while the children living in the same communal flat used up the actual archive, kept in a chest in the shared hallway, for 'firecrackers'. When Gerstein presented this story to Akhmatova, the two of them recalled the sled loaded heavy with folders. The fireworks from such a load would have been enough, one thinks, to burn down all of Petersburg. Mandelstam's papers, too, ultimately proved irrecoverable – a surreal fulfilment of his own fugitive wish for retreat (from imperilled life into prenatal security) in the so-called 'Wolfhound':

> Rather, stuff me away, like a hat in the sleeve
> Of a smothering Siberian fur coat.

The Finkelstein affair marks the beginning of a Mandelstam industry, which would thrive once the ban on the poet was officially lifted with the publication, in 1973, of the first posthumous edition, prepared by Nikolay

Khardzhiev with Nadezhda Mandelstam's assistance. The edition would instantly become emblematic of the hypocrisy that flourished under the regime, tainted as it were by Alexander Dymshitz's factitious preface, which turned years of Mandelstam's de facto homelessness in Moscow and his exile in Voronezh into an eccentric's penchant for changing places and residences. (Dymshitz was certain that compromise with the regime was necessary, if one wanted to publish anything of worth; others felt that such 'compromises' compromised the very heart of the endeavour.) Since then, it has become increasingly difficult to distinguish between selfless efforts to preserve 'literary heritage' and opportunism, between scholarship and the mass production of lucrative souvenir editions, between true friendship and self-seeking. It is not evident, for instance, what, precisely, separates the wish to purchase a purloined autograph from the wish to make a cast of a famous acquaintance's dead body – as was done, for purely personal use, by Boris Messerer and Bella Akhmadulina, members of Nadezhda Mandelstam's coterie of young Mandelstam aficionados. The two of them spoke of this on Radio Svoboda:

> BORIS MESSERER: Our rapport was not easy. But that image – that admiration that she elicited in our minds – would be very difficult to communicate to a present-day person. One would have to describe in great detail, very exactly, how much she resembled a thick stream of smoke, dwindling – her flesh had ceased to be significant. Only the spirit existed. Her fragile, delicate fingers, always holding a filterless 'Belomor' cigarette, are before my eyes even now. And the smoke streaming up from the cigarette obscures her face, and, so to speak, underscores the fragility of her image.

Nadezhda Mandelstam's smoking habit was insistently cast by her acquaintances as a metaphor of the woman's own immateriality. Oddly, it was Messerer who thought of capturing that evanescent image in plaster.

> BELLA AKHMADULINA: Boris Messerer told me to bring along a cast maker, to make a plaster cast of the face and hand. Those who were present said to me: 'This is contrary to religion.' I said: 'Not at all. Otherwise we would not have the death mask of Pushkin.' So here is the only copy, in plaster. I had to pour a drink for the cast maker because he kept saying, 'I'm afraid of the dead.' Now the only cast of Nadezhda Yakovlevna's face and her right hand is kept in our house. Her beautiful face, and her delicate, amazing hand.

Joseph Brodsky, who had frequented Nadezhda Mandelstam's flat, wrote of it, and of that same censer-like stream of smoke that appears to have fascinated everyone except her closest friends, Akhmatova and Gerstein, neither of whom engaged in such metaphorics with respect to Nadezhda. On the other hand, there is little that is said concretely about her in Brodsky's obituary, published in the *New York Review of Books*; instead, the piece is gripped by the idea of poetry's primacy over prose and man's primacy over woman (Akhmatova, a poet who, in a way, 'fathered' Brodsky, excepted). 'She was living in a small communal apartment', he writes, 'consisting of two rooms. The first . . . was occupied by a woman whose name . . . was Nietsvetaeva' (Tsvetaeva's opposite, with a negative prefix); 'the second was Mrs Mandelstam's'. 'It was eight square meters large, the size of an average American bathroom', he explains, cultivatedly, to the uncouth and ignorant readers of *NYRB* who wouldn't know, of course, that 'in educated circles, especially among the literati, being the widow of a great man is enough to provide an identity'.

> This is especially so in Russia, where in the Thirties and in the Forties the regime was producing writers' widows with such efficiency that in the middle of the Sixties there were enough of them around to organize a trade union.

As for Nadezhda Mandelstam, 'Of the eighty-one years of her life, Nadezhda Mandelstam spent nineteen as the wife of Russia's greatest poet in this century . . . and forty-two as his widow. The rest was childhood and youth'. This diminishment – for the insistent point is that the obituary's subject is *nothing* apart from her relation to Mandelstam and Akhmatova – is consistent and progressive, throughout the rest of the piece.

> The status of a non-person gradually became her second nature. She was a small woman, of slim build, and with the passage of years she shriveled more and more, as though trying to turn herself into something weightless, something easily pocketed in the moment of flight. Similarly, she had virtually no possessions: no furniture, no art objects, no library. The books, even foreign books, never stayed in her hands for long: after being read or glanced through they would be passed on to someone else – the way it ought to be with books.

> As a writer, as well as a person, she is a creation of two poets with whom her life was linked inexorably: Osip Mandelstam and Anna Akhmatova.

> repeating day and night the words of her dead husband was undoubtedly connected not only with comprehending them more and more but also with resurrecting his very voice... once set in motion, this mechanism of memorization won't come to a halt.... In both their content and style, her books are but a postscript to the supreme version of language which poetry essentially is and which became her flesh through learning her husband's lines by heart.

As for her own tragic abandonment by love, he could not be as much as moved to recognise it: 'If there is any substitute for love, it's memory. To memorize, then, is to restore intimacy.' (Problem solved?) And she herself, in his words, verges so close to symbolic non-existence that her actual non-existence as of 1980 becomes hardly anything to mourn.

> I saw her last on May 30, 1972, in that kitchen of hers, in Moscow. It was late afternoon, and she sat, smoking, in the corner, in the deep shadow cast by the tall cupboard onto the wall. The shadow was so deep that the only things one could make out were the faint flicker of her cigarette and the two piercing eyes. The rest – her smallish shrunken body under the shawl, her hands, the oval of her ashen face, her gray, ashlike hair – all were consumed by the dark. She looked like a remnant of a huge fire, like a small ember that burns if you touch it.

What is notable about this obituary for a nobody, callously obliterating the person it purported to praise and memorialize, is its way of making all of its points by means of metaphor. This is not in itself unusual, yet does not usually get the due attention, with the result that authors are able to imply metaphorically things that would not pass muster if put directly. It is safer, rhetorically, to liken so-and-so to a wisp of smoke than to say outright what this means: that she would be utterly insignificant save for being married to a famous man, and that we are only interested in wisps of smoke insofar as the flame itself is unavailable. We have already seen that Nadezhda Mandelstam herself deployed a clever array of rhetorical tactics to diminish and dismiss various people, and the reluctant publication of her private marginalia by Tatiana Levina in 1997 has only underscored the tension between preservation and destruction in each act of memorialization. 'N. Y. Mandelstam', Levina explains, gave me her personal copy of Volume 3 of the American *Collected* edition of Mandelstam (New York – München, 1969) in the fall of 1980, in late September or early October. On October 30, Nadezhda Yakovlevna's birthday, I brought the book with me, but was allowed to keep it until the next time. But the next time, December 29, there was no one left to return the book to. Nadezhda Yakovlevna's body lay in a coffin in the middle of the room, and the bookshelves were no longer holding the books that had stood there two months ago.

Having been left with this last memento, Levina would later be persuaded (by her own husband) to transcribe and publish Nadezhda Mandelstam's scribbled marginal notes in *Philologica*. As a result, seventeen years after Nadezhda Mandelstam's death, the limited world of Mandelstam scholarship gasped at such metaphors as 'a piece of shit' (scribbled next to the name of Nikolay Khardzhiev), or the triplet 'idiot – bitch – cunt', a memorial inscription next to the name of Nadezhda Pavlovich, whose characterization of Osip Mandelstam's face as 'unattractive' and 'insignificant' had been quoted in the edition. His widow took revenge on her and others, and even on Akhmatova, festooning the margins of a plate with Akhmatova's photo with the inscription: 'Idiotic dress – with her sagging breasts, bony shoulders, hyperthyroidal neck'; 'With breasts like hers – such décolletage!'; 'and that embroidery'. 'It's a good thing that Akhmatova had no money. She was remarkably tasteless. In her old age, very fat, she showed me a dress: "I designed it myself." A yoke, a baby-doll silhouette. Ruffles under the yoke. She was thick as a barrel.' All this invites the same perplexity that has been noted by H. J. Jackson in her study, *Marginalia*, which puzzles over the meaning and purpose of such notes, given that 'books are likely to outlive their owners' – something we might have expected to caution a writer of marginalia, who might, as did Mrs Piozzi, 'long to say something'.

> The writer of marginalia acts on the impulse to stop reading for long enough to record a comment. Why? Because it may be done and has been done; it is customary. Under certain conditions (subject to change) it is socially acceptable behavior. But it is seldom *required* behavior; not all readers write notes in their books. Those who choose to make the effort to register their responses must foresee some advantage for someone; so the question of motive resolves itself into another question, *cui bono*? For whose benefit is it done? And that in turn leads to the question of the addressee.

Yet, for the same pragmatic reason that 'books are likely to outlive their owners' the form may tempt us to finally say the things that we would not have said if expecting to face the consequences. It might be objected that Levina received her loan volume during Nadezhda Mandelstam's lifetime; yet the loan itself was a gesture so precious (and the edition was so rare) that it effectively precluded any possible remonstrations about the copiously scribbled obscenities. Levina, too, was baffled, and, in responding to the question of address in *Philologica*, wrote that the notes expressed an insistence on continuing to shape Mandelstam's biography:

> It appears that the marginal notes were addressed to the people (mainly members of N. Y.'s circle) who, in publishing and commenting on or simply in appreciating Mandelstam's writings, would realize her specific perspective and attitude toward events and their participants. The brief and catchy formulae such as the one used in the title of this publication were meant to aid the transformation of Mandelstam's biography into myth.

This, though partially plausible, does not sufficiently explain the notes that, if paused over, appear to indicate Nadezhda's resistance to the idea that all of her life should be swallowed up by her association with Mandelstam. 'I weighed 42 kilos being 165 cm tall'; 'I worked in the circus, under the cupola. Mandelstam saw it and was frightened to death'. True, her figure is once again accompanied by Mandelstam's, but in other instances, it is not, where the vignette itself bears no relation to literary biography – being a snatching not of biography but of life, as lived by Nadezhda.

> A huge lot of women's shoes was on sale, but they fit absolutely nobody. I had size 33–34 (now it's 35, and I am 77 years old). But not a single pair fit me. The Italian who had brought them offered them for free, but that was useless. It turned out that he had bought old toy and decorative shoes from store windows.

Next to the text of Mandelstam's letter – 'Your childish little paw covered in charcoal, your little blue robe – I remember everything, I forgot nothing . . .' Nadezhda's annotation, 'I drew', assented, in reply to him. The interlocutor was gone. What remained was not a 'remnant' but a lonely woman with her dead husband's book, and with her longing.

How different our world would be if female grief over loved men were felt, by all its inhabitants, to be real and tragic. But Mandelstam studies is largely a domain of *realpolitik*: its tones, metaphors and rhetoric, in English as in Russian, are predominantly inherited from the Cold War era, which means principally a denial of paradoxical ties between binaries seen as exclusive alternatives and of tensions among terms habitually grouped together by the propaganda. 'Truth and reconciliation', for instance (the title of Andrew Kahn's 2017 review, in the *Times Literary Supplement*, of Pavel Nerler's compilation of 'letters, reminiscences, testimonies' pertaining to Nadezhda Mandelstam) takes its two terms as fully compatible (non-contradictory), though the material in the book itself makes it rather plain that, however difficult it might be to achieve either 'truth' or 'reconciliation', achieving *both* might be well-nigh impossible. Yet it is in the nature of a cliché to squeeze its way into print, and the review itself can easily be encapsulated in the style of Flann O'Brien's *Catechism of Cliché*:

> What does this book about a famous woman do?
> It presents a *portrait* of her.
> What kind of portrait of her does it present?
> A *remarkable portrait*.
> What other kinds of portrait does it present?
> A *collective portrait*, a *cumulative portrait* and a *remarkable polyphonic portrait*.
> What was the woman famed for?
> She was famed for her *voice*.
> What kind of voice?
> A *powerful voice*.
> And precisely how powerful was it?
> *Singularly powerful*.

One of the remarkable features of this review, then, is its insistence on invoking portraiture and the notion of 'voice' – as in 'portrait of a woman famed for her powerful voice' – while taking no interest in the salient details of existing portraiture of Nadezhda Mandelstam, such as her actual 'quiet, pleasant voice', as remembered by Emma Gerstein. The concentration of stock phrases in the review once again creates the common impression of indifference to the subject, even as the piece praises Nerler's volume for memorializing her and itself recounts the canonical stations of her widowed life (referring to her throughout as 'Nadezhda Yakovlevna', unwittingly proposing a fictitious personal familiarity):

> After her husband's death in transit to the Gulag, Nadezhda Yakovlevna was barred from living in Moscow or Leningrad until the mid-1960s. Her survival in provincial teaching jobs over the twenty years between his disappearance and the official confirmation of his death in 1956, which brought a compensation of 5,000 roubles, was against the odds. (She immediately spent that sum acquiring a rare edition of her husband's first collection of poems annotated in his hand.) A room of her own was much less a priority than a roof over her head. The best-known fact about Osip Mandelstam's posthumous life is that his widow memorized, copied and preserved his writings (often exiguous scraps) with the help of a small group of devotees, including Akhmatova. Much anecdotal information here sheds light on how and when both his and her manuscripts circulated in underground literature. Nadezhda Yakovlevna built her acquaintances and friendships according to others' willingness to protect the archive. Her devotion was not only uxorious. She believed that literature was precious because it brought individuals into some form of compact that safeguarded humanity. She sized up potential curators instantly. Sergei Bernstein cleverly kept his part of the Mandelstam archive hidden in plain view at home, on a bookshelf easily accessible to the KGB if they had thought to open the box-file labeled 'Joseph Stalin, Questions of Leninism'. She broke off relationships with people who refused to assume the risk, leading to a temporary breach with Emma Gerstein, whose *Moscow Memoirs* were an eventual act of retaliation after decades of uneasy friendship (described in some letters here) in which the harder either woman tried to adopt the moral high ground and avoid being spiteful, the worse it got.

This is a well-worn, yet untrue, tale of triumphant survival under tyranny. It is untrue in the first place because there is no such thing as *triumphant survival*, regardless of the choice of words. What the notion of such 'triumph' denies is that time spent surviving, successfully or not, is irrecoverable, and that no decent idea of a good life (*eudaemonia*, human flourishing) would equate itself with the business of dodging a regime bent upon persecution. All this would have been fine in a spy novel, down to the familiar stock of tropes (the deprivations of Soviet life) and villains (Lenin, Stalin and the KGB). Yet criticism should know better than to glory in the resilience of 'underground literature', in the indestructability of people whose lives (we know) have unquestionably been destroyed, and in the erosion of friendships by the necessity of mercenary calculation. Above all, the passage is a gross distortion of the

Mandelstam–Gerstein relationship. Here, it is in collusion with the line taken by Pavel Nerler himself in editing the volume with the uneasy title *We'll see who outstubborns whom* . . . Though Kahn calls Nerler a dispassionate 'curator' of the volume (the value of the fashionable term 'curator', as opposed to 'editor', being its deflection of professional editorial questions), Nerler's copious interpolations throughout the collection bespeak a strong desire to instruct the reader on how to judge each witness and testimony. The metaphor of a trial, too, is explicit in the scornful remarks with which Nerler precedes a selection of Gerstein's letters:

> Emma Grigoryevna Gerstein is perceived by today's readers as the all but greatest opponent of N. Y. Mandelstam and denouncer of her books. Portrayed in less than attractive light in *Hope Against Hope*, after *Hope Abandoned* Emma Gerstein felt that she had been not only slighted but also slandered. Her reply to N. Y.'s books was her own book of *Memoirs* (first published in 1986 in Paris, the second edition appeared in 1998 in Saint Petersburg), where she not only replied to accusations against herself and others (B. Rudakov among them) but also acted as plaintiff in her own countersuit against her offender. While she was at it, she did not spare Osip Emilyevich either, 'bringing him out into the clear'. Emma Grigoryevna's responses were obviously inferior to Nadezhda Yakovlevna's texts.

There is nothing 'dispassionate' about this, and as for things that are 'obvious' ('Emma Grigoryevna's responses were obviously inferior'), they are the ones that speak for themselves, as Gerstein's writing does, even in this volume, bespeaking sentiments entirely other than a thirst for revenge. The first letter of the selection, dated June 7, 1943, begins:

> Dear Nadichka! I have discovered the secret of eternal friendships. For an old friend, a place is saved in the heart that can never be taken by anybody else.

'And so', she goes on, 'I remember you always. The loss of Osip, and partly even of you (for geographic reasons), I sense as if these things happened yesterday. Nothing like this will ever happen again'. 'If you and I were to meet', she acknowledged, 'in all probability, mutual displeasure and irritation would make themselves known. What kind of manner is it, for example, to insert barbs everywhere, to gloat over the wrinkles and gray hair of your friends, to make sexual insinuations?' This was truthfulness, reaching for a reconciliation, showing a loving willingness to try not only to understand but also to be understood. Even when mentioning revenge, as she did, this was done hyperbolically, for the sake of apology, and was never meant to be taken literally: 'I've had my revenge on you, and now feel relieved.' As for her feelings for Mandelstam himself, these we already knew from her *Memoirs*: 'I forgave Osip Emilyevich for his behaviour during the investigation.'

EPILOGUE

Criticism and the Fate of Poets

> Language, the element in which a poet works, is also the medium through which judgements upon his work are made.
> Geoffrey Hill,
> 'Poetry as "Menace" and "Atonement"'

One of the principal aims of literature is to offer the reader the imaginative means of liberation from the contingencies and constraints of her or his 'here and now'. Imaginative in the dual sense, first because of its being a fruit of the literary imagination, and second because it engages the reader's imagination in a way that augments her or his present world, in directions ranging across (and possibly beyond) space and time. This encounter of imaginations, the writer's and the reader's, liberates the reader's mind from the always-all-too-narrow constraints circumscribed by the circumstances of birth, history and individual opportunity that pin each of us to our stations. Liberal arts ennoble us because they set us free, imaginatively free – and this imaginative freedom should not be dismissed as merely imaginary, for imagination is not the opposite of life but a concomitant part of it. On the other side of the encounter, liberal arts also supply the means of liberation for the author – in one aspect, liberation from the tyranny of the present-day audience, into a wider readership afforded by the social change effected by time. Mandelstam contemplated this action of literature (which he delineated as 'poetry' nor in terms of form but according to the proprieties of communication between the writer and the reader) in his early essay 'On the Interlocutor', making a distinction between art and the work of the man or woman of letters or a public intellectual:

The fear of a concrete interlocutor, a listener from one's own epoch, that 'friend within my generation', has insistently pursued poets of all times. The greater a poet's genius, the more acutely he was plagued by that fear. Hence the notorious enmity between poet and society. What is true of a man of letters, a writer, is absolutely inapplicable to a poet. The difference between *belles lettres* and poetry is this: a man of letters is always addressing a concrete listener, a living representative of the times. Even when making prophecies, what he has in mind is a future contemporary. The man of letters transfers his contents into his contemporary on the basis of the physical law of communicating vessels. For this reason, a man of letters must be 'above', 'superior to', society. Moralizing is the nerve of *belles lettres*. This is why a man of letters requires a pedestal. Poetry is wholly different. A poet communicates only with a providential interlocutor.

Condescension has no place in the relations of a poet and this mysterious 'providential interlocutor'. (A 'poet' is understood here broadly as a 'literary artist', because it seems just to think that Mandelstam would have thought of, for instance, Pushkin's prose as the prose of a poet, not as *belles lettres*.) Their conversation across time is a conversation of equals, a reciprocal recognition defying the confines of lifetimes and of mortality itself. Defying, though not negating – yet this recognition should not render this undertow of the currents of oblivion negligible. Just as a poet follows a noble calling, a reader, too, has a calling – to become, for a particular poet, that 'providential interlocutor' who liberates the poet from being sealed in time, like a message in a bottle. The image is Mandelstam's own:

> In a critical moment, a sea-voyager tosses a sealed bottle containing his name and an account of his fate into the waters of the ocean. Many years later, wandering in the dunes, I find it in the sand, read its message, find out the date of the events and the last will and testament of the deceased. I had the right to do this. I did not unseal a letter addressed to another. A letter sealed in a bottle is addressed to the one who will find it. I found it, and therefore I am its mysterious addressee.

> My gift is meager, and my voice lacks power,
> And yet I live, and this my being
> Upon the earth is dear to someone.
> My far-away descendant will discover it
> Within my verses, and perhaps my soul
> Will find itself communing with his soul.
> And, as I found a friend within my generation,
> I, too, shall find a reader in posterity.

When I read Boratynsky's poem, I experience the very same feeling, as if such a bottle had landed in my hands. The ocean, with all of its colossal element, came to its help – assisting it in fulfilling its purpose – and the finder is seized by a sense of the providential. In the seaman's tossing of the bottle into the waves and in Boratynsky's sending off of his poem, there are two distinctive moments. The letter, and equally the poem, are not addressed to any specific, particular person. Nevertheless, both have an addressee: the letter being addressed to the one who finds it, the poem to the 'reader in posterity'. And I would like to know if there is a single person who, glancing upon the lines of Boratynsky, would not shudder with that joyful and ominous frisson that we feel when suddenly addressed by name.

In this way, Mandelstam became Boratynsky's 'providential interlocutor', all the more able to reciprocate sympathetically his address to 'a reader in posterity' because he, Mandelstam, was himself a poet, though in his homage to Boratynsky he acted as a critic. Among Mandelstam's own 'providential interlocutors', Geoffrey Hill stands out as a poet and critic who unsealed his message across considerable distance, both in time and space. Kenneth Haynes, in co-authorship with Andrew Kahn, made a moving study of Geoffrey Hill's fidelity to Mandelstam – which the two authors refer to as 'sustained engagement' – across decades of his own, now sealed, life. Once again, the sense of mystery attached to the 'providential interlocutor' and his response are resurrected by this study as the authors point out: 'When Hill was writing his elegy to Mandelstam, Clarence Brown's biography and the memoirs by Nadezhda Mandelstam were almost a decade away.' This elegy is 'Tristia: 1891–1938', written in 1965, the year of Brown's publication of *The Prose of Osip Mandelstam* – which does *not* contain Mandelstam's 'On the Interlocutor'. More than a decade, to elaborate this line of thought, would pass before Jane Gary Harris and Constance Link would make available the translations of their *Critical Prose and Letters* of Mandelstam, where Hill might have encountered Mandelstam's message-in-a-sealed-bottle figure. All the more prescient, then, the sympathetic intuition of 'The dead keep their sealed lives' in these lines:

> Difficult friend, I would have preferred
> You to them. The dead keep their sealed lives
> And again I am too late. Too late
> The salutes, dust-clouds and brazen cries.

Among the few things that Hill had to push off from, ice-skater-like, was Dimitri Obolensky's anthology of Russian verse, with its biographical note and translation of the closing lines of Mandelstam's *Tristia* (1918):

> So let it be: a small transparent figure lies, like a stretched out squirrel-skin, on a clean earthenware dish; a girl is gazing, bending down over the wax. It is not for us to tell fortunes about the Greek Erebus; wax is for women what bronze is for men. It is only in battle that the lot falls upon us; but to them it is given to die while telling fortunes.

The poem is concerned with things that take their shape in time, like molten wax and bronze that harden, where wax is used for prototyping works in bronze and also as a fluid medium for divining how the bronze of history will behave. The theme acknowledges Ovid as the source of the original *Tristia*, where divination is compared to critical judgement of a poet's future:

> This I learnt not from thunder
> on the left, or sheep's guts, or the cry
> or flight of a bird: reason's augury, my prediction
> for the future: thus I divined

In Mandelstam's recreation of the fortune-telling motif, the warmth of the household, where the night-time divination takes its place, is the microcosm to history's macrocosm of bronze weapons and monuments. (Mandelstam's Russian names his metal 'copper', the primary component of bronze. Similarly, Pushkin's poem 'The Bronze Horseman' might have been known, in a more technical translation, as 'The Copper Horseman', but at the loss of the historic connotations of the alloy sometimes casually referred to in Russian as 'copper' but understood to be bronze all the same.) There are advantages, the poem muses, to a private life whose knowledge is malleable and indeterminate, like wax. To restore some ambiguities to Obolensky's reliable but for that reason univocal translation, the final line of the poem might read: 'It is their lot to die while wondering' (since, in Russian, the verbs for 'divining' and 'wondering', and even 'guessing', are homonymous). And so, to have it as one's lot to die guessing about it, rather than to know one's lot all too well, death itself being its proof. The difference is subtle, susceptible to paradoxical reversals, as befits the relation of the private and the public, of life and history – yet in this opening onto paradox, Mandelstam's 'Tristia' became coextensive with Hill's apprehension of life and art as a paradoxical relation:

> And it seems to me that the poets one trusts most are those who seem to suggest that art is the totality of our life and simultaneously admit that art has no connection with life. I accept both halves of the paradox as being absolutely true. That is why it is a paradox.

In his 1966 talk at Leeds University, Geoffrey Hill accounted for his sudden recognition recorded in 'Tristia: 1891–1938'. The unpublished talk, reproduced by Haynes and Kahn as an appendix to their essay, acknowledges: 'I thought I saw my doppelganger walking towards me down the Nevsky Prospect.' Yet how does one *see* across such spatiotemporal chasms? Hill's account is that of sympathetic divination:

> By what right do I address Mandelstam as my friend? By the intuition that poets know what poets are getting at. An exclusive opinion that quite rightly irritates many and further exacerbates the already-strained relations between the poet and the public.

'The already-strained relations' that Mandelstam made his concern in 'On the Interlocutor'. Uncannily, this essay, too, reached Hill – days before the talk – in the form of a brief quotation from Mandelstam's essay in Helen Muchnik's book *From Gorky to Pasternak*: 'Fear of . . . the "epoch's" listener . . . has constantly pursued poets in all ages. The more gifted the poet, the more acutely has he suffered from this fear . . . Thence the proverbial enmity between the artist and society.' And, as a 'précis': 'The poet does not address himself to anyone in particular; his words are like the drowned man's letters sealed in a bottle and tossed into the sea; someone, someday will find it by mere chance and read it.' This thrilled Geoffrey Hill.

> Look, now, at the poem's second line: *The dead keep their sealed lives*, written two years before I knew of Mandelstam's 'sealed' message.

The felicity is, of course, made intelligible, like Mandelstam's own simile, by a whole tradition of similar similes that makes it possible for us to understand what is meant by a 'message in a bottle' or by a reference to something sealed off in time. This makes the particular recurrence of 'sealed' less improbable – which is why a felicity is not an aberration, but, rather, something that flowers on the seam between the probable and the unexpected. In jumping at the felicity, Hill acknowledges, too, that this sympathetic coextensiveness between poets cannot be taken for granted or claimed complacently. 'By what right', he interrogated himself, 'do I address Mandelstam as my friend?' – and with the same self-checked sense of propriety, nowhere does Hill adopt familiar terms in relation to Mandelstam, who remains for him always sealed as 'Mandelstam', not 'Osip' (though Akhmatova and Gerstein could call him so in writing, where their personal acquaintance was of pertinence), not 'Oska' (as revelled in by Rudakov, always behind Mandelstam's back, once familiarity had bred contempt), not 'M.' (Nadezhda Mandelstam's authoritative shortcut, adopted in places, imitatively but less authoritatively, by Pavel Nerler, not even the tasteless 'Osip Emil'yevich', employed by academics. Neither does Mandelstam take any liberties when writing of Batyushkov or Derzhavin, Kleist or Tasso, however vividly he imagines them, however boldly they are divined through time's opaque medium. By what right, we might ask, does Mandelstam address Batyushkov as a friend? ('Not for a moment believing our parting, / I think, I bowed to him: / A cold hand in a light-coloured glove – / I shake it, with feverish envy.') Mandelstam's answer preceded these poems of valediction: he enters the company of past poets by the right of a 'providential interlocutor' hoped for and needed by every poet, which makes this on first glance 'unreciprocable' friendship actively reciprocal, because welcome. And yet, if Mandelstam could write of 'that joyful and ominous frisson that we feel when suddenly addressed by name', what do the just-mentioned proprieties and improprieties of address have to do with dead poets?

If there is an answer to this question, it has to do with the conviction that literature and other arts enable us to live a larger life, one not confined to the company and ministrations of those immediately present. It is a life in the wider air encompassing closeness and distance, intimacy and strangeness, and the community of the living and the dead – a community whose proprieties should not be seen strictly as a province of religious thought, as it figures perennially in literary criticism and creation. No one today appears as alert to this 'interdisciplinary' connection as Olga Sedakova, a Russian poet, scholar and critic who has cogently framed 'death and the dead as a topic of social thought'. Reflecting on both the liturgical theology of death and on matters of decorum in the posthumous memorialization of poets – specifically, Dante and Mandelstam in their recent representations – Sedakova objects to a rhetoric that would invite the general reader's 'identification' with the great poets of the literary tradition. In discussing a new mass edition of Dante, Sedakova pointed out the implicit appeal of its cover design:

> I have brought with me this big book to show you the manner in which it has been designed. This is a remarkable edition, a cheap mass edition containing the entirety of Dante. But why – if not to avoid intimidating the reader – or for what purpose is Dante depicted here in such a caricatured, grotesque manner? This is significant. In the same way, by the way, that the monuments to Mandelstam, in Moscow and in Voronezh, are significant: good monuments, but they do the same thing. They turn a great person – they appear to *diminish* him somehow. They make him look funny. Mandelstam is made into a kind of street madman; and Dante here is not the kind of person that might inspire reverence. This seems to be the only way in which serious, great things can be shown to a person in a way that would not intimidate him.

In other words, in order to bring the poet closer to the mass reader, the publisher has attempted, visually, to displace the poet from his 'pedestal', suggesting that once 'depedestalized', the poet could be 'identified with' by the reader. This seems to be a common argument, aired in various forms more frequently than the objections to it, the first of which proceeds from Mandelstam's own observation, in 'On the Interlocutor', on the difference between *belles lettres* and poetry: 'A man of letters is always addressing a concrete listener, a living representative of the times. . . . Poetry is wholly different. A poet communicates only with a providential interlocutor.' A poet, then, already speaks to us as equals and needs not to be 'cut down to size' – on the condition that we approach the poetry as 'providential interlocutors', and not with the lukewarm curiosity of the 'mass reader' to whom mass editions are inevitably addressed by publishers, and therefore misaddressed from the perspective of the poet, if we are to believe Mandelstam's own perspective concerning 'the notorious enmity between poet and society'. This 'enmity', so frequently dismissed as yet another manifestation of self-serving elitism, needs to be allowed to make its case, as it happens to be the not-so-trivial distinction between 'identification' and sympathy. If the first term appears in prophylactic quotation marks, whereas the latter doesn't, it has to do with the conceptual nature of 'identification', as compared to 'sympathy', which refers to the experiential phenomenon itself, for which 'identification' is but one possible conceptual handle, as introduced by Freud:

> First, identification is the original form of emotional tie with an object; secondly, in a regressive way it becomes a substitute for a libidinal object-tie... and thirdly, it may arise with any new perception of a common quality which is shared with some other person.

It is the third form of identification that we normally refer to by the term as commonly used today – the dynamic arising 'with any new perception of a common quality which is shared with some other person', and this is the dynamic that the publisher of Dante singled out by Sedakova appears to encourage, by bridging the gap between the distant and recondite figure of Dante and the Russian mass reader in the epoch of Putin. This bridging is accomplished entirely, as Sedakova points out, at Dante's expense – a perennial problem in public relations, from the poet's point of view. 'I think that the goal of a scholar', Sedakova says,

> should be the opposite, which is to follow Pushkin's notes concerning the diary genre: they will say that Byron is as base as we are, etc., while he is indeed base, but not in the way that we are, there's something different about him. And this 'something different' is worthy of attention, because we need not delve into the materials of Mandelstam or Dante merely to discover the mundane.

Or to discover *ourselves* – and nothing beyond. Of course, there is Trilling's famously clever account of a life with books:

> A real book reads us. I have been read by Eliot's poems and by *Ulysses* and by *Remembrance of Things Past* and by *The Castle* for a good many years now, since

early youth. Some of these books at first rejected me; I bored them. But as I grew older and they knew me better, they came to have more sympathy with me and to understand my hidden meanings. Their nature is such that our relationship has been very intimate. No literature has ever been so shockingly personal as that of our time – it asks every question that is forbidden by polite society.

True, all this, but if what a book does is elicit from us the play of our own imaginative capacities, its greatness has to do with the feeling that it does so to an extent that we could not have imagined without it. And if through our encounters with literature we discover ourselves, that element of *discovery* depends on the recognition that we come to know things about ourselves that we did not know before the encounter. This breaks right out of the bounds of 'identification', a concept that takes no cognizance of the complacency involved in the experience circumscribed by seeing no more than one's own reflection, nor of the potential of seeing one's reflection to arouse feelings of profound alienation, for even our self-knowledge, in being incomplete, can be ruptured by unexpected new perceptions of ourselves. This latter sense of the exhilarating discovery of otherness in kinship is what animates Geoffrey Hill's statement: 'I thought I saw my doppelganger walking towards me down the Nevsky Prospect.' Compare this to the discovery of alienation in intimacy, recorded by the Russian philosopher Yakov Druskin, a lifelong investigator of the individual transcendental experience, in 'The Sight of the Unseeing':

> Recently I was exiting some building. As I came near the door, I lifted my head so as not to bump into anything, and suddenly saw an emaciated old man before me, who looked familiar in some way but also seemed a stranger to me. He was walking towards me and looking straight through me. I was frightened and almost right away understood: this is me.

'Why was I frightened?' Druskin inquires.

> I meet many strangers in the street without fearing them: they are not *very* strange, but the one I saw in the mirror seemed *very* strange to me. Why? I think because at the very same time he also seemed familiar to me in some way. It was precisely that familiarity that was the ground of my feeling of being his opposite – of alienation.

If these elaborations matter, it is because they prime not solely our negotiations of our readerly place with respect to literature, but also our critical understanding of the poets' sustained sympathetic engagement with unsympathetic historic figures, especially Mandelstam's and Robert Lowell's, the two poets who had the courage to centralize the 'ominous frisson that we feel when suddenly addressed by name' – within their experiences of their namesakes, Iosif Stalin, discovered by Mandelstam within 'Osip', and 'Cal' Lowell's Caligula. In that critical context, the matter of sympathy becomes politically charged, especially in Mandelstam's case, as sympathy opens the rhetorical floodgates for 'sympathizing' – the floodgates which those who do not wish to have the poet branded as Stalin's 'sympathizer' understandably strain to keep shut, but at the cost of sealing off the dangerous poems and laboriously insulating them to prevent the contamination of the whole *oeuvre* and the then-inevitable result: another case of 'tainted greatness'. The fear, summarized in this manner, has to do with the supposition that 'greatness' depends, somehow, on purity and immunity to aspersion, and the concomitant suppositions about what failures of principle can or should compromise a poet's reputation. Akhmatova's approach to building up a posthumous image for Mandelstam was in this regard decidedly conservative: 'He is guilty of nothing – not this, not that, nor the other', and matters that contradict this blanket exculpation are best not mentioned. That Gerstein was unable to see why this should be the policy, given its cost with respect to the truth of Mandelstam's biography, testifies not to Gerstein's meanness (as repeatedly represented by her detractors) but to her being, in actuality far more forgiving of incidents that, in Akhmatova's view, had to be wholly suppressed so as not to bring the whole memorial edifice to ruin. Because Gerstein could, and did, forgive, she did not have to forget or obfuscate matters like Mandelstam's production of a list of witnesses to his 'Epigram' to Shivarov. Yet even Gerstein chose not to consider at length the cycle of poems whose generous impartiality with respect to Stalin is so difficult to distinguish from a compromising partiality to the dictator. To broach these poems as part and parcel of Mandelstam's *oeuvre* is to be seen as a destructive tarnisher of the poet's reputation and a traitor to Mandelstam. To suggest that one sees them as valuable fruits of intensive philosophical thought on the subject of authoritarianism and history is to open oneself to accusations of Stalinism and fascism, particularly in a culture deeply polarized by strife and therefore increasingly insistent that each person pick a side and stick to one's station and one's guns, rather than, say, wander about the barricades making abstract remarks upon their various architectures. This type of climate increasingly demands a willingness to make oneself vulnerable to misconstrued accusations, in order to make statements that are true in any nuanced, unprejudiced way.

It has been more than once asserted that 'poetry is war'. Yet it would be good to rouse ourselves from the hypnosis of the sing-song phrases, and to recall that poetry isn't 'war' but can in many ways be conceived as its opposite, and that there is something we can do, other than *fight*, for justice, despite what the frequent invocations of various 'fights for justice' would have us believe. As for *justice*, it needn't be confined to the practical constraints of the courtroom, where its administration must, for practical reason, take the form of verdicts: 'guilty' or 'not guilty'. Literature itself supplies a model of pursuing justice through elaboration of various possibilities of seeing and understanding, as Lisa Rodensky, a legal and literary scholar, pointed out from her valuable dual vantage:

> Novels do not carry the responsibility of reducing the many possibilities they present to a single decision. They do not issue verdicts. But the law does. The practical and urgent necessities of the law require it to be guided by general rules and, in the end, to reduce the complexities and ambiguities of a case to a particular holding. This, among other things, distinguishes the work of law from the work of art.

However humane and comprehending, this is a minority opinion, easily drowned by the chorus that proclaims something opposite, and chiefly by means of metaphor. The latter fact makes direct objection impossible, as it must be primed by an examination of what relations are being intimated metaphorically. For instance (and an instance from which much of the chorus takes its cues), here is Czesław Miłosz in *The Captive Mind*:

> The work of human thought should withstand the test of brutal, naked reality. If it cannot, it is worthless. Probably only those things are worthwhile which can preserve their validity in the eyes of a man threatened with instant death.

'If the cant word "elitist" can now be applied anywhere', Geoffrey Hill retorted in 'Language, Suffering and Silence',

> it should be placed against this passage. Miłosz, in the opening sentence here quoted, purports to establish new terms of the utmost purity: the existential finality of things and moments; and with the apparent equity of 'work of human thought' he gestures towards the inclusive; a general redemption of the imagination through the witness of extreme experience, of survived extremity. What the quoted passage actually communicates is something different: the elitism of the man-of-the-moment. It excludes from aesthetic regeneration those works unbaptized by an arbitrary extreme experience of 'brutal, naked reality'.

Miłosz's biography suggests that his mistake was not arbitrariness but an over-generalization of his own predicaments and personality. But, to call on 'the witness of poetry', or, rather, the witness of literature at large, does literature itself have something to add to this critical debate? Does it anywhere test these assertions in a way germane to this Epilogue? Varlam Shalamov knew better than we do, better than Miłosz did, about the tests of 'brutal, naked reality'. His envisioning of Mandelstam's final hours in 'Sherry-Brandy' is informed by years spent within the 'brutal', 'naked' confines of the Soviet penal system, and by what he was able to learn from Nina Savoyeva, a camp doctor to whom Shalamov and many others had owed their survival in the GULAG. Savoyeva, in turn, had learned about Mandelstam's final death from physicians who had witnessed it. This is what Shalamov writes about 'the work of human thought' under those conditions.

> The poet was dying. His large hands – swollen from hunger, with bloodless white fingers and dirty, overgrown and tubular nails – were folded on his chest, no longer avoiding the cold. Earlier, he would shove them under his collar to warm them against his bare body, but too little warmth remained there now. The mitts had long been stolen; theft required no more than brazenness – it was a regular daytime business. (White day, the great polar day, reigned in this quarantine barrack.) The dim electric sun, fowled by flies and enclosed in a round wire cage, was affixed high up under the ceiling. The light fell towards the poet's feet: he lay in the murky depth of the lower bunk row. From time to time his fingers would move, snapping like castanets, feel a button, a loop, or a hole in the overcoat, brush off some clinging bits, and rest again. The poet had been dying for so long that he had ceased to understand that he was dying. At times, some simple and powerful thought would come, forcing itself

> painfully and almost palpably through the brain: that his bread, which he had placed under his head, had been stolen. This would burn him with such a terror that he felt ready to argue, to shout, to fight, to search, to demand. But he had no strength for any of this, and the thought of bread itself would fade... And immediately he would begin thinking about something else: that everyone there was waiting to be transported across the sea, but the steamer was late for some reason, and it was good for him to be here. And just as lightly and ephemerally he would go on to think about the birthmark on the face of the man on duty in the barrack. Most of the day he would think about those events that filled his life here. The visions that arose before his eyes were not visions of childhood, youth, or success. He had hurried somewhere his whole life. It was beautiful not to have to hurry, to have licence to think slowly.

The terrible effect of this passage rests on our recognition that all that really and truly mattered to the nameless poet has *not* withstood 'the test of brutal, naked reality' – and *had* it been able to endure, we would not have the same grounds to repudiate the regime responsible for this demise, as the grounds that we feel we have. Shalamov's indictment of the regime in this passage rests on the opposite possibility – that what really and truly matters is that which is crushed and thwarted by the 'brutal, naked reality' of the militaristic authoritarian state. In this, Shalamov is in implicit agreement with the lifelong documentarian of testimonies concerning the tests of 'brutal, naked reality' – Svetlana Alexiyevich. Shalamov gives us an authentic report of what happens to value and to 'the work of human thought' as the latter is being brutally extinguished:

> And he thought unhurriedly about the great monotony of the movements that precede death, about what had been understood and described by physicians before writers and poets. Hippocrates – humanity's death mask – was a face familiar to every medical student. This mysterious monotony of the movements preceding death gave Freud a foundation for some of his boldest hypotheses. Monotony, repetition – these are the necessary grounds of science. What is unrepeatable in death was sought out not by doctors, but by poets. He was pleased by the knowledge that he could still think. He had long got used to the hungry nausea. And everything was equal: Hippocrates, the man on duty, and his own dirty fingernail.

What is left lies entirely in the province of science, its repeatable physiological observations. What has vanished is the *hiatus irrationalis* of the individual – incalculable, unforeseeable and therefore surprising, thrilling even – the province of art. Nothing about the death of Shalamov's 'poet' indicates that the person dying *is* a poet, or anything at all for that matter, or that the death of a poet is in any way different from the death of, say, the man on duty, or the physician, or a criminal in the barracks. All distinctions have been lost, stripped away by suffering, and everything is 'equal', identical – *indifferent*. And value, too ('value' being closely involved with difference, as in 'gray-scale values', etc.) is not to be looked for here, at the ground zero of human experience, which does not encompass the realization that encompassed it, divined in these lines from Mandelstam's *Kamen*:

> Attack is balanced by attacks,
> And over me, a fateful pendulum
> Oscillates implacably
> And wants to be my fate.
>
> The spindle rushes but will stop
> abruptly, and will fall.
> And no arrangement can be made
> To evade what's to befall.

This imagined divining of a future that has since become the past invites us to a reciprocal imaginative effort of divination about the past: 'divination' in the sense of an art reliant not solely on every bit of discoverable evidence and responsible interpreting, but also on the sympathetic envisioning capacity in which we, too, can become Mandelstam's providential interlocutors – even as the earth edges 'closer to truth and terror'.

References

'*CCWL*' stands throughout for Osip Mandelstam, *Complete Collected Works and Letters* [Полное собрание сочинений и писем], edited by Alexander Mets (Moscow: Progress-Pleyada, 2010).

Epigraphs

Little book – no, I don't begrudge you . . . / . . . / never forget my sad estate: Ovid, *The Poems of Exile:* Tristia *and the Black Sea Letters*, translated and edited by Peter Green (Berkeley: University of California Press, 2005), 3.

The notion is that life involves maintaining oneself between contradictions . . . man being both animal and divine: *The Complete Poems of William Empson*, edited by John Haffenden (London: Allen Lane, the Penguin Press, 2000), 290.

Preface

he is guilty of nothing – not this, not that, nor the other: Anna Akhmatova, 'Poem Without a Hero', Part I, lines 178–79.

less than saintly behaviour: Virginia Rounding, 'Keepers of the Blame', *The Guardian*, May 14, 2004.

literary martyr par excellence: editor's phrase; Emma Gerstein, *Moscow Memoirs: Memories of Anna Akhmatova, Osip Mandelstam, and Literary Russia under Stalin*, translated and edited by John Crowfoot (New York: The Overlook Press, 2004), xiii.

As a matter of literary criticism . . . to know the normal lighting already, and to judge the difference: William Empson, 'Comment for Second Edition', *The Structure of Complex Words*, second edition (London: Chatto & Windus, 1977, first published 1952), 444–45.

Exhibits

I: Alexander Mets, *Chronicle of the Life and Letters of O. E. Mandelstam* [*Летопись жизни и творчества О. Е. Мандельштама*], second edition (Toronto: Department of Slavic Languages and Literatures, University of Toronto, 2016), 377.

II: *CCWL*, v. I, 184.

III: Pavel Nerler, *The Word and 'Deed' of Osip Mandelstam* [*Слово и 'дело' Осипа Мандельштама*] (Moscow: The Mandelstam Society, 2010), 45.

IV: *CCWL*, v. I, 308.

V: Images courtesy of Mandelstam Society (Moscow) and Pavel Nerler; originals in the Central Archive of the Federal Security Service (*CAFSB*).

VI: Peter B. Maggs, *The Mandelstam and 'Der Nister' Files: An Introduction to Stalin-era Prison and Labor Camp Records* (New York: M. E. Sharpe, 1996), Document M–9.

Prologue

what quality went to form a Man of Achievement . . . irritable reaching after fact & reason: *The Letters of John Keats*, edited by Hyder Edward Rollins (Cambridge, Mass.: Harvard University Press, 1958), v. I, 193.

love lyric: Pavel Nerler, *Osip Mandelstam in Heidelberg* [*Осип Мандельштам в Гейдельберге*], Annals of Mandelstam Society [*Записки Мандельштамовского общества*], v. 3 (Moscow: Art-Business Centre, 1994), 46.

Prologue

И пальцы тонкие дрожат, / К таким же, как они, прижаты: CCWL, v. I, 258.

In Moscow, this elegant and sophisticated man . . . the ineffable and the mystery of silence: Nerler, *Mandelstam in Heidelberg*, 35.

tremendous ribs: CCWL, v. I, 62.

the individual, the subject matter of history, is 'irrational' . . . the hiatus irrationalis: Frederick Beiser, *The German Historicist Tradition* (Oxford: Oxford University Press, 2011), 445–46.

Political nonconformist Osip Mandelstam's opposition . . . in the face of oppression and terror: *Stolen Air: Selected Poems by Osip Mandelstam*, translated and edited by Christian Wiman (New York: Ecco, 2012).

He was particularly tempted . . . 'Could I really have said that? Nonsense, dog's ravings!': Boris Kuzin, *Memoirs, Works, Correspondence* [Воспоминания, произведения, переписка], edited by N. I. Kraineva and E. A. Perezhogina (St. Petersburg: Inapress, 1999), 176.

Any expositor of Windelband's philosophy . . . ideas which he would later abandon or retract: Beiser, 368.

The lives of Russian poets are like the lives of saints . . . Some have been hailed as martyrs, others cast as prophets: Darra Goldstein, *Nikolai Zabolotsky: Play for Mortal Stakes* (Cambridge: Cambridge University Press, 1993), 1.

Tormented by spiritual thirst . . . set the hearts of men on fire with your Word: *The Penguin Book of Russian Verse*, translated and edited by Dimitri Obolensky (Harmondsworth, Middlesex: Penguin Books, 1962), 92.

the side of the 'I' has decisively and unjustly outweighed the side of the 'not-I' . . . proven to be too light: CCWL, v. II, 9.

made a simple but seminal distinction . . . intoxicating for a later generation: Beiser, 369.

The doctrine of validity of practical reason . . . the realm of action: Ibid., 453.

there are grounds for supposing that Lask's figure and his fate are reflected in the 'Verses to German Prosody': *Mandelstam Encyclopedia* [Мандельштамовская энциклопедия], edited by Pavel Nerler et al. (Moscow: Rosspen, 2017), v. I, 305.

When rowan in the spring develops / The leaves whose fate is to be dead: CCWL, v. I, 261.

The verdant ivy by the window: Ibid.

not to be a hero is not the same thing as to be a scoundrel: Kuzin, 178.

This myth is tidy and vivid . . . *Mandelstam of the epigram, and not of the ode*: Mikhail Gasparov, *Mandelstam: The Civic Poems of 1937* [Мандельштам: Гражданская лирика, 1937] (Moscow: Russian State University for the Humanities, 1996), 17–18.

an independent and very talented belletrist . . . *describing Mandelstam's heroic self-flagellation very convincingly*: Ibid.

It is entirely obvious that Mandelstam . . . *had to do considerable violence to himself in his work on the 'Ode'*: 'Osip Mandelstam's Fate and Word' ['Судьба и весть Осипа Мандельштама'] in *Averintsev and Mandelstam* [Аверинцев и Мандельштам], edited by Mikhail Gasparov et al. (Moscow: Russian State University for the Humanities, 2011), 107.

must be accepted . . . *on their own terms*: 'Why Mandelstam?' ['Так почему же все-таки Мандельштам?'], Ibid., 124.

it is better to be a sinner in a world ruled by God . . . *The only prospect is one of death and destruction*: W. R. D. Fairbairn, *Psychoanalytic Studies of the Personality* (New York: Routledge, 1994), 66–67.

what makes on you the most sinister impression of madness . . . *we underscore our interest towards one another every single minute*: CCWL, v. II, 5.

all real literature in modern history is . . . *against established style and direction of literature*: Andrey Sinyavsky, 'Dissidence as a Personal Experience' ['Диссидентство как личный опыт'], *Sintaxis*, No. 15, 1985, 133.

It has been a quarter of a century of my looming before Russian poetry . . . *changing something in its structure and contents*: CCWL, v. III, 548.

The existing monuments form an ideal order . . . *great difficulties and responsibilities*: T. S. Eliot, 'Tradition and the Individual Talent', *Selected Essays* (London: Faber and Faber Limited, 1932), 15.

We dwell with satisfaction upon the poet's difference . . . *the period of full maturity*: Ibid., 14.

It involves, in the first place, the historical sense . . . *conscious of his place in time, of his own contemporaneity*: Ibid.

the programmatic 'Stanzas' of 1935 . . . *never take the position of opposing it*: Gasparov, *Mandelstam: The Civic Poems*, 18.

The intervention of the European powers . . . *these daily homages became a necessity for him*: Kornei Chukovsky, *The Poet and the Hangman (Nekrasov and Muravyov)*, translated by R. W. Rotsel (Ann Arbor: Ardis, 1977), 24–26.

Someone is walking down Nevsky . . . *children who might become impaled on them*: Ibid., 76–77.

Chapter 1

this betrayal seems such a great crime . . . the Russian society of the time was just as guilty as he: Ibid., 23.

An all too familiar Russian picture . . . crushed by the same boot one and all: Kornei Chukovsky, *Diary, 1901–1969*, edited by Victor Erlich, translated by Michael Henry Heim (New Haven: Yale University Press, 2005), 430.

the difficult and elaborate logic of poetic thought: Gasparov, *Mandelstam: The Civic Poems*, 65.

Twixt devil and deep sea, man hacks his caves / . . . / Dance, like nine angels on pinpoint extremes: William Empson, 'Arachne', *The Complete Poems of William Empson*, edited by John Haffenden (London: Allen Lane, the Penguin Press, 2000), 34.

There was nothing mad about Coleridge except a peculiarly severe conflict . . . a kind of suicide: William Empson, '*The Ancient Mariner*' in *Argufying*, edited by John Haffenden (Iowa City: University of Iowa Press, 1987), 305.

When the individual is involved in an intense relationship . . . he cannot make a metacommunicative statement: 'Toward a Theory of Schizophrenia' in Gregory Bateson, *Steps to an Ecology of Mind* (Northvale: Jason Aronson, 1987), 208.

Be simple answer'd, for we know the truth: Shakespeare, *King Lear*, III, vii, *The New Nonesuch Shakespeare*, ed. Robert Farjeon (London: The Nonesuch Press, 1953), v. III, 796.

There are many people who appreciate the expression of sincere emotion in verse . . . The emotion of art is impersonal: Eliot, 22.

Anna Akhmatova once said that Mandelstam . . . as near to Keats as to any other English poet: Henry Gifford, 'Mandelstam Whole', *New York Review of Books*, March 9, 1978.

Chapter 1

best if no light had shone / on my creations! . . . / . . . / . . . the author's / own morals had no truck with these 'arts': Ovid, 21.

Curiously, the poem's two final lines . . . the memories of those who heard it recited in the distant year of 1934: José Manuel Prieto, 'Reading Mandelstam on Stalin', *The New York Review of Books*, June 10, 2010.

The principal difficulty in doing this . . . Gothic architecture, properly so called: John Ruskin, *The Stones of Venice*, v. II in *The Works of John Ruskin*, edited by E. T. Cook and Alexander Wedderburn (London: George Allen, 1904), v. X, 181.

We have, then, the Gothic character . . . Gothic architecture, properly so called: Ibid., 182–83.

Psychologists tell me that they do not recognise the term 'neurotic guilt' . . . a kind of suicide: Empson, 'The Ancient Mariner', *Argufying*, 305.

Sir Thomas Browne (who liked epigrams and epitaphs) . . . 'short and sweete poems, framed to praise or dispraise': Geoffrey Grigson, *The Faber Book of Epigrams and Epitaphs* (London: Faber & Faber, 1977), vii.

Point, it can be claimed . . . a good epigram has simply to be a good poem: Ibid., viii.

'I'm warning you: not a soul! If this gets where it may, I'll be . . .': Emma Gerstein, *Memoirs* [*Мемуары*] (St. Petersburg: Inapress, 1998), 51.

The poem interrogates the conjunction of the body politic and the body personal . . . Behind the sequential hatred is the loving convention which itemized the beauties of the loved one's person: Christopher Ricks, *T. S. Eliot and Prejudice* (Berkeley: University of California Press, 1988), 148.

his words like measures of weight: *The Selected Poems of Osip Mandelstam*, translated by Clarence Brown and W. S. Merwin (New York: New York Review Books, 2004), 70.

monstrous infantilism: Ricks, 150.

He plays with them: Robert Lowell, 'Stalin' in *Collected Poems*, edited by Frank Bidart and David Gewanter (New York: Farrar, Straus and Giroux, 2003), 915.

his thin-necked, drained advisors: Ibid.

They make touching and funny animal sounds. He alone talks Russian: Ibid.

the rusty Roman medal where I see / my lowest depths of possibility: Lowell, 'Caligula', *Collected Poems*, 360.

you wish the Romans had a single neck: Lowell, 'Caligula', *Collected Poems*, 445.

Stalin? What shot him clawing up the tree of power . . . / . . . / The large stomach could only chew success: Lowell, 'Stalin', *Collected Poems*, 540.

Animals / ripened for your arenas suffered less / than you . . . yours the lawlessness / of something simple that has lost its law: Lowell, 'Caligula', *Collected Poems*, 445.

Chapter 1

their lives and the lives of their families . . . the group to which they happened to belong: Hannah Arendt, *The Origins of Totalitarianism* (London: Harcourt, 1973), 320.

well-nourished: Mets, 301.

unpardonable mistake: Pavel Nerler, 'The Battle at Ulenspiegel' ['Битва под Уленшпигелем'], *Znamya*, No. 2, 214.

In revising an old translation . . . Instances of complete creative revision are rare . . . in being excessively individual. Mets, 335–36.

there is no method but to be very intelligent: T. S. Eliot, 'The Perfect Critic', *The Sacred Wood* (New York: Alfred A. Knopf, 1920), 10.

against the entirety of my literary earnings: Mets, 315.

Ulenspiegel *has been published . . . but I remain, for the time being, severe*: Ibid., 312.

Poor devil – his shenanigans have helped me . . . I would never again place that translation! Ibid., 318.

Literary Paper *asked me to write a feuilleton . . . so much noise would arise because of it*: Ibid., 325.

repeated purges which invariably precede actual group liquidation: Arendt, 323.

it is obvious that the most elementary caution demands that one avoid all intimate contacts . . . they are in danger of their own lives: Ibid.

in the face of the Federation of Soviet Writers . . . a dramatization of a scandalous criminal process: *CCWL*, v. III, 486.

If one could collect everything that I have written . . . the rank smell of death and decomposition: Ibid., 491.

In mid-winter he had the stupidity and the misfortune . . . I am a philistine, and we nearly fell out after one particular conversation: Mets, 325.

I dispute the right of the editors . . . what sharpness of tone and phrasing have been permitted therein': *CCWL*, v. III, 479–80.

is in a terrible state, hates everyone around . . . has torn up all his publishing contracts: Ibid., 332.

telephoned Zaslavsky and said approximately the following . . . you are a scoundrel: Ibid.

A young man who had fairly well recovered . . . following her departure he assaulted a orderly and was put in the tubs: 'Toward a Theory of Schizophrenia', Bateson, 217.

the victim is caught in a tangle of paradoxical injunctions . . . that he should do something . . . or that he should do something else incompatible with it: R. D. Laing, *Self and Others* (Harmondsworth, Middlesex: Penguin Books Ltd., 1969), 144–46.

trouble in identifying and interpreting those signals . . . what sort of a message a message is: 'Epidemiology of a Schizophrenia', Bateson, 194.

traumatic situation which involves a metacommunicative tangle: Ibid., 195.

When the individual is involved in an intense relationship . . . he cannot make a metacommunicative statement: 'Towards a Theory of Schizophrenia', Bateson, 208.

if this pathology can be warded off or resisted, the total experience may promote creativity: 'Problems of Cetacean and Other Mammalian Communication', Bateson, 278.

I have no manuscripts, no notebooks, no archive . . . all around me the mangy curs are writing away: *CCWL*, v. II, 350.

The book is of signal value . . . as an attempt . . . to break the continuous chain of the monistic Marxist worldview: Mets, 317.

a clot of bitterness about the vanishing of the past: Ibid., 322.

Mandelstam is solving one of the most difficult problems . . . older theorists warn against conflating 'harmony' with 'melody': Ibid., 320.

a sophisticated 'dish' suitable for the enjoyment of bookworms and philologists: Ibisd., 332.

Considering the art of Pasternak and Mandelstam . . . enemy ideas under a benign guise (the topic of objective sabotage in poetry and prose): Ibid., 376.

Certain individual representatives of the class vanquished by the proletariat . . . It is on this despondency that Mandelstam's muse feeds: Ibid., 333.

antiquarian rarity: Ibid., 347.

Pasternak, Antokolsky, and the old men, Mandelstam and Andrey Bely, need our help . . . by means of systematic comradely criticism: Ibid., 371.

the bourgeois and counterrevolutionary character of acmeism . . . on the eve of the proletarian revolution: Ibid., 373–74.

Chapter 1

Here lies the dreadful danger for contemporary poetry... a product of exceptionally high culture: Ibid., 374–75.

To reissue them at present (even with a critical introduction) would be a large-scale political misstep... but also a disservice to Mandelstam himself: Ibid., 379.

The old Petersburg poet O. Mandelstam has missed the abundantly blossoming Armenia that joyfully builds socialism: Ibid., 386.

period feeling: William Empson, *The Structure of Complex Words* (London: Chatto & Windus, 1951, Second Impression 1952), 158.

Now I look with bitterness over my past life. A dog's jubilee was my reward... you've managed not to have even noticed it: Osip Mandelstam, *Collected Works* [Сочинения], edited by Pavel Nerler and A. Nikitayev (Moscow: Art-Business Centre, 1993), v. IV, 125.

This wolfhound age throws itself upon my shoulders, /.../... like a hat in the sleeve / Of a smothering Siberian fur coat: CCWL, v. I, 156.

angry, greedy, savage, mad, cruel: Alberto Manguel, 'Dante's Dog', *PN Review* 192, March–April 2010, xxxvi, 4, 14–18.

The word plays an unusual trick... very mixed feelings are there to be drawn upon: Empson, *The Structure of Complex Words*, 163.

Four hours of questioning... Colossal patience: CCWL, v. III, 496.

Dearest Nadinka! I am completely lost... I keep wishing to brush off the lies – and cannot, keep trying to wash off the dirt – and that, too, is impossible: Ibid., 497–98.

Mandelstam called on me... I gave him an advance... against the prose: Mets, 359.

Some days ago, O. MANDELSTAM has returned from Crimea... He is depressed by the scenes of hunger... and by his own literary misfortunes: Ibid., 385.

we hear the voice of class enemy: Ibid., 387.

Mandelstam has the reputation of a madman... the essence of the European way of life: Ibid., 388.

He astonished me with the news... Then we recalled Baratynsky's brilliant 'Laughing epigram': Ibid., 388.

I understood that he had written something new... it took a year for the poem to reach its destination: Kuzin, 176–77.

Così gridai colla faccia levata: Dante, *Inferno*, XVI, 76.

Chapter 2

Since the created mind . . . he will never understand that other completely: Nicholas of Cusa, *On Conjecture*, translated from *The Works of Nicholas of Cusa* [*Николай Кузанский: Сочинения*] (Mysl: Moscow, 1979), v. I, 188.

most plausible addressee: Lada Panova, 'The Friend of Dante and Petrarch. Article 2. The Russian Trills of an Italian Nightingale (Once Again about Petrarch's Sonnet 311 in Mandelstam's Translation)' ['Друг Данте и Петрарки друг. Статья 2. Русские трели итальянского соловья (еще раз о 311-м сонете Петрарки в переводе Мандельштама'], in *Roots, Shoots, Fruits . . . Osip Mandelstam and Poland* [*Корни, побеги, плоды . . . Осип Мандельштам и Польша*] (Moscow: Russian State University for the Humanities, 2015), 364–410.

Where I seek the traces of beauty and honour / That disappeared, like a moulten falcon, / Leaving its body in an earthen bed: CCWL, v. I, 188.

It is no wonder for an old man to be as young again. When a falcon is moulten many times over, he . . . will let no one offend against his nest: L. V. Sokolova, '"A Moulten Falcon"' ['"*Sokol v mytekh*"'] in *The Works of the Ancient Russian Literature Department of the Institute of Russian Literature of Russian Academy of Sciences*, v. 50 (St. Petersburg: Institute of Russian Literature of Russian Academy of Sciences, 1996), 454–65.

Sometimes a falcon soars so high that he can barely be seen, and only as a dark speck in the sky: Ibid.

the sight is in birds vastly more perfect . . . equal accuracy and clearness: Anita Albus, *On Rare Birds* (Guilford, Connecticut: Lyons Press, 2011), 230.

Our bird's-eye views . . . with one glance comprehend the whole: Ibid., 232.

And, furrowing my brow, I now wonder, / How well she looks, and with what crowd mingles, / And how the storm of gathers swirls around her: CCWL, v. I, 190.

How the bereaved nightingale proclaims / . . . / Melting the silence of the countryside: Ibid., 189.

When the earth falls asleep and the heat dies down, / . . . / I sense, burn, yearn and cry – yet she doesn't hear: Ibid., 190.

Wisely created am I, be my witness: / . . . / And sleep forever to awaken: Konstantin Batyushkov, *Collected Works* [*Сочинения в 2 т.*], edited by V. Koshelev (Moscow: Khudozhestvennaya literatura, 1989), v. I, 426.

nothing but a flimsy silken garment . . . the voluptuous forms of her limbs: E. H. Gombrich, *Symbolic Images* (London: Phaidon, 1972), 47.

She strides but slightly overtaking / . . . a youth a year younger than herself: CCWL, v. I, 243.

I shall note another moment, little-known in Russian love lyrics . . . John the Baptist before Christ: Olga Sedakova, 'Mandelstam's Lyrics of Farewell' ['Прощальные стихи Мандельштама: "Классика в неклассическое время"'], <http://www.olgasedakova.com/Poetica/1584>.

Venus placide commoversi . . . voluptuous sound of the flute: Gombrich, 48.

Let us not unambiguously tie the verses about a 'clear conjecture' . . . the 'conjecture' exceeds the bounds of one person's destiny: Irina Surat, 'A Clear Conjecture' ['Ясная догадка'], *Zvezda*, No. 10, 2013.

Dipping against her will down to the empty earth, / . . . / Of an inspired defect: CCWL, v. I, 243.

Some women are akin to humid earth, / . . . / . . . the first to greet the newly dead: Ibid., 244.

Not long before our 'journey' around the wine cellars . . . And he handed me the paper: Natalia Shtempel, *Mandelstam in Voronezh* ['Мандельштам в Воронеже'] (Moscow: Mandelstam Society, 1992).

A diptych, two independent poems . . . as stanzas of a canzone their Italian theme opens up before me: Sedakova, 'Mandelstam's Lyrics of Farewell'.

I am convinced and hope to convince you . . . That was the main event of his life: Ibid.

In the Italian key . . . The human soul . . . comes out of its chambers, revealing itself on the balconies of the gait, gaze, smile, and speech: Ibid.

I am wondering in earnest . . . Each step is a conclusion, vigilant like a syllogism: CCWL, v. II, 159.

An ice-skater, a first-born, thrown out by his time / Under the frost-dust of declensions formed anew: CCWL, v. I, 191.

his collar in its beaver braiding / glitters with hoar-frost all about: Alexander Pushkin, *Eugene Onegin*, translated by Charles Johnston (London: Penguin Classics, 2003), 14.

That if I then had wak'd after long sleepe, / . . . / I cri'de to dreame againe: Shakespeare, *The Tempest*, III, ii, *The New Nonesuch Shakespeare*, v. I, 42.

Rome was not the first ancient culture to link thinking and walking . . . a typically Greek kind of accident: Mary Beard, 'Walk Like a Roman', *Times Literary Supplement*, May 11, 2012.

The diptych is organized as a palimpsest . . . if not on earth, then in heaven: Lada Panova, 'Dante', *Mandelstam Encyclopedia* [Мандельштамовская энциклопедия], v. I, 219.

I am certain that the word 'sladkaya' ('sweet') . . . A lady who lacks dolcezza *. . . cannot be said to be beautiful*: Sedakova, 'Mandelstam's Lyrics of Farewell'.

This kind of love has a cultural history . . . this is fin amor: Ibid.

How he would peel a pear with his fine long-fingered hands: Gerstein, 12.

But I would restrain myself, afraid to appear ridiculous: Ibid., 16.

He lay on his side . . . seemed to be afloat in blissful repose, as if listening to something: Ibid.

heels together, toes apart. This accounted for his gait . . . the equilibrium of his whole body when in motion: Ibid., 21.

He knew how to create both the outer and the inner likeness of a woman, very much as an artist, not an infatuated lover who had 'lost his head': Ibid., 438.

was planning to divorce her husband . . . (this I learned . . . from shared acquaintances): Ibid., 422.

A young man came to the bureau . . . in the role of a supplicant: Ibid., 49.

Beginning with that day, Lyova . . . alarmed Anna Andreyevna: Ibid., 203.

That will be you . . . Especially not Lyova: Ibid., 51.

Until Mandelstam's conviction . . . initiated into the secret: Ibid., 52.

Not Hippocrene but a jet / . . . / Will break through the ramshackle walls / Of mean Moscow housing: CCWL, v. I, 183.

brought Lyova along to Gosizdat . . . 'It was interesting all the same': Gerstein, 49.

This morning I had a visit from Leonid Lavrov . . . a wise old Jew with a stick: Nerler, *The Word and 'Deed' of Osip Mandelstam*, 37.

I have still a ways to go before becoming / A patriarch; my age is half-revered. / . . . / Without changing inwardly a bit: CCWL, v. I, 165–66.

And now and then, I'll go and run errands / . . . / Like swallows skimming over Yangtze river: Ibid.

And I would want so much to shake my doldrums, / . . . / Be gentle – for we're going the same way: Ibid.

Chapter 3

once a thing is put in writing, the composition . . . drifts all over the place . . . being unable to defend or help itself: Plato, *Phaedrus*, 275d-e, in *Collected Dialogues* (Princeton: Bollingen Series LXXI, Princeton University Press, 2002), 521.

I have a taste for the secret . . . we are in a totalitarian space: Jacques Derrida and Maurizio Ferraris, *A Taste for the Secret*, translated by Giacomo Donis (Cambridge: Polity, 2001), 59.

the most elementary caution demands . . . they are in danger of their own lives: Arendt, 323.

the would-be controller . . . cannot have a simple lineal control: 'Conscious Purpose versus Nature', Bateson, 443.

Lubyanka: The Organs of VChK – OGPU – NKVD – NKGB – MGB – MVD – KGB, 1917–1991, A Reference Guide [Лубянка: Органы ВчК — ОГПУ — НКВД — НКГБ — МГБ — МВД — КГБ, 1917-1991, справочник] (Moscow: MFD, 2003).

During the 1930s and 1940s . . . the People's Comissariat of State Security (NKGB) became the Ministry of State Security (MGB): Maggs, 7.

said to M. that it was useful for a poet to experience fear . . . the use of the future tense: Nadezhda Mandelstam, *Hope Against Hope*, translated by Max Hayward (London: The Harvill Press, 1999), 80.

In supplement to my prior testimony . . . promising, however, to destroy the copy later: Nerler, *The Word and 'Deed' of Osip Mandelstam*, 45.

On the fifth and sixth lines . . . I had read that work to him: Ibid.

For O. E. friendship was a necessity . . . Narbut was probably closer to him than anybody else: Kuzin, 168.

trilled like a nightingale: Nerler, *The Word and 'Deed' of Osip Mandelstam*, 34.

basketfuls of nonsense: Ibid.

My reception of the October revolution . . . my acute revulsion against the White Guard: Ibid., 46.

In 1930 a deep depression sets in . . . O. Mandelstam: Ibid.

Question: *Do you acknowledge yourself guilty . . . Anna Akhmatova, in whose presence he had first heard the poem*: Ibid., 46–47.

If only I could survey the twenty years that followed . . . But that day I had other things on my mind: Gerstein, *Memoirs*, 55.

In 1934 O. E. was sent into exile . . . had then moved to Moscow: Kuzin, 177.

I always thought it unjust to demand heroism . . . not to be a hero is not the same thing as to be a scoundrel: Ibid., 178.

Question: *How did Anna Akhmatova respond . . . a greatly potent propaganda poster*: Nerler, *The Word and 'Deed' of Osip Mandelstam*, 47.

Question: *Does your counter-revolutionary lampoon . . . can be used by any social group whatsoever*: Ibid.

As far back as 1934, Anna Andreyevna and I heard of the writer Pavlenko's stories . . . writhed like a fish in a frying pan, and so forth . . .: Mandelstam, 104.

Taciturnity does not have an absolute value . . . lie somewhat lightly upon the tongue: Geoffrey Hill, 'Language, Suffering, and Silence', *Collected Critical Writings*, edited by Kenneth Haynes (Oxford: Oxford University Press, 2008), 395.

Shortly after the already described events . . . I set out for Voronezh: Gerstein, 63.

But in the face of Mandelstam's increasing demands . . . my particular feelings for L. Gumilyov: Ibid., 65.

It is fairly sad to realize that you had been chosen to be sacrificed . . . It was Pavlenko: Ibid.

Why are we supposed to be brave enough to stand up to all the horrors of twentieth-century prisons and camps? . . . the writing of verse in a state of fury and indignation? Mandelstam, 85.

Chapter 4

The after-math seldom or neuer equals the first herbage: Andrew Marvell, *The Rehearsal Transprosed* in Andrew Marvell: *The Rehearsal Transpros'd* and *The Rehearsal Transpros'd: The Second Part*, edited by D. I. B. Smith (Oxford: Clarendon Press, 1971).

liked the verses so much . . . read them to Bukharin: Nadezhda Mandelstam, *Memoirs* [*Воспоминания*] (Moscow: Vagrius, 2006), v. I, 102.

Vyshinsky: *Tell us, traitor Yagoda . . . do not feel any regret for what you have done?* Vladimir Bychkov, 'Andrey "Jaguar'yevich" Vyshinsky: the prosecutor's revolutionary conscience', *Radio Sputnik*, December 10, 2018, <www.radiosputnik.ria.ru>.

the victim is caught in a tangle of paradoxical injunctions . . . in which he cannot do the right thing: R. D. Laing, 144.

One person conveys to the other that he should do something . . . to get out of the situation, or to dissolve it by commenting on it: Ibid., 145–46.

this result could have been avoided . . . though she comments on his and forces him to accept and to attempt to deal with the complicated sequence: 'Toward a Theory of Schizophrenia', Bateson, 217.

Methods like these are possible . . . and by no means everybody is allowed to receive packages: Mandelstam, *Hope Against Hope*, 78.

it is better to be a sinner in a world ruled by God . . . The only prospect is one of death and destruction: W. R. D. Fairbairn, *Psychoanalytic Studies of the Personality* (New York: Routledge, 1994), 66–67.

The interrogator's approach . . . one could constantly sense his hatred for Stalin: Mandelstam, 81.

His obvious purpose was to impress on me his view . . . on how the whole thing should be seen: Ibid., 74.

M.'s cellmate tried to frighten him . . . his 'fellow prisoner', who gave him ne respite: Ibid., 75.

will provoke the patient . . . he feels that he is being deceived: 'Toward a Theory of Schizophrenia', Bateson, 225.

'What touching concern!' O. M. only managed to insert: Mandelstam, *Memoirs*, v. I, 94.

At the interview I saw that M. had bandages on both wrists... M. persuaded a cobbler he knew to secrete a few blades in this way for him: Mandelstam, 77.

an experience of being punished precisely for being right in one's own view of the context: 'The Group Dynamics of Schizophrenia', Bateson, 236.

severe pain and maladjustment can be induced... in the wrong regarding its rules for making sense of an important relationship with another mammal: 'Epidemiology of a Schizophrenia', Bateson, 194.

His metacommunicative system... determined to demonstrate that he could not be deceived: 'Toward a Theory of Schizophrenia', Bateson, 211.

he invited O. M. to accompany him on his rounds... The doctor and the patient parted as friends: Mandelstam, *Memoirs*, v. I, 149.

Broca's area... one of the speech centers of the brain... went offline whenever a flashback was triggered: Bessel van der Kolk, *The Body Keeps the Score: Brain, Mind, and Body in the Healing of Trauma* (New York: Penguin Books, 2014), 43.

come up with what many of them call their 'cover story'... a narrative with a beginning, a middle, and an end: Ibid.

Oh horror, horror, horror, / Tongue nor Heart cannot conceive, nor name thee. / ... / Confusion now hath made his masterpiece: Shakespeare, *Macbeth*, II, iii, *The New Nonesuch Shakespeare*, v. III, 512.

The thaw in St. Petersburg... barely paying attention to what was going on around them: Van der Kolk, 77.

Behaviors to avoid or escape from danger... reciprocals of avoidance and escape: Ibid., 75–76.

Pavlov showed that after exposure to extreme stress, animals find a new internal equilibrium... startle reactions in response to... approaching laboratory assistants: Ibid., 77.

take much longer to return to baseline... most vulnerable in a particular individual: Ibid., 46.

After trauma the world is experienced with a different nervous system... a whole range of physical symptoms: Ibid., 53.

On one of those first days Osip Emilyevich stood facing the window... This was the character of those times: Gerstein, 66.

Interlude

Two things fill the mind with ever new and increasing admiration and reverence . . . the starry heavens above me and the moral law within me: Immanuel Kant, *Critique of Practical Reason*, translated by Mary Gregor (Cambridge: Cambridge University Press, 2015), 129.

the total experience may promote creativity: 'Double Bind, 1969', Bateson, 278.

I remember that I myself began to shout at the interrogators . . . who were then failing in their attempts to dishonour me: Nikolay Zabolotsky, *The history of my imprisonment [История моего заключения]*, *Ogonyok*, 1991. Cp. N. A. Zabolotsky, 'The Story of My Imprisonment', translated by Robin Milner-Gulland, *Times Literary Supplement*, October 9, 1981.

Once we were not given water for about three days . . . able to forget that New Year's feast: Ibid.

the very crucial 'balance – deadlock' opposition where balance suggests a man walking on a tightrope . . . and deadlock two men fighting and neither getting what he wills: *Selected Letters of William Empson*, edited by John Haffenden (Oxford: Oxford University Press, 2006), 59.

What this means, as the context makes clear, is . . . to accept the injustice of society as we do the inevitability of death: William Empson, 'Proletarian Literature', *Some Versions of Pastoral* (London: Chatto & Windus, 1935, Second Impression 1950), 4.

The beauty of the image of 'fair constellated foam' . . . there is a silent joy at their arrival: Hill, 'Poetry as "Menace" and "Atonement"', *Collected Critical Writings*, 14.

Ideally, my theme would be simple . . . instinctive assent to such statements: Ibid., 4.

Hill's search for at-one-ment has led him to two descriptions . . . the two of which are finally irreconcilable, tonally and totally: Christopher Ricks, 'Geoffrey Hill 2: "At-one-ment"', *The Force of Poetry* (Oxford: Oxford University Press, 1984), 319–20.

I washed myself at night in the yard. / . . . / And the Earth more truthful and terrible: CCWL, v. I, 122.

No purpose, view, / / Or song but's weak if without the ballast of fear. / . . . to get // Out by a rival emotion fear: Empson, 'Courage means Running', *The Complete Poems*, 76.

There was an old man, timid as a boy, / . . . / Like a tendril, sink into the foam: CCWL, v. I, 171.

As I was washing myself in the dark / . . . / The earth edged closer to truth and terror: George Kalogeris, 'Mandelstam #126', *Dialogos: Paired Poems in Translation* (Champaign: Antilever Press, 2012), 25.

'And things are worse than ever', thought the poor child . . . 'and in that case I can go back by railway', she said to herself: Lewis Carroll, *Alice's Adventures in Wonderland*, quoted in Empson, 'Alice in Wonderland: The Child as Swain', *Some Versions of Pastoral*, 255.

The only passage that I feel sure involves evolution . . . ontogeny then repeats phylogeny, and a whole Noah's Ark gets out of the sea with her: Empson, 'Alice in Wonderland: The Child as Swain', 255.

He nothing common did or mean / . . . / But bow'd his comely Head / Down as upon a Bed: Andrew Marvell, 'An Horatian Ode upon Cromwel's Return from Ireland', *The Poems and Letters of Andrew Marvell*, edited by H. M. Margoliouth (Oxford: Clarendon Press, 1951), v. I, 88–89.

I slept, and blank as that I would yet lie. / . . . / The heart of standing is you cannot fly: Empson, 'Aubade', *The Complete Poems*, 69.

Chapter 5

and at last for the highest event in ethics, the moral discovery, which gets a man called a traitor by his own society: William Empson, 'The Ancient Mariner' in *Argufying*, edited by John Haffenden (Iowa City: University of Iowa Press, 1987), 305.

Ballance thy Sword against the Fight: Andrew Marvell, 'A Dialogue Between the Resolved Soul, and Created Pleasure', *The Poems and Letters of Andrew Marvell*, v. I, 9.

These Walls restrain the World without, / But hedge our Liberty about. / . . . / The Cloyster outward shuts its Gates, / And, from us, locks on them the Grates: Andrew Marvell, 'Upon Appleton House', *The Poems and Letters of Andrew Marvell*, v. I, 62.

There is much that is paradoxical in the nature of colour . . . while being in itself green, envelops itself, so to speak, in red: Kuzma Petrov-Vodkin, *Euclydian Space* in *Khlynovsk, Euclydian Space, Samarcandia* [Хлыновск. Пространство Эвклида. Самаркандия] (Leningrad: Iskusstvo, 1970), 492.

The world's inception . . . / In the green night, a black fern. / . . . / Single, continuous, indisputable: CCWL, v. I, 307.

Midnight in Moscow . . . / . . . / . . . in the repose of smallpox: CCWL, v. I, 162.

verse properly called metaphysical is that to which the impulse is given by an overwhelming concern with metaphysical problems . . . the problem of the Many and the One: James Smith, 'On Metaphysical Poetry', *Scrutiny*, v. II, No. 3, December 1933, 228.

'Metaphysical' is a somewhat misleading term . . . Without sharp North, without declining West? Poets of the English Language: Elizabethan and Jacobean Poets, edited by W. H. Auden and Norman Holmes Pearson (Harmondsworth, Middlesex: Penguin Books, 1950), xxxi–xxxii.

it is Donne's verse that is disturbed, and his lines that are the battleground between the difficulty of belief and the reluctance to doubt . . . so that they seem to be alive: Smith, 225.

Metaphysical thought *depends on what is held in suspension . . . it is this precipitate that the disciples collect, and of it they make their 'neat' display*: Ibid., 226.

This problem is at the same time the most difficult and the latest to be solved . . . after many fruitless attempts: *Kant's Idea for a Universal History with a Cosmopolitan Aim: A Critical Guide*, edited by Amélie O. Rorty and James Schmidt (Cambridge: Cambridge University Press, 2009), 16.

The double Wood of ancient Stocks / Link'd in so thick, an Union locks: Andrew Marvell, 'Upon Appleton House', *The Poems and Letters of Andrew Marvell*, v. I, 74.

Schubert on the water, Mozart in the din of birds, / . . . / counted the crowd's pulse, and believed the crowd: CCWL, v. I, 186.

Could I have thought that from you I would hear the Bolshevik sermon? . . . Yesterday is gone, and what remains is only the very ancient and the future: CCWL, v. III, 504.

I must live, although I have twice died. / Of swollen water, the town is in half-mind: CCWL, v. I, 198.

Unhappy is the one, who, shadow-like, / . . . / Pleads for alms with his own shadow: Ibid., 218.

The stockings of these barking lanes, / . . . / . . . the dark bewhiskered cornerers... Ibid., 221.

What street is this? / Mandelstam street. / . . . / . . . that Mandelstam... : Ibid., 198.

Near the window in the room at the seamstress's . . . he had not been able to smother his own poems, and they had broken loose and conquered the evil spirit. 'Mandelstam's "Ode" to Stalin', *Slavic Review*, *34*(4) (1975), 683–91.

Osip Mandelstam and the Stalin Ode, by J. M. Coetzee: *Representations* No. 35, Special Issue: Monumental Histories (Summer, 1991), 72–83.

There are such things as living mosques – / . . . / We, too, might be an Hagia-Sophia / With a countless multitude of eyes: CCWL, v. I, 187.

The Commonwealth then first together came, / . . . / Into the Animated City throng: Andrew Marvell, 'The First Anniversary of the Government under O. C.', *The Poems and Letters of Andrew Marvell*, v. I, 105.

The Common-wealth does through their Centers all / . . . / Knit by the Roofs Protecting weight agree: Ibid.

Foliated *Architecture, which uses the pointed arch for the roof proper, and the gable for the roof-mask*: Ruskin, 260.

Egyptian and Greek buildings... throughout every visible line of the building: Ibid., 240.

When Gothic is perfect . . . the pointed arches must be built in the strongest possible manner: Ibid., 255.

the forms of arch thus obtained . . . the utmost strength and permanency obtainable with a given mass of material: Ibid., 256.

reciprocal harmony, like that of a bow or a lyre: Heraclitus, *Fragments: A text and Translation with a Commentary by T. M. Robinson* (Toronto: University of Toronto Press, 1987), 37. Fragment 51, Hippolytus, *Refutation of all Heresies* 9.9.2: 'They do not understand how, while differing from (or: being at variance), (it) is in agreement with itself. (There is) a back-turning connection, like (that) of a bow or lyre.'

And slender fingers tremble, / Pressed against their own counterparts: CCWL, v. I, 258.

Acmeism is for those who, possessed by the spirit of workmanship . . . 'I build, therefore I am right': CCWL, II, 23.

Tytchev's stone . . . asked to be taken into the cross-vault, to partake in the joyous interaction with others of its own kind: Ibid., 24.

mountain brotherhood between the cathedral and the Alp: Ruskin, 188.

magnificence of sturdy power: Ibid.

The more attentively, O rock of Notre Dame, / I contemplated your tremendous ribs, / . . . I, too, some day / Would create beauty from a sinister mass: *CCWL*, v. I, 62.

By an architectonic I mean the art of systems . . . the form of the whole congruent with this purpose: Kant, *Critique of Pure Reason*, translated by Werner S. Pluhar (Cambridge: Hackett, 1986), A832, B860, 755.

I, dear comrades, am not an angel in starched vestments . . . my right to failure, my right to have a breakdown: *CCWL*, v. III, 488.

It seems a fantastic paradox . . . as noble as the intellect of the age can make it: Ruskin, 202.

in the mediaeval, or especially Christian, system of ornament . . . a stately and unaccusable whole: Ibid., 189–90.

Wherever the workman is utterly enslaved . . . whether the several parts of the building are similar or not: Ibid., 204.

the backdrop of poetic Staliniana of 1937: Oleg Lekmanov, 'The Stalin "Ode": Mandelstam's poem "If I were to pick up the charcoal in high praise" against the backdrop of poetic Staliniana of 1937' [Сталинская 'ода': Стихотворение 'Когда б я уголь взял для высшей похвалы' на фоне поэтической сталинианы 1937 года]: *Novyj Mir*, No. 3, 2015.

Not me, and not the other, but his kin, / His Homer-people triples praise upon him: *CCWL*, v. I, 309.

There are such things as living mosques – / . . . / We, too, might be an Hagia-Sophia / With a countless multitude of eyes: *CCWL*, v. I, 187.

And the first beast was like a lion . . . Holy, holy, holy, Lord God Almighty, which was, and is, and is to come: Revelation 4:8, King James Bible.

Perhaps it is the point of madness, / . . . / By the diligent spider, light, / . . . gathered again into a single bundle: *CCWL*, v. I, 235.

Twixt devil and deep sea, man hacks his caves / . . . / Dance, like nine angels on pinpoint extremes: William Empson, 'Arachne', *The Complete Poems*, 34.

As aortas swell up with blood / . . . / . . . and the centuries / Encircle me with their flames: *CCWL*, v. I, 231.

Crushing the charcoal intersecting all, / ... / I shall crumble the coal in hunting for his features: CCWL, v. I, 310.

His desperate Pencil at the work did dart, / ... / What all thy softest touches cannot do: Andrew Marvell, 'The last Instructions to a Painter', *The Poems and Letters of Andrew Marvell*, v. I, 141.

both are signs of something very different from the certainty to be found in Dante and Lucretius ... it seems impossible that it should not possess both: Smith, 228.

There are good lines in the 'Verses about Stalin'... much in it that is muddled, which has no place in a Stalin theme: Nerler, *The Word and 'Deed' of Osip Mandelstam*, 98.

as if over the meadow ... walk mad mowers; the downpour mows the meadow in a bow: CCWL, v. I, 250.

Chapter 6

No human face is exactly the same in its lines on each side ... to banish imperfection is to destroy expression: Ruskin, 203.

she treated the poet's widow with great attention ... a tendentious work in their own right: Gerstein, 416.

following Akhmatova's wishes, I began to put my scattered notes about Mandelstam in some order ... 'because Osip was in the wrong!' Ibid.

There was prior agreement ... this supposedly ennobling deception becomes translated into the crudest of untruths: Ibid.

Had I continued my relations with N. Y. . . . the cult of Mandelstam: Kuzin, 178.

utterly confounded ... influenced by the guiding hand of Nadezhda Yakovlevna: Gerstein, 418.

Here's what I can tell you about Mandelstam ... I tried to be unfaithful to him, but it never worked. Because he was the best: audio transcript, Radio Svoboda, <www.svoboda.org>.

He had a bunk in a room ... We only smiled, and tried not to hurt his feelings: Mandelstam, 271–73.

Linusya, is this clear or not? Lika, this is Mandelstam ... inviting us and Anna Andreyevna to visit at the dacha (they'll be just outside Voronezh 20–25/IV): This and all other excerpts from the correspondence: *O. E. Mandelstam in the letters of S. B. Rudakov to his wife (1935–1936)* [*О. Э. Мандельштам в письмах С. Б. Рудакова к жене (1935–1936)*], edited by E. A. Toddes and A. G. Mets, *Annual of the Manuscript Department of the Pushkin House* (St. Petersburg: Akademicheskiy proekt, 1997). Further excerpts from the correspondence can be located by date.

Everything's intact: Gerstein, 76.

I stayed with Lina Samoylovna ... 'There's never been and never will be anybody better than Seryozha': Ibid., 77.

Rather, stuff me away, like a hat in the sleeve / Of a smothering Siberian fur coat: CCWL, v. I, 156.

Boris Messerer: *Our rapport was not easy . . . underscores the fragility of her image*: audio transcript, Radio Svoboda, <www.svoboda.org>.

Bella Akhmadulina: *Boris Messerer told me to bring along a cast maker . . . her delicate, amazing hand*: Ibid.

She was living in a small communal apartment . . . Nietsvetaeva: Joseph Brodsky, 'Nadezhda Mandelstam (1899–1980): An Obituary', *New York Review of Books*, March 5, 1981.

N. Y. Mandelstam gave me her personal copy . . . the books that had stood there two months ago: Tatiana Levina and A. T. Nikitayev, eds, '"He loved me but was sometimes a little bit unfaithful": The marginalia of N. Y. Mandelstam on the American edition of Mandelstam's *Collected Works*', *Philologica* 4, 1997, No. 8/10, 169–99.

The writer of marginalia . . . the question of the addressee: H. J. Jackson, *Marginalia: Readers Writing in Books* (New Haven: Yale University Press, 2001), 88.

It appears that the marginal notes were . . . to aid the transformation of Mandelstam's biography into myth: Levina, 169.

After her husband's death in transit to the Gulag . . . the harder either woman tried to adopt the moral high ground and avoid being spiteful, the worse it got. Andrew Kahn, 'Truth and Reconciliation', *The Times Literary Supplement*, March 17, 2017.

Emma Grigoryevna Gerstein . . . obviously inferior to Nadezhda Yakovlevna's texts: 'We'll see who outstubborns whom. . .': Nadezhda Yakovlevna Madelstam in Letters, Reminiscences, and Testimonies [*Посмотрим, кто кого переупрямит. . .': Надежда Яковлевна Мандельштам в письмах, воспоминаниях, свидетельствах*], edited by Pavel Nerler (Moscow: Ast, 2015), 84.

Dear Nadichka! I have discovered the secret of eternal friendships . . . a place is saved in the heart that can never be taken by anybody else: Ibid., 85–86.

I forgave Osip Emilyevich for his behavior during the investigation: Gerstein, 60.

Epilogue

Language, the element in which a poet works, is also the medium through which judgements upon his work are made: Hill, 'Poetry as "Menace" and "Atonement"', *Collected Critical Writings*, 3.

The fear of a concrete interlocutor . . . A poet communicates only with a providential interlocutor: *CCWL*, II, 9–10.

In a critical moment, a sea-voyager tosses a sealed bottle . . . we feel when suddenly addressed by name: Ibid., 7.

When Hill was writing his elegy to Mandelstam, Clarence Brown's biography and the memoirs by Nadezhda Mandelstam were almost a decade away: Kenneth Haynes and Andrew Kahn, '"Difficult Friend": Geoffrey Hill and Osip Mandelstam', *Essays in Criticism*, 2013, 63 (1), 51–80.

Difficult friend . . . / The salutes, dust-clouds and brazen cries: Geoffrey Hill, *Broken Hierarchies: Poems 1952–2012*, edited by Kenneth Haynes (Oxford: Oxford University Press, 2013), 58.

So let it be: a small transparent figure . . . to die while telling fortunes: Obolensky, 358.

This I learnt not from thunder / . . . / . . . my prediction / for the future: thus I divined: Ovid, 21.

And it seems to me that the poets one trusts . . . That is why it is a paradox: From Geoffrey Hill's Leeds talk, Haynes and Kahn, 54.

I thought I saw my doppelganger walking towards me down the Nevsky Prospect: Ibid.

By what right do I address Mandelstam as my friend? . . . relations between the poet and the public: Ibid.

Look, now, at the poem's second line: The dead keep their sealed lives, *written two years before I knew of Mandelstam's 'sealed' message*: Ibid.

I have brought with me this big book . . . great things can be shown to a person in a way that would not intimidate him: transcript of a book presentation, 'Olga Sedakova on the book *Podskazano Dantom*', <http://ru.duh-i-litera.com>.

First, identification is the original form of emotional tie . . . a common quality which is shared with some other person: Sigmund Freud, 'Group Psychology and the Analysis of the Ego', *Civilization, Society and Religion* (Penguin Freud Library 12), 137.

I think that the goal of a scholar should be the opposite . . . we need not delve into the materials of Mandelstam or Dante merely to discover the mundane: 'Olga Sedakova on the book *Podskazano Dantom*'.

A real book reads us . . . it asks every question that is forbidden by polite society: Lionel Trilling, 'On the Modern Element in Modern Literature', *Partisan Review*, January–February, 1961, collected in *The Liberal Imagination* (first published by Viking, 1950; New York: NYRB, 2008), 118.

Recently I was exiting some building . . . I was frightened and almost right away understood: this is me: Yakov Druskin, 'The Sight of the Unseeing' [Видение невидения'], *Jacob's Ladder: Essays, Tracts, Letters* [Лестница Иакова: Эссе, трактаты, письма] (St. Petersburg: Academicheskiy proekt, 2004), 35–36.

Novels do not carry the responsibility of reducing the many possibilities they present . . . This . . . distinguishes the work of law from the work of art: Lisa Rodensky, *The Crime in Mind: Criminal Responsibility and the Victorian Novel* (Oxford: Oxford University Press, 2003), 31.

The work of human thought . . . a man threatened with instant death: Czesław Miłosz, *The Captive Mind* (New York: Knopf, 1953), quoted by Geoffrey Hill in 'Language, Suffering, and Silence', *Collected Critical Writings*, 402.

If the cant word 'elitist' can now be applied anywhere, it should be placed against this passage . . . unbaptized by an arbitrary extreme experience of 'brutal, naked reality': Ibid.

The poet was dying... beautiful not to have to hurry, to have licence to think slowly: my translation, Varlam Shalamov, 'Sherry-Brandy' ['Шерри-бренди'], *Kolyma Tales* [*Колымские рассказы*] (Moscow: Khudozhestvennaya literatura, 1989), 60.

And he thought unhurriedly about the great monotony of the movements that precede death... and his own dirty fingernail: Ibid., 61.

Attack is balanced by attacks, / ... / To evade what's to befall: *CCWL*, v. I, 47.

closer to truth and terror: Kalogeris, 25.

Perspectives in English

An Annotated Bibliography

The arrangement of this bibliography follows the sequence of ideas as presented in this book, with the aim of further contextualizing its claims in the body of existing work. Most of the readings suggested below are not usually associated with Mandelstam's name but, nevertheless, explore questions germane to his art and biography. The inclusion of works constitutive of 'the usual lighting' on the subject is, then, more the exception than the rule, as these are easily discoverable by the usual methods of library research.

Nadezhda Mandelstam, *Hope Against Hope* (New York: Atheneum, 1970) and *Hope Abandoned* (New York: Atheneum, 1974). Both books of memoirs, although indispensable, call for constant critical vigilance in interpreting the writer's own interpretations of her world.

Emma Gerstein, *Moscow Memoirs: Memories of Anna Akhmatova, Osip Mandelstam, and Literary Russia under Stalin*, translated and edited by John Crowfoot (New York: The Overlook Press, 2004). Crowfoot's translation is not always reflective of Gerstein's Russian prose style and its period character. It can acquaint us with a range of biographic facts but does not allow for close reading.

Oleg Lekmanov, *Mandelstam* (Boston: Academic Studies Press, 2010). This biography, translated from the Russian, collates the basic facts of the narrative.

Peter B. Maggs, *The Mandelstam and 'Der Nister' Files: An Introduction to Stalin-era Prison and Labor Camp Records* (New York: M. E. Sharpe, 1996). The edition reproduces sequentially the key documents of Mandelstam's penal-system dossier, with a commentary.

William Empson, *Using Biography* (Cambridge, Massachusetts: Harvard University Press, 1984). Organized as a series of critical studies of poets in terms of biographical contradiction, this study implicitly argues against the critical implications of W. K. Wimsatt's and M. C. Beardsley's views in 'The Intentional Fallacy' (published in *The Sewanee Review*, v. 54, No. 3, July–September 1946, 468–88).

The Neo-Kantian Reader, edited by Sebastian Luft (New York: Routledge, 2015), is representative of Mandelstam's formative curriculum during his Heidelberg year.

Frederick Beiser, *The German Historicist Tradition* (Oxford: Oxford University Press, 2011). Valuable as a commentary, accessible to a non-specialist, on the varieties of scepticism accommodated by the neo-Kantian tradition.

T. S. Eliot, 'Tradition and the Individual Talent', in *Selected Essays* (London: Faber and Faber, 1932). The essay is indicative of a Bergsonian sensibility, whose affinities with Mandelstam's own sense of the poetic tradition intimate further parallels between the two poet-critics, who had both been students of Henri Bergson in Paris.

Examples of investigating Bergson's philosophy in relation to the Modernist tradition include:

Robert McParland, *Philosophy and Literary Modernism* (Newcastle upon Tyne: Cambridge Scholars Publishing, 2018);

Corey Latta, *When the Eternal Can Be Met: The Bergsonian Theology of Time in the Works of C. S. Lewis, T. S. Eliot, and W. H. Auden* (Eugene, Oregon: Pickwick Publications, 2014);

Paul Douglass, *Bergson, Eliot, and American Literature* (Lexington, Kentucky: University Press of Kentucky, 1986).

William Empson, *Seven Types of Ambiguity* (London: Chatto & Windus, 1930) makes a number of analytic distinctions of lasting value to interpreting 'difficult poets'. Empson's later work, *The Structure of Complex Words* (London: Chatto & Windus, 1952) extends his early ideas to the study of lexicography, its historic dimension and ambiguity on the scale of a word.

Truth, edited by Simon Blackburn and Keith Simmons (Oxford: Oxford University Press, 1999) surveys three major approaches to the idea of truth in the twentieth century.

J. L. Austin, *Philosophical Papers* (Oxford: Clarendon Press, 1961) and *How to Do Things with Words* (Cambridge, Mass.: Harvard University Press, 1962). Austin disambiguates, with immaculate patience, a variety of utterances (e.g. performatives), helping bring into focus irreducible ambiguities, such as those analysed by Empson in the *Seven Types*. Austin appears to be a philosopher *par excellence* in relation to F. R. Leavis's *The Critic as Anti-Philosopher* (Athens, Georgia: University of Georgia Press, 1983).

Jacques Derrida, *Rogues: Two Essays on Reason* (Palo Alto: Stanford University Press, 2005) and *The Politics of Friendship* (Brooklyn: Verso, 2006). Two works pursuing the notion of reversal in politics. Derrida's idea of 'auto-immunity' is continuous with Gregory Bateson's cybernetic analyses of social transactions.

Rebecca West, *The Meaning of Treason* (New York: Viking Press, 1947). This historically informed discussion of political crime supplies the grounds for contrasting the Soviet notion of 'counter-revolution' with British conceptualizations of citizenship, allegiance, and treason.

Frank Kermode, *The Genesis of Secrecy: On the Interpretation of Narrative* (Cambridge, Mass.: Harvard University Press, 1979). Kermode reflects critically on secrecy in relation to the concepts of privacy and political crime.

Sigmund Freud, *The Psychopathology of Everyday Life*, translated by James Strachey (New York: W. W. Norton & Company, 1989). An early psychoanalytic investigation of disavowed wishes and impulses – secrets we keep from ourselves.

W. R. D. Fairbairn, *Psychoanalytic Studies of the Personality* (first published 1952; New York: Routledge, 2001). An influential analysis of social pressure, anxiety and conformity. Fairbairn's observations regarding military psychology suggest some implications for situations involving imprisonment.

R. D. Laing, *Self and Others* (first published in 1961; reissued with substantial revisions, Harmondsworth, Middlesex: Penguin Books Ltd., 1969). A key text on the role of the double bind in psychopathology. Laing did not recognise the role of the 'tertiary injunction' as a necessary constituent of the double-bind situation, as posited by Gregory Bateson the same year, in 'Double Bind, 1969'. The collection *Steps to an Ecology of Mind* (Northvale, New Jersey: Jason Aronson Inc., 1987) charts the development of Bateson's double-bind theory.

Alan Sinfield, *'Lear* and Laing', *Essays in Criticism*, v. XXVI, No. 1, January 1976, 1–16. An early attempt of applying Laing's description of the double bind to literary criticism, the essay did not take into account the role of a tertiary injunction in securing the double-bind structure, occasioning Christopher Ricks's revisions of Sinfield's argument in his own notes on the double bind in *King Lear*.

Bessel van der Kolk, *The Body Keeps the Score: Brain, Mind, and Body in the Healing of Trauma* (New York: Penguin Books, 2014). This popular book discusses the current state of neurological knowledge about trauma and post-traumatic stress, resurrecting the idea of conflict among contradictory impulses as the basis of traumatic psychopathology.

M. H. Abrams, *The Mirror and the Lamp: Romantic Theory and the Critical Tradition* (New York: Norton, 1958). A meditation on the boundaries of art and life as conceptualizations that inform criticism.

Christopher Ricks, *Allusion to the Poets* (Oxford: Oxford University Press, 2002). 'Metaphor' is an essay that revisits the ontology of metaphoric figures, supplying the analytical background for examining complex (conceptual) metaphors and the special difficulties arising where metaphor involves a universal. Other essays in the collection investigate the application of New-Critical principles to varieties of allusion. The reader is at liberty to contrast this approach with the methods adopted in the well-known philological studies of allusion in Mandelstam:

Kirill Taranovsky, *Essays on Mandelstam* (Cambridge, Mass.: Harvard University Press, 1976);

Omry Ronen, *An Approach to Mandelstam* (Jerusalem: Hebrew University, 1983);

Gregory Freidin, *A Coat of Many Colors: Osip Mandelstam and His Mythologies of Self-Presentation* (Berkeley: University of California Press, 1987);

Charles Isenberg, *Substantial Proofs of Being: Osip Mandelstam's Literary Prose* (Columbus, Ohio: Slavica Publishers, 1987); and

Nancy Pollak's *Mandelstam the Reader* (Baltimore: Johns Hopkins University Press, 1995).

Donald Davie, *Purity of Diction in English Verse* (London: Chatto & Windus, 1952). Davie's analysis of metaphor as a species of relation is coextensive with Ricks's argument in 'Metaphor' and, where he makes a distinction between 'living' and 'dead' metaphors, with Empson's approach to lexical analysis in *Complex Words*.

A study of opposition, in the context of language and lexicography, is implicit in the design of the earlier editions of *Roget's Thesaurus of English Words and Phrases* (first published in 1805, 'so as to facilitate the expression of ideas') – P. M. Roget's monument of Victorian 'structuralism', graphically organized as a presentation of both synonyms and antonyms of the language. Later editions, including those presently in print, have lost much of the *Thesaurus's* former value and function by abolishing and disassembling the oppositional structure of antonyms formerly presented on the opposite sides of the page.

Martin Gardner, *The Ambidextrous Universe* (New York: Basic Books, 1964). Symmetry is recurrent concept in rhetorical figures; Gardner's investigation of the paradoxes of symmetry is helpful in tracing related paradoxes in the language.

William Empson, *The Face of the Buddha* (Oxford: Oxford University Press, 2016). The monograph (lost in manuscript in 1947) explores facial asymmetry as a convergence of feeling and ambiguity.

J. M. Coetzee, *Giving Offense: Essays on Censorship* (Chicago, Illinois: University of Chicago Press, 1996). Coetzee's 'Osip Mandelstam and the Stalin Ode' can be read profitably in conjunction with J. L. Austin's 'Pretending' (collected in the *Philosophical Papers*), which discusses the criteria and the boundaries of dissimulation.

Lionel Trilling, *Sincerity and Authenticity* (Cambridge, Mass.: Harvard University Press, 1972). This critical study places Austin's and Coetzee's considerations of pretence in a broader cultural and historical context.

Clare Cavanagh, *Osip Mandelstam and the Modernist Creation of Tradition* (Princeton, New Jersey: Princeton University Press, 1995). The scholar reflects, among other things, on 'cathedrals' as a figure significant to Modernist poetry.

Judith Deborah Haber, *Pastoral and the Poetics of Self-Contradiction: From Theocritus to Marvell* (New York: Cambridge University Press, 1994). A monograph on the central concept of the present work.

William Empson, *Some Versions of Pastoral* (London: Chatto & Windus, 1935). On the political ramifications of the contrasts inherent in the genre.

Lydia Chukovskaya, *The Akhmatova Journals (1938–41)* (New York: Farrar Straus & Giroux, 1994). An important witness of the social circle close to Mandelstam, Chukovskaya is a discerning critic and commentator.

Beth Holmgren, *Women's Works in Stalin's Time: On Lidiia Chukovskaia and Nadezhda Mandelstam* (Bloomington: Indiana University Press, 1993). A monograph on the relations within the two Mandelstams' circle of friends.

Ian Hamilton, *Keepers of the Flame: Literary Estates and the Rise of Biography from Shakespeare to Plath* (Boston: Faber and Faber, 1994). A critical study of literary estates and their influence upon biographical narratives.

Stanley Plumly, *Posthumous Keats* (New York: W. W. Norton, 2008). An elegant and penetrating study of the poet's posthumous reputation as a creation of surviving witnesses – a model investigation of its kind.

Witness Literature: Proceedings of the Nobel Centennial Symposium, edited by Horace Engdahl (River Edge, New Jersey: World Scientific Publishing Co., 2002). The volume displays an array of rhetoric inherent in the critical phenomenon of 'witness literature', and can be read as a backdrop to Geoffrey Hill's 'Poetry as "Menace" and "Atonement"' or to Svetlana Alexievich's inquiries into the rhetoric of heroism employed by the coercive apparatus of the state and by the proponents of 'witness literature' alike. This view is perhaps best expressed in *The Unwomanly Face of War: An Oral History of Women in World War II*, translated by Richard Pevear and Larissa Volokhonsky (New York: Random House, 2017).

Czesław Miłosz, *The Witness of Poetry* (Cambridge: Harvard University Press, 1983) is representative of the political thought inherent in the notion of 'witness literature'.

Reuben A. Brower, *Hero and Saint: Shakespeare and Graeco-Roman Heroic Tradition* (Oxford: Oxford University Press, 1971). A historical study of the two figures most frequently employed in the language of 'witness literature'.

Lisa Rodensky, *The Crime in Mind: Criminal Responsibility and the Victorian Novel* (Oxford: Oxford University Press, 2003). Contains a shrewd discussion of the metaphor of justice and its limitations, as applied to the literary imagination.

John MacKay, *Inscription and Modernity: From Wordsworth to Mandelstam* (Bloomington: Indiana University Press, 2006). The volume's final chapter takes a Hegelian perspective on Mandelstam's metaphysics.

Andrew Kahn, 'Canonical Mandelstam' in *Twentieth-Century Russian Poetry: Reinventing the Canon*, edited by Katharine Hodgson et al. (Cambridge: Open Book Publishers, 2017). Traces the political patterns of Mandelstam's reception in England and the United States, by surveying a range of literary periodicals.

Henry Gifford, *Poetry in a Divided World* (Cambridge: Cambridge University Press, 1986). A principled reflection on poetry as an international force, and its responsibilities.

Carmen Bugan, *Seamus Heaney and East European Poetry in Translation: Poetics of Exile* (London: Legenda: Modern Humanities Research Association and Maney Pub, 2013). Opens with a carefully considered chapter on Mandelstam's influence on Heaney.

Donald Davie, *Slavic Excursions* (Chicago: University of Chicago Press, 1990). A model of responsible, humane and capacious critical encounter with the Russian and Soviet literature, from a liberal English perspective.

Geoffrey Hill, *Collected Critical Writings*, edited by Kenneth Haynes (Oxford: Oxford University Press, 2008). Essays in this volume probe the continuities and discontinuities of the language of art and criticism respectively, stringent in addressing their moral and political responsibilities.

Index

Akhmadulina, Bella 204, 249
Akhmatova, Anna:
    Gifford's dissent to 44
    losing papers via Finkelstein 202–10
    mother to Gumilyov 110, 115
    nuances of address 218
    'Poem Without a Hero' 194–95
    shaping M.'s posthumous reputation 193–95, 222
    witness to 'The Stalin Epigram' 87, 122, 126–28, 133
Alexiyevich, Svetlana 225
ambiguity 83
anapaest 56–57, 80, 121
animal: Empson 42
    Kant 175
    Lowell 60–61
    Zabolotsky 151–52, 155, 159
    see also beast; birds; cockroach; Darwin, C.; dog; scorpion; spider; wolf
antinomies 42, 59
    see also contradictions; irony; opposition; paradox
anxiety:
    epistemic 29
    in detainees 139
    M.'s while in Voronezh 176, 200
    see also double bind; Mandelstam, O., suicidality; trauma
Aquinas, Thomas 174, 192
Arc de Triomphe: *see* Paris
arch:
    a 'complex word' 83
    Marvell 183

Ruskin 183–84
    seen in Thode's fingers 22–23
    see also architectonic; architecture
architectonic 22, 181–90
    see also arch; Gothic architecture
archive (M.'s) 197–98, 201–03, 210
    M.'s denial of having one 76, 80
    see also Finkelstein, L.; Rudakov, S.
Arendt, Hannah 63, 67, 118
Armenia 70, 79–80
atonement 154–56, 197
Auden, W. H. 172, 174, 245, 254
audience: *see* interlocutor
Averintsev, Sergey 32–33, 41

Babel, Isaac 40
Baikal (lake) 150–51
balance 152, 167
'balconies of the soul' 102
    see also Italian poetry; Sedakova, O.
Balmont, Konstantin 29
Baltrušaitis, Jurgis 164
Baratynsky, Yevgeny 51, 86, 89, 107
Bateson, Gregory:
    control systems 119
    double bind 72–76, 136–52
    views compared with Laing's 137
    see also double bind
Batyushkov, Konstantin 96–97, 105, 218
Baudelaire, Charles 'Le Cygne' 161, 164
Beard, Mary 106
beast:
    Apocalypse 189–90
    Empson 43, 190

M.'s versions of Petrarch 91, 96
Pushkin 28–29
Zabolotsky 155, 159
see also animal
Beatrice 98, 102, 107–08
Beiser, Frederick 23, 27, 29
belles lettres 214, 219
Bely, Andrey 79, 103–05, 113
Bergson, Henri 36–37, 55
biography:
    the problem of irrationality 42–44
    the question of motives 49
    see also Mandelstam, O.; memoirists
birds 43, 176, 216
    eagle 28, 189
    falcon 91–95
    nightingale 94–95, 124, 145
    snipe 151–53
    swan 96, 104, 161–64
'The Birth of a Smile' 174
birthmark 225
Bolshevik 166–71, 175–79
Botticelli, Sandro: *see Primavera*
bourgeoisie: *see* class
Brodsky, David 121–22
Brodsky, Joseph 38, 205
Brown, Clarence 58, 215
Browne, Thomas 52–53
Buddhism 153
Buffon, Comte de 92
Bukharin, Nikolay 70, 134
Byron, *The Giaour* 49–50, 54

Camden, William 53
canzone 100–01
Carlisle, Olga 60
Carroll, Lewis 161
Cherdyn 120, 130, 132, 144
Christian ideas 152, 187, 197
Chukovsky, Korney 38–41

class 63
    bourgeoisie 78
    class enemy 51, 86
    kulaks 125
    see also proletariat
cliché 25–26
cockroach 9, 178
coercion 32–33, 42, 132
Coetzee, J. M. 181
Coleridge, Samuel Taylor 43, 50–51, 154
colour 168–70
Communism 24, 26, 125–26, 166
    Emil Mandelstam 177
    Ruskin 180
concepts 23–24, 42, 173–75, 186
    see also metaphor; metaphysical poetry; universal
contradictions 21–45
    causing internal conflict 177–78
    Empson 42, 197
    in metaphysics 192
    in poetry 192
    misunderstood as undesirable 107
    of Bolshevism 165–67, 172
    of control 119
    of Stalin's injunction 49
    productive of a dialectic 103–04
    see also antinomies; double bind; Mandelstam, O., *c.* of biography; opposition; paradox
Conversation About Dante 63, 86, 102–08, 113
Copernican revolution 30
    see also neo-Kantianism
Coster, Charles de 63
    see also '*Ulenspiegel* affair'
counter-revolution 51, 111, 117, 122–30
    paradox of 166–69
creativity: *see* double bind
Crimea 86, 125, 126

criticism 210, 213–26
    'comradely criticism' 79
Cromwell, Oliver: *see* Marvell, A., 'An Horatian Ode'
crystal 47, 190
    see also system
crystallography 186
    see also crystal; system
Cusa, Nicholas of 89

Dante 62, 82, 192, 219–20
    Divine Comedy 101, 106, 174
    Inferno 114, 170–71
    Vita Nuova 98, 102, 106–08
    see also Beatrice; *Conversation About Dante*
Darwin, Charles:
    The Expression of Emotions in Man and Animals 146
    On the Origin of Species 159
Davie, Donald 173
'The Dawn of Acmeism' 103, 185
    see also arch; Gothic architecture
deadlock (psychodynamics) 50, 72–73, 147, 152, 157, 159, 183
    see also balance; double bind
Derrida, Jacques 118
Derzhavin, Gavriil 218
Devil: *see* Fairbairn, W. R. D.
dialectic 103–05, 113, 168
dialogue 89, 103–05, 113
    see also Marvell, A., 'A Dialogue Between the Resolved Soul, and Created Pleasure'; Plato
dilemma: *see* double bind
dissent 33–38, 104–05, 179–80
    see also heresy; heterodoxy; opposition
diversity: *see* monoculture
divination 216–17

Divine Comedy: *see* Dante
dog 27, 76, 111, 191
    'complex word' 80–83
    Pavlov 146–47
    wolfhound 80–83, 203
Donne, John 172–74, 192
    see also metaphysical poetry
double bind: defined by Bateson 75
    may lead to creativity if averted 73, 76, 149–50, 159
    Laing's view 137
    M.'s situation 72–76, 136–52
doubt (as a value) 21, 29, 44, 174
    see also anxiety; scepticism
Druskin, Yakov 221
duel 49–51, 158
duress 24–25, 88, 131–32, 147, 160
Dymshitz, Alexander 26, 204

e pluribus unum 183
    see also Kant, I., 'crooked wood'; unity
eagle: *see* birds
editors of M. and Mandelstamiana: *see* Khardzhiev, N.; Maggs, P.; Mets, A.; Nerler, P.; Rudakov, S.
Efros, Abram 86
The Egyptian Stamp 63
Eliot, T. S. 220
    'Tradition and the Individual Talent' 35–37, 44
    'The Three Voices of Poetry' 156
Empson, William:
    'Arachne' 43
    'Aubade' 163
    Buddhism 101, 153
    'balance and deadlock' 152, 161
    'Courage Means Running' 157
    on Gray's 'Elegy' 152–53
    on the pastoral 162

'neurotic guilt' 50–51
note to 'Bacchus' 42
The Structure of Complex Words 81–83
epigram: *see* Baratynsky, Y.; 'The Stalin Epigram'
eroticism 96, 108–09
exile 81–82, 120–21, 127, 130, 145, 148, 165
    see also Cherdyn; Rudakov, S.; Voronezh; Voronezh poems
eye: *see* pun, 'eye' in English

Fairbairn, W. R. D. 33, 37, 43, 75, 139
falcon: *see* birds
feuilleton: Herzen 39
    Gornfeld 65
    M. 66
    Zaslavsky 68–72, 84
Fichte, Johann Gottlieb 24, 29
figure-ground distinction 61, 169, 196
fin amor 108
    see also Platonic love
Finkelstein, Lina 198–203
    see also Rudakov, S.
foot: *see* metre (in verse); walking
forest 150–55, 159
FOSP ('Federation of Unions of Soviet Writers'): *see* '*Ulenspiegel* affair'
The Fourth Prose 76, 194
Frederick the Great 30
freedom 25, 131–32, 175, 213
    see also liberty
Freud, Sigmund 220
friends of the Mandelstams 127, 132
    see individual entries, including Akhmatova, A.; Finkelstein, L.; Gerstein, E.; Gumilyov, L.; Kuzin, B.; Petrovykh, M.; Rudakov, S.; Shtempel, N.
friendship 112, 122, 204, 210–11, 215–18

Galilei, Galileo 173
Gasparov, Mikhail 31–33, 37–38, 42
genre definition 47–48, 52
    see also 'The Stalin Epigram', genre attribution
Gerstein, Emma:
    declined *ménage-a-trois* 109
    forgave M. 212, 222
    friendship with N. Mandelstam 209–12
    gifted memoirist 108, 110, 209, 222
    hosted the homeless Mandelstams 71
    memories of M.'s trauma 132–33, 148
    on Rudakov 198, 202–05
    protocols of M.'s interrogations 11, 126, 127
    resisted Akhmatova's policies 193–96
    relationship with Gumilyov 110–13
    took dictation from M. 66
    witness to 'The Stalin Epigram' 52, 54, 111–12
Gifford, Henry 44
Ginzburg, Lydia 86
Gladkov, Aleksandr 114
Goethe, Johann Wolfgang 176
Goldstein, Darra 28
Gombrich, E. H. 97–98
Gornfeld, Arkadiy 64–66, 69, 194
Gosizdat 79, 113
Gothic architecture 47–48, 181–90
    see also arch; architectonic; Ruskin, J.; 'The Dawn of Acmeism'
graft (metaphor) 100, 174
Gray, Thomas, 'Elegy Written in a Country Churchyard' 152
Green, Nina 111
Grigson, Geoffrey 52–53
guilt:
    Byron's insight 49–50
    'neurotic guilt' 43, 49–51, 133
    relation to criticism and justice 223

Index

'the artisan of guilty looks' 110
  see also Akhmatova, A., 'Poem Without a Hero'
Gulag 26, 210, 224
Gumilyov, Lev ('Lyova') 55, 110–15, 126–27, 133, 203
Gumilyov, Nikolay 199, 202

H. J. Jackson, *Marginalia* 207
Hagia-Sophia 182, 189
handwriting 76, 80, 198
Haynes, Kenneth 215–17
Heidelberg 21–37, 184
Heraclitus 183–84
  harmonia 23
  lyre 23
  'reciprocal harmony' 174
heresy 35, 77, 180
  see also heterodoxy; orthodoxy
hero 31
  see also Akhmatova, A., 'Poem Without a Hero'
heroism 40, 128, 131
Herrick, Robert, *Hesperides* 53
Herzen, Alexander 39
  writers' house named after 110
heterodoxy 35, 166–67
hiatus irrationalis 24, 42, 55, 149
  see also neo-Kantianism; scepticism
Hill, Geoffrey 31, 131, 213–24
  'at-one-ment' 154–59
  'cant' 43, 224
  contra Miłosz 215–24
  'taciturnity' 131
history 22, 184, 186
  the problem of 23–24
  see also Lask, E.; Lowell, R., *History*
Homer 37, 83, 189
House, Humphrey 154

'I washed myself at night ...' 156–57, 160–61, 164
identification 125, 176, 219–21
ideology 27, 32, 35, 79, 105, 165
  see also Bolshevism; class; Communism; Soviet regime; Socialism; totalitarianism
imagination 96, 149–50, 213, 224
imprisonment 24, 28, 150, 188
  inherently pathogenic 142, 147
  paradox of 82, 163
impulse:
  basis of behaviour 146–47, 157, 162
  behind 'The Stalin Epigram' 47–48, 66, 86, 89, 134
  in Bergson 55–56
  in dialectic 103
  in love poetry 107
  in metaphysical poetry 172
  in marginalia writing 207
Ingram, John 131
interlocutor 113, 115, 118, 141, 208, 214–22
  see also 'On the Interlocutor'
internal conflict:
  Batyushkov 105
  Byron 50
  Chukovsky 40–41
  Coleridge 43, 51
  Fourth Prose 194
  Pavlov 146
  Zabolotsky 149–57
  see also double bind; madness
interrogation: as a rhetorical situation 131, 135, 138, 142
  M. 31, 46, 54, 84, 117, 121–29, 141
  Zabolotsky 150
Ionov, Ilya 71
irony 59, 62, 117, 153
Irrationalitätsproblem 23
  see also hiatus irrationalis

Italian poetry 53
    the gait of the beloved 98–108
    see also Dante; Petrarch
Izvestiya (News) 66, 68

John the Baptist 98
Johnston, Charles 105
The Journey to Armenia 79

Jugashvili 13, 58
    see also Stalin, J.

Kahn, Andrew 38, 209, 211, 215, 217
Kalogeris, George 160–61
Kamen (Stone) 21, 30, 226
Kanatchikov, Semyon 69
Kant, Immanuel 29, 37, 149, 186
    'crooked wood' 166–67, 175–76
    see also neo-Kantianism
Karyakin, Vasiliy 64, 70
Keats, John 21, 44
kettlebells 58, 60
KGB 45–46, 119–20, 210
    see also Lubyanka
Khardzhiev, Nikolay 204, 207
Kharms, Daniil 55
Khazin, Yevgeniy 11, 71, 126
Khlebnikov, Velimir 199
Kiev 55, 84, 125
Kipling, Rudyard, 'Rikki-tikki-tavi' 73, 136
Kleist, Ewald Christian von 30, 218
Klychkov, Sergey 86, 87
Klyuyev, Nikolay 86
Kniga i Revolyutsiya (Book and Revolution) 78
Kolokol (The Bell) 39
Kolyma 127

Komsomolskaya Pravda (Komsomol Truth) 69–70
Kovarsky, Nikolay 79
Krasnaya Gazeta (The Red Newspaper) 65
Kremlin 170–72
    compared to the pit of Dante's hell 114
    Stalin as 'the Kremlin highlander' 54, 56, 111
    see also Moscow; Muscovites
Krylov, Ivan, 'The Swan, the Pike and the Crawfish' 104
Küchelbecker, Wilhelm 200
kulaks: *see* class, *kulaks*
Kuzin, Boris 26–27, 31, 87, 112, 117, 122, 126–27, 133, 142, 195
Kvitko, Lev 41

Laing, R. D.: *see* double bind
'Lamarck' 158–59, 162
Lamarck, Jean-Baptiste 158, 162
    see also Kuzin, B.
Lapshin, Ivan 27
Lask, Emil 23–31, 55
Latini, Brunetto 82
Laura 107–08
    see also Beatrice; Sedakova, O.
Lay of Igor's Campaign, The 91
Lekmanov, Oleg 188
Lenin, Vladimir 77, 124, 168, 188, 210
Leningrad 68, 115, 150, 202, 210
    see also Petersburg; Petrograd
letters 39, 44, 65, 66, 69, 135, 152, 156, 198–99, 201, 202
    M.'s 35, 37, 54, 67–69, 81, 84, 109, 176, 187, 208, 209–15, 217
    see also 'On the Interlocutor'
Levina, Tatiana 206–08
liberty 45–88, 131–32, 163, 168
line ending 87, 90, 99, 101, 114

Index

literary language 2, 26, 35, 160, 197, 213
  see also criticism
Literaturnaya Gazeta (*Literary Paper*) 66–72
Literaturnyy Leningrad (*Literary Leningrad*) 86
Literaturnyy Sovremennik (*Literary Contemporary*) 79
Lotze, Herman 29–30
  see also neo-Kantianism; scepticism
love lyric 21–23, 96–109
Lowell, Robert 58–64, 143, 176, 222
Lubyanka 117–48
Lucretius 174, 192
lyre: *see* Heraclitus

madness 34, 43, 85, 190, 192, 201
  see also sanity
Maggs, Peter B. 120
Mandelstam, Alexander 71
Mandelstam, Emil 177
Mandelstam, Nadezhda:
  assaulted by Sargijan 110
  assisted Khradzhiev with M.'s first posthumous edition 204
  Brodsky's obituary 205–06
  disparaged by Rudakov 199–200
  dissemination of 'The Stalin Epigram' 111
  dictating the interpretations of the 'Ode' 179, 181, 189
  in Voronezh 132–33, 179
  influential witness of M. 32, 35, 193, 195, 215, 218
  marginalia 207–08
  M.'s letters to 84
  on M.'s imprisonment and Shivarov 121–22, 127, 129, 134, 139–41, 144
  on Pavlenko 129
  on Petrovykh 109
  on Rudakov 197–98
  posthumous reputation 205–06, 209–12
  'sexual accomplishments' 196
Mandelstam, Osip:
  arrest 121
  contradictions of biography 21, 41–42
  disavowal of writing 76, 80
  eyelashes 109, 132
  forgiven by Gerstein 212
  homelessness 71
  internal conflict 33, 43, 51, 54, 69–73, 189
  manners 70, 85–87, 171, 187, 198–20
  nonconformity examined 24–27, 31
  peeling a pear 108
  philosophical education 22–24, 27, 29–31, 36–37, 55
  philosophical mindset 27, 29, 37, 44, 172, 180
  posthumous reputation 21, 24–27, 38, 45–46, 131, 180, 193–96
  saintliness questioned 131, 134
  suicidality 43, 50–51, 85, 88, 132, 141–42, 144, 177, 201
  see specific entries for particular works and aspects of biography
Manguel, Alberto 82
marginalia: *see* Mandelstam, N., marginalia
Martial 53
martyr 28, 131, 197
Marvell, Andrew:
  'after-math' 131
  'A Dialogue Between the Resolved Soul, and Created Pleasure' 167
  'An Horatian Ode' 163
  Buddhist sensibility 101
  'Last Instructions to a Painter' 191–92
  'The First Anniversary' 182

'Upon Appleton House' 167–68,
    173, 176
Mazurin, Vasily 79
memoirists: *see* Akhmatova, A.; Gerstein,
    E.; Kuzin, B.; Mandelstam, N.;
    Shtempel, N.; Zabolotsky, N.
memorization 111, 134, 206, 210
Merwin, W. S. 58
Messerer, Boris 204
metaphor:
    in propaganda 166, 183
    ice-skating 104
    in 'witness literature' 28, 204–06,
        209–11, 223
    locomotion in Dante 83
    running 159
    see also dog; metaphysical metaphor;
        walking
metaphysical metaphor 172–76, 183–88,
    193, 197
metaphysical poetry 172–76, 190
metaphysics 167, 173, 192, 197
    see also metaphysical poetry
metre (in verse) 56–57, 80, 102–03, 106
Mets, Alexander 30, 63, 77, 198
Mikhailov, Mikhail 40
Miłosz, Czesław 197, 223–24
Mirsky, Dmitry (D. S.) 40
modulation (in verse) 57, 106, 108
Moscow 54, 67–70, 105, 112–14, 127,
    133, 148, 165, 170–71, 198–99,
    203–10, 219
    see also Kremlin; Lubyanka;
        Muscovites
mower 188, 192
    mowth as 'after-math' in Marvell 131
Mozart, Wolfgang Amadeus 158, 176, 192
Muchnik, Helen, *From Gorky to
    Pasternak* 217
Muravyov, Mikhail 38–40
Muscovites 148

Na Literaturnom Postu (*On the Literary
    Watch-post*) 77
names (nuances of usage) 41, 195–
    99, 214–22
'Cal' Lowell 60
'maiden names' 119
M. 179
M.'s interrogation 126–28, 133
Stalin 56–58, 172, 188
Vyshinsky's nickname 135
Narbut, Vladimir 121–22, 126–27
Nature 151–54, 158–59, 174, 175, 188
negative (photography) 169
Nekrasov, Nikolay 38–40
neo-Kantianism 23–29, 79
Nerler, Pavel:
    conjecture concerning Lask 30
    commentary on M.'s
        interrogation 124
    editor of *We'll see who outstubborns
        whom*... 209–11
    following conventions established by
        N. Mandelstam 218
    misattribution of 'love lyric' genre 21–22
    on the '*Ulenspiegel* affair' 64, 66
Nevsky Prospect 39, 217, 221
New York Review of Books 45, 205
nightingale 94–95, 145
    M. under interrogation compared to 124
Nikisch, Arthur 22
Notre Dame: *see* Paris
'Notre Dame' 185
Novy Mir (*New World*) 77

O'Brien, Flann, *Catechism of Cliché* 209
obituary: *see* Mandelstam, N., Brodsky's
    obituary
Obolensky, Dimitri 28, 216
obscenity: *see* Mandelstam, N.,
    marginalia

'Ode' 165–92
    first English publication 179
    M.'s regrets 200
    reception 31–33, 37–38, 41, 179, 181, 194
    text in English 13–15
    see also Marvell, A., 'An Horatian Ode'
OGPU 52, 85, 119–21, 130, 134, 194
    see also Lubyanka
Olesha, Yuriy 68
'On the Interlocutor' 23, 29, 34, 37, 89, 176, 213–26
opposition:
    conceptual 23, 35, 104, 152
    in lexicography 167
    in metaphysical poetry 174, 183
    political 2, 24–25, 28, 35
    rhetorical uses of 25, 28, 41, 168
    see also contradictions; metaphysical poetry; paradox
orthodoxy:
    Communist 27, 166, 168, 177
    Darwinist 26
    nature of 35
    reception of the 'Ode' 179–80
    see also heresy; heterodoxy
Ossetian 9, 52–62
Ovid 45, 216
    M. compared to 201
Owen, Wilfred 191
Oxford English Dictionary 123, 185

Panova, Lada 90, 94, 106–07
paradox 97, 105
    biographical 1, 3, 43, 76, 187
    constituent of a double bind 74, 137
    denial of, in Cold War rhetoric 209, 217
    of control over a system 49, 118–19, 138, 166–68, 170, 176
    of irrelation 167–68
    of 'The Stalin Epigram' 46, 61
    see also antinomies; contradictions; double bind; irony; opposition
paralysis: see deadlock; double bind
parasitic plants: 'bourgeois poets' compared to 78
Paris 211
    Arc de Triomphe 191
    Notre Dame 22, 185
particular (philosophical category) 24, 107, 171, 173
    see also concepts; metaphor; universal
Pasternak, Boris:
    letter to Tsvetaeva concerning M. 68, 81
    not denounced by M. 133
    ruled out as M.'s denouncer 87
    subject to proposed 'liquidation of the bourgeoisie as a class' 78–79, 86
pathetic fallacy 153, 162
patronage 171, 175, 177, 182
Pavlenko, Pyotr 129, 134, 192
Pavlov, Ivan 146–47, 199
Pavlovich, Nadezhda 207
penal system 120, 131–32, 138, 147, 224
Petersburg 27, 203, 211
    mistakenly identified as Mandelstam's birthplace 26
    Pavlov's experiments in 146
    symbol of bourgeois sensibility 80
    walking in 170–71
    see also Leningrad, Petrograd
Petrarch 89–107
    see also Italian poetry
Petrograd 170
    see also Leningrad, Petersburg
Petrov-Vodkin, Kuzma 168–69
Petrovykh, Maria ('Marusya') 96, 109–10, 121, 126–27

Philologica 207–08
Philomela (Greek myth) 145
philosophy: *see* Mandelstam, O., philosophical education, philosophical mindset; metaphysical poetry; neo-Kantianism; paradox; scepticism; *see also* entries for specific concepts
plagiarism 65–68
Platonic love 106–07
  see also 'balconies of the soul'; *fin amor*
poetic address: *see* 'On the Interlocutor'; Panova, L.; Shtempel, N.; Vaksel, O.
Pogodin, Mikhail 38, 39
Poland 38–39
Polevoy, Nikolai 40
political system 41, 68, 112, 140, 166
  as depersonalized locus of responsibility 41
Polonsky, Vyacheslav 77, 85
polyphony 3, 189, 209
Pope, Alexander 83
Popova, Elikonida 37–38
Postupalsky, Igor 77
power 41, 49, 93, 102, 138, 166, 182
  the power of art as cliché 24–25, 209, 214
  see also double bind; interrogation; Kant, I., 'crooked wood'; Lubyanka; 'Ode'; 'The Stalin Epigram'
Pravda (*Truth*) 71, 80, 86
presentiment of death 178–79
Prieto, José Manuel 45–46
Primavera (Botticelli) 91, 97–98
privacy 118
proletarian literature 40, 51, 80, 165
  see also proletariat
proletariat 78–80, 125, 135

ideology 105
  in relation to Stalin 172–75
  see also class
pronoun in poetry 51, 57, 99, 160
prophet 28–29
prophylaxis (in criticism) 4
proprieties of address: *see* names
protocol (interrogation record) 11, 46, 117, 121–29
psychosis 132, 134, 144, 147
  see also double bind; trauma
publishing: *see* '*Ulenspiegel* affair'
pun 58
  'eye' in English 154
  'graft' in Russian 174
Pushkin, Alexander 33, 101, 204, 214
  Eugene Onegin 105
  Mozart and Salieri 192
  Pushkin House 100, 201
  'The Bronze Horseman' 216
  'The Prophet' 28

Radio Svoboda 204
radish: *see* Trotsky, Leon
raznochintsy 23, 37
Reid, Mayne 66
relationship, parent-child 73–76
reviews (of M.) 77–80
revolution 7, 33, 77, 120, 124, 144, 168–70
  'revolutionary conscience' 135
  see also counter-revolution
Revolyutsiya i Pechat (*Revolution and Print*) 77
rhetoric:
  in criticism 2–3, 28, 31
  memorial uses 32, 41, 196, 206, 209, 219–22
  of Gothic architecture 183–86
  probed by 'The Stalin Epigram' 59
  with respect to M. 1–3, 195

rhyme 87, 100–03, 108, 114
  see also line-ending
Richards, I. A. 152
richness 26, 80, 92–93, 113, 187
Ricks, Christopher 58, 156–59
Rodensky, Lisa, *The Crime in Mind* 223
Roget's Thesaurus of English Words and Phrases 167–68, 173
Rounding, Virginia 131
Rudakov, Sergey 197–202, 211, 218
  see also Finkelstein, L.
Ruskin, John 47–48, 180, 183–88, 193

saint 28, 38, 197
  see also Mandelstam, O., saintliness questioned
sanity (as a function of social relations) 176
  see also double bind; Fairbairn, W. R. D.; Laing, R. D.; *raznochintsy*
sarcasm 59, 189
Sargijan, Amir 110
satire: *see* 'The Stalin Epigram'
Savoyeva, Nina 224
scepticism 23–37, 44, 197
schizophrenia 73, 141, 144
Schubert, Franz 176
scorpion 49–54
secrecy 118
secret police 1, 31, 46, 111, 115, 117–19, 134–35
  see also Lubyanka
Sedakova, Olga 97–108, 219–20
Shakespeare, William 21, 105, 145
Shalamov, Varlam 224–26
Shivarov, Nikolay 11, 62, 121–30, 131–32, 140–42, 222
Shklovsky, Viktor 79
Shtempel, Natalia ('Natasha') 98–101, 106–07

silence (political metaphor) 22, 28, 38, 131–32
simile 92, 188, 218
  see also metaphor
sin 197
  see also Akhmatova, A., 'Poem Without a Hero'; Fairbairn, W. R. D.; guilt
Sinyavsky, Andrey 34–36
sleep 147, 188
  in poetry 96, 97, 105, 151
  M.'s manner 108–09, 148, 196
  M.'s sleep deprivation 132
Smith, James 172–74, 190
Socialism 27, 80, 166
  see also Communism
Sokolova, Lydia, 'A Moulten Falcon' 92–93
solitary confinement 141
sonnet: *see* Petrarch
Southwell, Robert 131
Soviet dissidence 32–35
Soviet literature 7, 175, 188
  see also '*Ulenspiegel* affair'
Soviet regime 28, 32, 46, 166
  M.'s relations with 37–38, 41–42, 51, 63, 86, 124–25, 175, 200
  see also interrogation, M.; 'Ode'; Shivarov, N.; 'The Stalin Epigram'
spider 43, 60–61, 190
St Petersburg: *see* Petersburg
'The Stalin Epigram' 45–88, 89, 94, 189
  dissemination 31, 111, 115, 117, 134
  genre attribution 47–54
  reception 24, 45–46
  text in English 9
  see also Baratynsky, Y.; interrogation, M.; Lowell, R.; Stalin, J.
Stalin, Joseph (Iosif) 41, 120
  M.'s relation to 1, 24, 26, 49, 86, 222
  'isolate but preserve' 148
  see also 'Ode'; 'The Stalin Epigram'

'Stanzas' 37
stars 149, 154–56, 160–64
Stepun, Fyodor 22
Stone: see *Kamen*
'Streams of Hackwork' 66
suffering: *see* Hill, Geoffrey, 'cant'
suicidality: *see* Mandelstam, O.,
    suicidality
Sukhum (modern Sukhumi) 63
Surat, Irina 98, 102
sweetness, in Russian and Italian 107–08
sympathy 220–22
system:
    concept 79, 122, 167, 183–87, 197
    of language 64
    psychophysiology 143, 147

taciturnity: *see* Geoffrey Hill
Tager, Elena 7
Talov, Mark 86–87
Tarasenkov, Anatoliy 77
Tarsis, Valeriy 78–79
Tasso, Torquato 105, 218
Tbilisi: *see* Tiflis
Ter-Gabrielyan, Sahak 70
    see also Armenia
terror:
    cliché 24–25
    emotion 56, 146, 156, 225
    metaphysical 160, 164
    policy 49, 56, 118, 120
Thode, Henry 22, 184
Thomas, Dylan 50
Tiflis (Tbilisi) 156, 160–61
Times Literary Supplement 209
'To German Prosody' 30
Todes, E. A. 198
Tolstoy, Aleksey 55, 110
torture: *see* duress; double bind; trauma
totalitarianism 3, 24–25, 32, 118, 132

tradition (literary and critical) 23, 44,
    98, 128, 213–26
    M.'s sense of belonging 35–36
    Eliot 35–37
translation 89–95, 160–61, 215–16
    see also Lowell, R.; '*Ulenspiegel* affair'
trauma 75, 143–48
    traumatic situations 74, 143–48
    post-traumatic behaviour 132,
        134, 150
    see also double bind
Trilling, Lyonel 220
Tristia 30, 215–16
    Hill 215–16
Trotsky, Leon:
    M.'s sympathies 125
    compared to a radish 168
Tsvetayeva, Marina (also 'Tsvetaeva') 41,
    45, 52, 68, 81, 205
Tuscan poetry 101
    see also Italian poetry
Tynyanov, Yuriy 35, 37, 77, 200

'*Ulenspiegel* affair' 63–73, 136, 187, 194
unity 91, 104, 106, 157, 160, 182–83, 186
    see also arch; contradictions; *e
        pluribus unum*; richness
universal (of philosophy) 24, 25, 42, 101,
    113, 173, 176
    in 'Verses For the Unknown
        Soldier' 191
    Stalin viewed as 170, 172

Vaksel, Olga 90, 94, 98
validity (philosophical concept) 29–31, 37
van der Kolk, Bessel 144–47
Vandysh 130
variant 46, 64, 111, 126
Vechernyaya Moskva (*Evening Moscow*) 66

Index

Venus 54, 98, 237
'Verses for the Unknown Soldier' 190–92
'Verses to Natalia Shtempel' 98–101
Virgil 103, 158
voice:
    metaphor xi, 3, 9, 26, 28, 38, 86, 185, 206, 209, 214
    M.'s voice 7, 199
    nonverbal communication 137, 140, 143
    significance to M. 7, 76, 84, 134, 188–89, 201
    see also Eliot, T. S., 'The Three Voices of Poetry'
Voronezh 41, 107, 133, 144, 165
    see also Voronezh poems
Voronezh poems 165–92
Vtoraya Rechka 19
Vygodsky, David 70
Vyshinsky, Andrey 135–38

walking:
    deeply individual 98–107, 113–14
    linked with breath, dialectic and versification 82, 98–107
    M.'s manner 54, 109
Warsaw 26
    see also Poland
Whewell, William 186
White Guard 125

Wiman, Christian 24
Windelband, Wilhelm 27, 29, 37
    see also neo-Kantianism; philosophy; scepticism
witness 97, 111–12, 118, 127
    false 67–70
    paradoxes of 46, 145
    textual 3–4, 23, 35, 37, 54, 81, 117, 141
    see also voice
witness literature 28, 224
wolf 81–82
wolfhound: *see* dog

Yagoda, Genrikh 121, 135–38
Yakhontov, Vladimir 37
Yasensky, Bruno 41
Yeats, W. B. 156, 159
Yesenin, Sergey 40

Zabolotsky, Nikolay 28, 150
    'The Forest Lake' 151–55, 159
Zaslavsky, David 66–76
Zelinsky, Korneliy 86
Zemlya i fabrika (*ZiF*, *Land and Factory*) 63–66, 84
Zhdanov, Andrey 202
Zoschenko, Mikhail 68
Zvezda (*Star*) 63–64

www.ingramcontent.com/pod-product-compliance
Lightning Source LLC
LaVergne TN
LVHW021951060526
838201LV00049B/1665